Discovering
Real Business Requirements for
Software Project Success

For a listing of recent titles in the *Artech House Computing Library,*
turn to the back of this book.

Discovering
Real Business Requirements for
Software Project Success

Robin F. Goldsmith

Artech House
Boston • London
www.artechhouse.com

Library of Congress Cataloging-in-Publication Data
A catalog record for this book is available from the U.S. Library of Congress.

British Library Cataloguing in Publication Data
Goldsmith, Robin F.
    Discovering real business requirements for software project success.
    —(Artech House computing library)
    1. Computer software – Developement   2. Computer software – Design – Methodology
    3. Business – Computer programs
    I. Title
    005.1'2

Cover design by Igor Valdman

© 2004 ARTECH HOUSE, INC.
685 Canton Street
Norwood, MA 02062

International Standard Book Number: 1-58053-770-7

10 9 8 7 6 5 4 3 2 1

To my requirements:
Janice, Christian, and Tudor Noel,
who sometimes give me the business

Contents

3   Real requirements 31

4   Evaluating requirements form 51

14   Measuring proof of the pudding 195

Appendix: Summary of 21+ ways to test requirements 203

Introduction

"It's not right."
"It's what you said you wanted."
"Well, it's still not right."

Every system developer I've ever met has experienced some similar frustrating dialog with his or her user. Those of us who are charged with developing systems—including analysts, programmers, testers, and their managers—continue not to get it right for those who depend on systems to help them do the business' work.

Our problems start with the requirements, *what must be delivered to provide value*. The requirements set the tone and parameters for a system that is to be developed. A system isn't likely to be better than its requirements. When we don't get the requirements right, getting the system right becomes much more challenging.

Routinely, projects proceed with only partial requirements, the degree of which seldom is recognized at the time. Progress is uneven—the more and wider diversions from "right," the less adequate the requirements are. Consequently, much of project effort consists of course-correcting adjustment iterations that often also identify new and changed requirements, again with varying adequacy. This continual addition and changing of requirements generally is called "requirements creep" or "scope creep[1]." It's enormously expensive because it usually entails throwing out and redoing previously completed work.

In information technology (IT), which I'm using synonymously with "systems" to embrace development and support of software and/or hardware solutions, for internal and/or external use, the virtually universally accepted conventional wisdom holds that such creep is inevitable and unavoidable. Developers generally feel they reasonably do know the right requirements as they begin implementation, but they also believe ongoing market, business, and legal/regulatory changes mean the requirements are no longer right by the time they finish. Almost all developers further agree

---

1. While attending a presentation by the author at the System Management/Applications of Software Measurement SM/ASM 2002 Conference, fellow speaker Dale Emery asked, "Who is this requirements creep, and why is he on my projects?" I'll bet he's on your projects too.

that requirements creep still more as users (applying the term broadly to include all sources of business requirements, not just those who personally use a system) seem to change their minds, which is attributed mainly to the "fact" that "users don't know what they want."

As an industry, we've been at system development for 50 years and still don't get it right. Let me suggest maybe we just don't get *it*, period. Our customary approaches don't work very well, and they need a lot more help than the mere tweaking usually offered as advice.

The conventional wisdom above and many other similarly accepted truths often are not helping us. In fact, they are quite likely to be hurting us, in ways that are all the more insidiously damaging, because we follow them under the illusion we're applying wisdom. I'm sure most conventional wisdom probably does start with some measure of truth and with the best of intentions, but then it's prone to getting out of hand. We tend to miss some of the story, often the important part. It's so much easier just to accept generalizations and reassurances that relieve us of responsibility for our results.

Yes, *requirements* change, but they *don't have to change nearly to the extent that we've grown content with*. Some methodologies even treat requirements change as sort of a virtue, often making it a self-fulfilling prophecy and masking its true cost. *We can do a lot better*—maybe not perfection, but a lot better—*but not by continuing to think and do things the same old ways*. Requirements creep and projects fail, not because of some cosmic inevitability that we're powerless to confront, but mainly because of the practices that we routinely and usually intentionally apply.

We receive the results we create. As an industry, we keep doing the same things and expecting a different result. That's the definition of insanity.

This book presents a different way of thinking about and defining requirements. It challenges some conventional wisdom, and furthermore it challenges the reader to take more active responsibility for changing their results.

✖ Warning

Some readers may find these challenges troubling and may be tempted to reject out of hand my suggestion that some customary methods may not be so effective as they presume. Many colleagues, clients, and others hearing these ideas for the first time express similar reservations. *Those who are open to new ways of looking at familiar things, hearing out the ideas in full, and experiencing them in action (as we'll do in this book) then often say they wish they'd known and used these ideas all along.*

How this book differs

This book presents numerous practical techniques woven together within a more effective way to approach requirements where "It's not right" is *not* inevitable:

1. This book is about *business requirements*. Business requirements are the REAL requirements that the systems we create are meant to satisfy. As an industry, we tend to delude ourselves into thinking the products we build are what the business requires. *The REAL reason for much of software project difficulty is the failure of our products' requirements to meet the business requirements.* Such failure indeed is practically inevitable because our supposed conventional wisdom and good practices generally distract us from adequately identifying the REAL, business requirements. Requirements creep and projects overrun as we inefficiently go back into finally identifying the REAL, business requirements we didn't know to identify earlier.

2. This book emphasizes how to *discover what* the REAL business requirements are—their *content* or substance. This is perhaps the hardest part of system development and gets little attention compared to the amount spent on the form and storage of requirements. These other "requirements management" and "requirements engineering" concerns are important, and we'll address them *after* we've addressed the more important matters of getting the content right. To aid the reader in discovering the REAL requirements content, this book introduces a very powerful tool called a Problem Pyramid™ that helps avoid common requirements pitfalls[2].

3. This book describes more than 21 practical and effective ways to *test* that the requirements have been defined appropriately. Testing as we're using the term in this book includes static test methods, such as reviews and inspections. Twenty-one ways may sound overwhelming or possibly nitpicking, but I think you'll find these tests workable and powerful aids to complement discovery. To make it clear when the book is discussing ways to test requirements, each of the 21+ ways is designated by a ✪ star symbol. The more ways you use, the more requirements issues you detect when they are easiest to fix. We address not only the commonly relied-upon but surprisingly weak ways that test requirements' form, but also additional less well-known, more powerful ways to identify overlooked requirements and check the accuracy of content.

4. This book places *responsibility* on those of us charged with discovering requirements to do a much better job, rather than falling back on the tired old excuses. We truly can identify REAL requirements much more accurately, completely, and early than conventional wisdom would have us believe.

---

2. Throughout this book you'll see several terms designated with trademarks on their initial mentions in the text. These are trademarks owned by me and my company, Go Pro Management, Inc. The purpose of a trademark is to identify a specific unusual use of a term which is proprietary to the trademark holder. These are valuable pieces of intellectual property which the law protects against misappropriation. You are welcome to use the terms, just please include the trademark symbol and proper attribution. Thank you.

REAL requirements

This book uses the term "REAL" (in all capitals solely for emphasis and not as an acronym) with regard to requirements. By REAL, we're embracing two important related meanings. The first is one that developers generally can identify with. It's common for developers to get requirements from users, only to discover that the user actually wanted something different. In my experience, developers routinely refer to the user's *re*defined requirements as the "real requirements."

The second meaning for REAL is more subtle and less likely to be one that people recognize consciously. Quite simply, a user seldom actually requires *the* system that the developer provides. Rather, the system is a means for meeting the user's REAL requirements for accomplishing their business purposes. This book is about discovering these frequently unarticulated business requirements, so that developers in fact can provide the proper systems to meet them.

Applicability to various methodologies

As I write this book, the methodological fad du jour is "agile development." Not surprisingly, therefore, a reviewer asked how this book fits with it.

This book is not about agile development but fits well with it. The book also fits well with other approaches. *The need to know the business requirements is universal and is not a function of job title, development methods, programming languages, hardware/software platform environments, application involved, nature of user, external visibility of implementation, importance or size of the problem/ opportunity.*

Moreover, this book's approach is not heavy on formality. Rather, I emphasize content. I do not believe in busywork for its own sake. That is not to say, though, that I am against writing things down, which alas I fear is some people's definition of "agile." Overattention to form can be a real problem and is not limited to requirements. For example, some prominent software testing gurus actively advocate not spending time writing test plans, because they feel the time would be better spent executing tests to hunt down bugs in the system.

I agree, to an extent, and preface my Proactive Testing™ seminars with, "Write no more than is helpful—and no less." This book adopts the same philosophy. It emphasizes practical methods that real people can implement; and it provides a breadth of methods that facilitate scaling to the size and shape of one's own situation.

The most well-known agile method, eXtreme Programming (XP), actively enlists users in creating user stories, which are a format for briefly documenting the requirements for the code that will be programmed [1]. I salute XP and any other technique which actually does promote meaningful user involvement. The XP community seems pretty convinced that user stories are the business requirements. Just because they originate from the user doesn't mean user stories, or any other requirements, necessarily are the

REAL, business requirements. User stories, and other touted techniques, will become even more valuable when used in conjunction with this book's approaches and methods for discovering business requirements.

Objectives

After reading this book, readers should be able to:

- Effectively discover business requirements at both high and detailed levels.
- Distinguish the nature, role, and importance of business requirements from system requirements and use cases.
- Apply the Problem Pyramid tool to guide reliable identification of the REAL problem/opportunity and business requirements.
- Use interviewing and other well-known practices more effectively to better discover relevant data concerning requirements.
- Selectively apply more than 21 ways to test the accuracy and adequacy of business requirements from perspectives of:
  - Assessing suitability of form;
  - Identifying overlooked requirements;
  - Evaluating substance/content.
- Enlist appropriate models and formats for analyzing and understanding the requirements data.
- Apply 7 guidelines for documenting and communicating the business requirements.
- Differentiate the scope of the business requirements from the scope of implementation.
- Manage the process of iteratively discovering, testing, and negotiating business requirements without analysis paralysis.

In short, I want you to be able to experience the "You understand us better than we do" type of feedback which I've been fortunate to receive many times from clients in a variety of businesses.

Who needs to know

This book is for:

- Analysts, project managers, consultants, developers, and others who are involved with identifying requirements.
- Quality assurance, testing, auditing, and process improvement professionals who have, or would want to have, occasion to assure the REAL requirements have been defined accurately and completely.

> • Users and business managers, including marketing staff, who seek an explanation for why the technical people repeatedly fail to understand what the business' requirements really are and need ways to be sure they are defined appropriately.
>
> • Instructors and students, whether in universities or professional training situations, who need to learn these important lessons before joining the above ranks.

Caveat: No methods work by themselves. Your skills applying the methods and knowledge of your business, as well as system development, greatly influence the value you'll get from these or any methods. Practice and review for improvement are essential for developing proficiency.

What's in it for you

Organizations that learn to identify business requirements well can gain an insurmountable advantage over competitors that persist in getting conventional results with conventional approaches. This is not just my perception. Recently, the heads of both IBM and Hewlett-Packard have announced independently that success today in the information systems industry demands primary attention to understanding the needs of the customer, in other words, the business' requirements.

Isn't this old news? We've been talking for decades about how necessary it is for IT to align with the business. Surely alignment demands first that IT understand what the business needs—its requirements. Aren't we already doing it?

If anyone in IT is understanding business needs, it would be the outsourcing vendors, who after all command premium pay in part because of being perceived as more businesslike. Yet, in a recent issue of *CIO*, Mohanbir Sawhney writes, "Before a vendor starts designing your solution, make sure it understands your real problem"[2]. I'd guess the author, along with most of the rest of us, has encountered solutions-for-pay that didn't meet the REAL business requirements because they hadn't been understood.

I'd further suggest that IT trails business in general in this realm, and business in general still seems to be having trouble. Just for example, let me cite two articles from the March 2003 *Quality Progress* (the current issue as I write this), the magazine of the American Society for Quality. One article is titled, "The Shift to Customer Focus"[3]. Shift! I thought total quality management (TQM) made that shift ten years ago. Apparently not.

Even more telling is what Editor Debbie Phillips-Donaldson writes: "One member of a conference panel commented that with ISO 9000:2000, this is the first time companies actually have to worry about their customers' needs [4]." It takes the new ISO 9000 standard to get companies to care about customers' needs?

Origins and structure

This book is based upon more than 35 years of hands-on experience performing, managing, and advising business and systems professionals on the development, acquisition, testing, support, and use of systems to meet business needs. I've captured those lessons in the various seminars I present regularly for business and systems professionals. The seminars have provided a valuable means for organizing, testing, and refining the concepts and techniques.

The structure of the book draws primarily upon two complementary seminars that I conduct: a two-day *Defining and Managing User Requirements* [5] and a one-day *21 Ways to Test Business Requirements* [6], (which is also the first day of a two-day seminar entitled *Testing Early in the Life Cycle* [7]). My two-day *Managing Systems Projects with Credibility* [8] seminar also presents the methods described in this book for defining scope that doesn't creep.

As with the seminars, this book reinforces concepts and techniques by applying them all to the same real case situation. The case comes from a company whose name (which I will not reveal—I don't reveal any of my clients' names) is synonymous with world-class excellence. Even the best organizations have trouble defining business requirements well.

Whereas my individual seminars deal separately with discovery and with testing, in this book we'll intertwine discovery and testing techniques. Here is how the chapters proceed. Chapter 1 sets the stage with fundamental information about requirements and their challenges, including why it is hard to test that requirements are right. Chapter 2 presents the case's initial requirements definition and the regular ways that organizations conventionally rely on to test requirements, but which are weaker than usually is realized.

Chapter 3 explores why business requirements are the REAL requirements and differentiates them from other uses of the term requirements. Chapter 4 describes a number of ways to test requirements form, which represents the main type of testing techniques ordinarily portrayed in the requirements literature.

Then we get to the heart of the book. Chapter 5 describes methods for discovering the business requirements content, and Chapter 6 introduces the powerful Problem Pyramid tool that Chapter 7 applies to the case. Chapter 8 explains data-gathering techniques and uses the case situation to work through realistic examples of interviewing dos and don'ts.

Chapter 9 examines modeling formats that serve both discovery and testing roles to help understand the requirements better. Chapter 10 identifies the keys to making sure the requirements are dealing with the complete story.

Only after discovering the REAL content, not until Chapter 11, do we get to documenting the business requirements. This chapter further describes a multilevel iterative approach that can drastically reduce scope creep while also avoiding analysis paralysis. Chapters 12 and 13, respectively, subject these seemingly suitable requirements to two other very powerful and too-seldom used categories of testing that reveal overlooked requirements and content inaccuracies. Chapter 14 concludes with methods and tools for managing the requirements process and controlling changes.

Some authors offer advice in the Introduction on how to jump about the book and skip chapters selectively. I'm not going to do that. Instead, I encourage reading this book in sequence from front to back for the following reasons:

> ‣ Each chapter builds on the prior chapters. They're not isolated standalone pieces. The place to be selective is later in deciding which methods to apply and to what extent, not which ones to read about.

> ‣ The usual rationale for skipping chapters is that they contain only information that experienced readers already know. Well, *this book was necessary because I've found the industry doesn't know the ideas in it, but often presumes that it does.* Moreover, I think one of the main reasons our industry doesn't get better at requirements is because many of us misjudge how well we already do. It's exactly the material that an experienced person thinks he knows that may be most important to read in the (I think you'll find different) context I present it.

> ‣ If you're in a skipping mode, you may be most prone to skip past the business case and related exercises, since very often the cases and exercises presented in books seem superficial and contrived. I don't use the case merely to illustrate foregone conclusions, which often initially seem so obvious, but then are hard for readers to replicate in their own projects. This book is different. The business case has real substance. *Working through the case exercises is the best way I know to gain true useful understanding not only of the concepts and techniques, but also of the thought processes needed to apply them, that often are difficult because they probably represent new ways of thinking.*

You'll learn a lot more by doing the exercises than just by reading about them in the textual analysis. Trying the methods with the case's fact situation at the suggested times, and stumbling sometimes, makes the methods come alive and be much more meaningful than merely passively reading about them. If you do try the methods, you may stumble at first, because they are unfamiliar and often hard. Some people don't like trying things they're not good at right away, but I've never found a substitute for trying, making mistakes, and then most importantly analyzing, correcting, and learning from them.

I've honed these concepts and exercises with thousands of experienced business and systems professionals throughout the world from many different industries, roles, and backgrounds. I believe they form a representative sample of common experiences with systems projects and requirements. Therefore, throughout the book I draw upon reactions, behaviors, and comments from clients and seminar participants with the assumption that they will be similar to those of most readers. Consequently, the analysis in the book probably will identify most of the issues you encounter. If you bump into something that I've missed, or have any other comments or suggestions about the book, please let me know at www.gopromanagement.com. That's how I continually improve.

What's not in this book

This is *not theory*, which is the opposite of practical. The purpose of this book is to present to practitioners a set of useful concepts and techniques that have evolved through extensive practical systems development and acquisition experience, which I've been able to refine within the context of highly interactive seminars. In addition to specific techniques, I do emphasize understanding how and why the techniques work. I find that understanding the concepts underlying the practical techniques is key to adapting the techniques to one's own situation.

This book is *not thick*. On the premise that a book is more useful if it's actually read, and that the likelihood of being read is inversely proportional to its girth, this book is relatively short. Thus, for example, I've skipped the seemingly obligatory prosaic opening that goes on at length about how important information systems are.

This book is *not attempting to survey the literature on requirements or provide extensive footnote references*. If you want them, a number of other books include summaries of many prior requirements writings. While I certainly give credit to sources of ideas where I can, I'm only giving citations for ideas that I actually took from a particular identifiable source or represent good sources of added information. I apologize in advance for not always knowing where I heard or read something, perhaps years ago (which may be an affliction of the practitioner as contrasted with an academic, or maybe it's just a sign of growing ripe).

A number of other books offer valuable information relevant to some aspects of requirements. In fact, since 1999 a veritable plethora seems to be coming on the scene after a long period with relatively few books about requirements. I developed the concepts and approaches in this book before most of the other books were written, and I admit back then I was busier discovering clients' REAL requirements than reading those few books that did exist on the subject.

I indeed have read many of the other writings and have not found any which address my key emphases on discovering and testing the content of REAL business requirements. Some of the specific techniques I describe, though, indeed are well known and may appear in other writings. I don't feel compelled to acknowledge every possible place which may describe them too.

Finally, this book does *not debate with previous writings*. I endeavor to point out when I am presenting approaches which differ from those found in other books, but I'm not going to dwell on what the other books say, and my reasons for disagreeing should be apparent.

Thanks

This book is about getting things right and has a hearty respect for testing. So too do I have a hearty respect and gratitude for the colleagues, clients, and seminar participants who have been kind enough to test my work and provide excellent valuable feedback to help me get the ideas first, and then secondly the book, right.

I chose to solicit advance feedback from a small select group of colleagues whose opinions I value. None of them is the author of a book on requirements, because some colleague authors have suggested that any author of a related book inevitably would approach a review of this book from the standpoint that it should be the same as theirs. I'm writing this book to say something different, ideas I think need to be said. Colleagues Tom Belanger, Ross Collard, Carol Dekkers, Bob Galen, Dorothy Graham, John Lisle, Gary Mogyorodi, Rebecca Staton-Reinstein, and Linda Westfall: Thank you all for your invaluable advice. Thank you also to Tim Pitts and Tiina Ruonamaa of Artech House Books for their patience, support, and assistance.

References

[1]   Beck, K., *eXtreme Programming Explained*, Boston, MA: Addison-Wesley, 2000.

[2]   Sawhney, M., "The Problem with Solutions," *CIO*, February 15, 2003, pp. 42–44.

[3]   Lindborg, H., "The Shift to Customer Focus," *Quality Progress*, March 2003, pp. 84–85.

[4]   Phillips-Donaldson, D., "Pathos and Progress," *Quality Progress*, March 2003, p. 6.

[5]   Goldsmith, R. F., *Defining and Managing User Requirements*, Needham, MA: Go Pro Management, Inc., 2003.

[6]   Goldsmith, R. F., *21 Ways to Test Business Requirements*, Needham, MA: Go Pro Management, Inc., 2003.

[7]   Goldsmith, R. F., *Testing Early in the Life Cycle*, Needham, MA: Go Pro Management, Inc., 2003.

[8]   Goldsmith, R. F., *Managing Systems Projects with Credibility*, Needham, MA: Go Pro Management, Inc., 2003.

Value up-front

You can't make a silk purse from a sow's ear.

Defining business requirements is the most important and poorest performed part of system development.

The time-honored silk purse saying sums up why I say defining business requirements is the most important part of system development. Since some people might not be familiar with this saying, let me explain that a sow is a female pig. The saying says that what we start with sets the limits on what we'll end up with. We're not likely to produce a system that is better than what has been defined as its requirements.

Nonetheless, many of our systems projects begin with requirements that bear amazing resemblance to pigs' ears. No methods or technology that I'm aware of can turn those requirements into the system equivalent of a fine silk purse. We pay to build wrong stuff, then pay to find what's wrong, and pay again to fix it. What a brilliant business model! What's left when all the defects are removed: time, money, credibility? Certainly not the system we would have built if we'd done it right from the start.

If we're going to end up with the systems we need, for reasonable expenditure of time and resources, we've got to start with requirements that suit the result we want. Pig's ear requirements won't do in a competitive world demanding silk-purse systems.

Preaching to the choir

Everyone I've ever heard says good requirements are extremely important. Yet, on every project I've ever seen, developers, testers, and others routinely complain that they

1

waste far too much time doing wrong things and things wrong because the requirements are not adequate. They also complain that someone else has made decisions, such as shortcutting the requirements definition process, which strongly indicate that *those* people obviously don't recognize the importance of requirements.

There's a disconnect somewhere. Actions don't match words. Everyone claims to appreciate the essential importance of good requirements, but we're constantly frustrated that nobody seems to have the time, resources, or support to make sure the requirements really are good.

As individuals, we can be very aware informally of issues with the specific requirements themselves. However, our organizations usually don't detect or maintain measures that reveal the quality of the requirements process. Even those few development organizations that do monitor defect metrics seldom classify requirements errors as defects or record them in a defect tracking system. Without such measures, we can't tell the impact of poorly defining requirements or even whether we're getting any better at it. Moreover, albeit unconsciously, our organizations often employ a variety of mechanisms to rationalize the requirements attitudes and actions that result in our current situation. Consequently, we virtually assure perpetuating ineffective practices, while continuing to complain about time, cost, and quality problems due to poor requirements. We're stuck in a loop.

I assume the fact that you are reading this book means you genuinely believe requirements are important and endeavor to act in a manner consistent with such a belief. I'll also guess that you're like many of my clients and seminar participants and feel you work with some people whose actions do not seem to reflect sufficient appreciation for requirements. Whatever has been said throughout the years about requirements doesn't seem to have registered. (Some of the more cynical amongst us have suggested that some coworkers intentionally leave requirements vague so they can't be pinned down to anything. I'll not attempt attributing intent to anyone and just stick with observable behavior.) That's why this chapter is devoted to providing you, the choir of true believers, with some perhaps new ways to help get the requirements-awareness message through to the other folks.

It still may not work. While necessary, awareness alone probably won't suffice; you need to know how to identify requirements too. The following chapters describe numerous techniques that don't depend solely on awareness to get better requirements. In the long run, though, the benefits of those techniques will be lost if the organization does not also maintain meaningful measures, both from data the techniques provide and more importantly of their impact on the complete cost, time, and value of resulting systems.

Definition

Let's start by getting clear on what we mean by business requirements. In this book, we'll use this simple definition of requirements: *What must be delivered to provide value.* Figure 1.1 shows graphically how the definition relates to business requirements.

Let's discuss the Figure 1.1 diagram as it relates to the *what must be delivered to provide value* definition. Three of the definition's seven words are especially important. When I ask systems professionals in my seminars which three of the words they think are most important, participants generally agree that *value* is one of the three. I agree too. Unless something provides value, there is no reason to require it. The source of value varies depending on the type of requirement, but value is achieved by meeting an objective. The diagram shows that *business* requirements achieve value by meeting *business* objectives. Note that we're using "business" in the broad sense of purpose, as opposed to some form of legal entity or financial function. For example, relieving pain and suffering is the business of a hospital, as well as furnishing facilities, employing professional and administrative staff, and billing for services.

Often the value is expressed in money, such as increasing revenues or reducing expenses, but value also can be in terms of intangibles. However, even such a noble intangible as relieving pain and suffering ultimately may be reduced to dollars and cents, because someone has to decide whether the intangible value is worth the tangible expenditure to achieve it. Stand-up comedians continually remind us that HMOs have a reputation for putting money over care, but in fact even the most noble organization has to make very hard choices about how best to use scarce resources.

Seminar participants tend to agree much less on which are the two remaining most important words in the definition of requirements. One popular choice is *must*. *Must* connotes something mandatory, which is

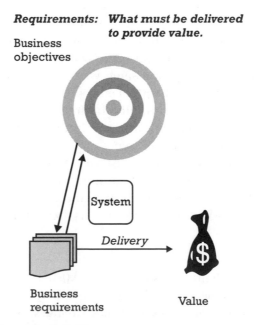

Figure 1.1 Requirements definition.

basically synonymous with "required." Yes, *must* is important, but I don't think it's nearly so important as two of the other words.

Another popular choice is *system*. This is quite understandable, since systems tend to be very important to us. After all, many of us make our livings providing systems, usually ones involving computers. Moreover, it's probably the creation or modification of a system that necessitates our trying to find out requirements. But wait, "system" isn't even in the definition. However, it is in the diagram. How come?

The system is not the essence of the business requirements. Rather, as the diagram shows, the *system* is the extraneous means for delivering (or accomplishing, meeting, or satisfying) the business requirements. Note that we're using *system* in its generic sense as a means of delivery, and not just referring to a set of computer hardware and/or software.

It's now probably pretty obvious that *delivered* must be one of the three most important words in the definition. As the diagram shows, requirements provide value only when delivered. Consequently, business requirements must be deliverable, even when their value is intangible. This situation is a common source of confusion when defining business requirements. Although the value may be intangible, the requirement itself cannot be intangible, for that would preclude the ability to deliver it.

What is the third most important word in the definition. Pardon the Abbott and Costello (Who's on first?) play on words. Requirements are *what*; design (the system for delivery) is *how*. As we can see in the diagram, business requirements are *what* is deliverable and provide *value* by contributing to accomplishing business objectives when *delivered* by the system. This *what* versus *how* distinction seems very straightforward yet in fact can be exceedingly difficult. *Hows* can seem like *whats;* and *whats* can seem like *hows*.

My perception is that one of the few points of unanimity among requirements authorities is that requirements are *what*, as opposed to *how*. Despite essentially universal citation of this distinction, people can use the same definition words, yet mean considerably different things. While seemingly defining *"what"* the same way, one person's *what* in fact may be another person's *how*. The problem comes not only from having different meanings for the same terms, but also from not realizing one's own meaning differs from how someone else may interpret the term. A key purpose of this book is to create such awareness.

The problem becomes compounded because *what* versus *how* confusion occurs at two levels of abstraction. Let me give a concrete example of the lower, more frequently recognized of the two levels. You'll quickly understand why this example is very fresh in my mind.

I'm drafting this book using Microsoft® Word 2002. To see changes to a document, I can pull down the Tools menu choice at the top of the screen and click on Track Changes. A toggle function, it turns off by clicking it again. When on, changes appear in a different color and modified text shows in marginal annotations. At first, I couldn't turn off the display of changes; but later I found a toolbar pull-down box to change display mode.

However, I couldn't figure out how to create a copy of a document that no longer contained the tracked changes. I literally hunted for hours to no avail. Help didn't help. My colleagues all told me to go to the Tools menu, then Track Changes and click Accept or Reject Changes. When I clicked Track Changes, it only toggled. My menu didn't offer Accept, Reject, or any other choices. The Help information about tracking changes didn't mention these choices or possible differences among menus, either.

Finally, just by accident, my mouse went over an icon on some toolbar I'd never noticed before and caused display of the label, Accept Changes. This turned out to be what I needed to get rid of the tracked changes. To confirm my understanding, I looked up Accept Changes in Help. After hunting a bit, I found a somewhat cryptic explanation, which told me that I first had to display the Reviewing toolbar, which I'd never heard of before, including in my reading of Help about Tracking Changes. By accident, I apparently had displayed it and also mouse-overed its icon.

I'm pretty certain that developers at Microsoft would say a Track Changes toggle, a Reviewing toolbar, a display/hide changes pull-down menu, an Accept Changes icon, and Help text were user requirements. I'll suggest those are merely *how* the design of MS Word endeavors (unsatisfactorily in my opinion) to meet my business requirement *whats*, such as having the abilities to:

- Identify, and not further identify, changes to an existing document.
- Easily and reliably learn of and use consistent and intuitive product features that meet my needs.

The *what* versus *how* distinction is often hard. As we go forward in this book, we'll examine the *what* versus *how* confusion in more detail and especially address it at the higher level of abstraction. It's common to have difficulty making the distinction, which is a fundamental source of many of our requirements problems. In turn, this book is directed largely toward helping avoid problems that commonly occur when people think *hows* are *whats*. Making *whats* explicit provides the context for delivering them with suitable system *hows*.

Throughout this book, we'll continually keep returning to the *"What must be delivered to provide value (to the business)"* definition of business requirements with more and more examples that should help make clearer the elements and their distinctions.

Requirements impact

Figure 1.2 shows how the quality of the requirements impacts the system that is developed. Please note that this diagram is *not* meant to say that all requirements should be defined before any design or that all design must be completed before programming any code. Rather, it's saying that *whatever code is implemented, of whatever size, needs to be based on a design which in turn needs to be based on requirements.*

The diagram shows that development starts by defining the requirements. Some of those are defined appropriately, and some are in error. The error could be that a requirement has been overlooked, or that something extra is included which should not be considered a requirement, or that the requirement is wrong (or likely to be interpreted incorrectly).

Some of the appropriately defined requirements are translated into an appropriate design, and some are lost in translation. Just as meaning can be lost when translating from one language to another, meaning can be lost when translating from one phase of development to another. In the diagram in Figure 1.2, we can see that some of what was defined appropriately in one phase moves into the error column when translating into the next phase's deliverables. Thus, some of the appropriate design is translated into

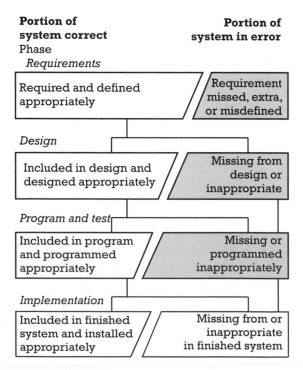

Figure 1.2   Error sources by phase.

appropriate program code, and some is lost in translation; and the slippage continues all the way through implementation.

Notice, though, that once something hits the error column, it tends to stay an error. At any given point, those involved focus mainly on their direct inputs and may have limited awareness of or access to prior-phase information. For instance, it's very unlikely that a programmer will detect a requirements error. The programmer probably has little information to even suggest that a requirement is erroneous, let alone missing.

Independent testers often are somewhat closer to the business and may be more likely to detect some possible requirements issues, but just having testers (and many organizations don't) does not assure accurate requirements. Many of my testing colleagues routinely complain of not becoming involved until the code has been written, not having suitable access to requirements or design information, and having defect reports dismissed as "coded as designed." Moreover, regardless of role (including users and developers), we all can improve greatly at both defining and testing requirements. Thus this book.

An example most people are familiar with was the Y2K problem. I'll admit right off that I was a cause of it. To save human and computer processing time and computer storage space, I and other programmers stored a year such as 1999 as 99. In view of how expensive computer capacity was at the time, even for those few who actually anticipated the century change, saving space then far outweighed some reprogramming costs decades in the future. (No, contrary to current explanations, at the time I never heard programmers express any expectation that their programs would be replaced or fixed prior to the year 2000. Y2K demonstrated that a lot of those programs were still around.)

Two-digit dates worked fine for more than 50 years of the computer age, until the century changed. Then, the year 2000 would have been stored as 00, and much of the logic in existing programs would have interpreted it incorrectly as being the year 1900 instead. Who would have expected it? The requirements obviously must have changed! Was this a programming error or a design error? Clearly it was a design error that had been programmed quite adequately. The fact that it didn't become an issue until 2000 doesn't diminish the realization that it was a design error nonetheless.

It turns out Y2K is not at all an isolated example of "correctly" programming incorrect designs. For example, I'm confident the MS Word Track Changes function was tested to make sure it met the requirements as perceived by Microsoft (the developer), but their requirements were really a high-level design that do not satisfy all my requirements.

Looking objectively at errors in software, about two-thirds are already in the design before the programmer programs it and the testers test it. Traditional software development and testing are mainly concerned with assuring that programmed code conforms to the design. As such, traditional methods are unlikely to find up to two-thirds of the errors. Moreover, guess what is the major contributor to design errors: requirements errors. They are the sow's ear and can't possibly turn into the desired silk-purse design.

I recognize that many developers and testers may protest that *they* are basing their programs and tests on the requirements as well as on the design. While undoubtedly true, at best it's only to the extent they know the requirements, and most development proceeds knowing perhaps only half the requirements, which is reflected in so much creep.

As we can see graphically in Figure 1.2, the portion of a system in error grows as we progress through development. Quality and other success factors continue to deteriorate. Although probably not our normal perception, people generally agree it's really happening once they see this diagram.

But something else must be happening too, because systems usually do get better as we proceed through development. Programs that didn't exist ultimately take form and work, though sometimes only after multiple tries. The gaps between what should be and what is keep getting narrowed. Let's look a little closer at what's happening, and what's not.

There are basically three ways (along with the method discussed in the Warning below) to narrow the quality gap depicted in Figure 1.2:

1. By far the most common way is to repeat the full requirements-through-implementation process, though usually for selected smaller pieces. That is the ordinary response to "It's not right." This is very expensive because a lot of work already must have been done to create an observable "it," programs, which then are tested to catch errors. Traditional software testing is largely testing the translation from design into program code. Too often, though, we don't find out that "it's not right" until after another translation—from programming to implementation. With each error, we zero in a bit more finely on which part is not right and then start over defining the requirements for just that part. This cycle may get repeated over and over again, each time with newly added requirements ultimately getting closer and closer to being "right." This sequence of events is classic *creep*.

2. Prevent inappropriate coding by using various testing techniques (using "testing" in the broad sense which includes reviews, static analysis and modeling, and prototyping) to reduce the loss when translating requirements into design. Such postrequirements tests are much less expensive than iterative recoding but are outside this book's focus on requirements.

3. Prevent the most waste by using more effective discovery and testing methods to get more of the requirements right in the first place. This is the most productive and economical way to get the system right, and it *is* the subject of this book.

✖ Warning

Conventional wisdom often encourages using administrative sanctions, such as user sign-offs and requirements "freezes" to prevent the gaps that cause creep. I don't think such sanctions ever work, but they do frequently infuriate the people who need the system and pay our salaries. We've got to learn to deliver value, not finger pointing; to deliver value we've got to learn what the requirements are, even though it's hard.

A related bit of conventional wisdom is that requirements keep changing and can't possibly be known up-front. Well, when we look at these changes from a different perspective, we realize that *it's really our awareness of the requirements, rather than the requirements themselves, that accounts for much of the apparent change.* That is, *we could have identified and anticipated* (perhaps not all, but) *a lot more* of what we call requirements changes than we typically do identify.

Consider Y2K. I certainly knew of organizations that continued to build systems with two-digit years into the late 1990s, long after the century change issues had become publicized. Not fixing those lurking problems until the deadline neared added considerably to the already enormous remediation expense. The Y2K requirement didn't change, it had been there all along. People just weren't aware of it. Think how much easier and cheaper it would have been for companies if they had become aware, and acted, say in 1990.

Using the methods in this book enables us to identify more of the requirements—including ones such as Y2K—correctly in the first place and to use various types of testing to detect errors that do exist in the requirements after they've been defined, so the errors can be corrected most economically before being perpetuated in incorrect designs and code.

What it's worth

Regardless of topic area (e.g., software engineering and project management, as well as requirements), practically every author cites Barry Boehm's 1981 classic *Software Engineering Economics* [1], which said that the cost of fixing an error rises by a factor of about 10 for each additional later stage at which the error is fixed. The oldest and most expensive error is a requirements error that is not found until the system is in production. Almost everyone in the industry accepts this concept intellectually, yet almost every one of them then acts as if the concept doesn't exist. I've mentioned Boehm, now I'll describe the same concept in terms that perhaps will register better with those whose actions continue to seem impervious to Boehm's revelation, even after more than 20 years.

When a programmer writes code to implement an incorrect requirement, and then the requirement error is detected and corrected, the programmer typically has at least 10 times as much work to do compared to the work needed had the requirement been corrected before it was coded. The programmer may have to throw out some of his code, write new code to implement the corrected requirement, and retest the revised program. These are all very time-consuming, labor intensive, intensely disliked activities that are intimately familiar to all programmers.

If that requirement error is not detected until after the program goes into production, implementing the corrected requirement ordinarily will take 75 to 1,000, or more times, greater effort than if the requirement had been corrected before it was coded. It takes so much more effort for a variety of reasons. The programmer who is fixing it probably is less familiar with the code, either because he is a different programmer from the one who wrote the code originally or simply because over time he's forgotten how it was written. (Many programmers have shared the experience I've encountered of fixing a program and making disparaging comments about the quality of the code, only to discover that I was fixing my own code.) Lack of familiarity makes it more difficult to figure out how to fix the code. Fixing it will take longer and be more error-prone, so several tries may be necessary, which take even more time.

Also, once a program is in production, it's likely that other things also may have to be changed. Data may exist that has to be corrected or replaced, and other programs may be affected. When a program is changed, not only must it be retested, but it probably also will need additional integration retesting to make sure it still works correctly with other programs, and regression testing is needed to assure that the fix didn't break anything else that already was working.

Then there's the cost of installing the revised program. In a mainframe environment, the revised program needs to be installed in one place, on the mainframe. In a distributed environment, the revised program must be installed in every place where the program had been installed previously.

I have a client who reports that it costs them $7 million to create and distribute a new release of their software on CD discs to all their customers. New releases are needed when requirements change, which often may be due to not identifying or anticipating them adequately. That substantial figure doesn't include the cost that their thousands of customers must incur actually loading and trying out the revised software on their own computers. *It especially doesn't take into account the potentially huge costs to a customer's business when the system fails to perform its functions.* I'd guess that my client's customers' total costs exceed my client's $7 million many times over, and each new release could cause questioning of whether they want to continue with my client.

Whether we recognize it or not, the quality of our requirements is a major determinant of the extent and frequency of such production system impacts. In my experience, few organizations have in place any measurement mechanisms that enable them routinely to see objectively the source and cost of changes. If yours does, then well done!

Frankly, my client was fortunate they knew any costs of revision. They knew the direct cost of the CDs, but so far as I'm aware, like most software organizations, they did not measure the cost of fixing the software or relate that cost to the practices that necessitated the changes. They surely didn't relate that $7 million back to requirements errors that could have been found and fixed a lot cheaper before they got implemented in code that went to thousands of clients. Consider the direct and indirect value to my client, and especially to their clients, of reducing the number and frequency of revisions, even by one! That sounds to me like a pretty high payoff for getting better at defining requirements.

If your organization does not routinely and accurately identify where errors occur and what it costs to fix them, they are not alone; nor are they very likely to realize what is happening. Problems get assigned to be fixed, but few organizations count them; fewer of them track the cost of fixing. Even rarer are organizations that tie errors back to their source and identify what those errors are costing them. If they did, they'd see the enormous number and cost of revisions that were needed because the requirements were not as accurate and complete as they could have been with a far smaller cost and effort.

Reconsidering iterative development

When I mention requirements, I commonly hear some technique touted as THE panacea, all that needs to be done. Sometimes it's sign-offs or reviews, but most often iterative development is presumed to cure all. There is no magic bullet, but iterative development—and many other practices—can be valuable.

Iterative development is a practical alternative to spending months developing a system in its entirety before checking whether the system is right or continuing to develop code after learning "it's not right." Though perhaps unfairly, the industry usually equates such inflexible, wasteful practices with the waterfall model of development.

To counteract such waste, most popular development techniques have adopted some form of iteration, whereby development is broken into smaller pieces that then can be checked sooner. If the piece of code is wrong, only a relatively small amount of effort must be redone, and overall project progress can be corrected before getting so far off track. Iteration is an effective supplement, not a substitute, for the various requirements discovery and testing methods described in this book's subsequent chapters.

Is XP an eXception?

Several reviewers have cautioned me against devoting much attention to any particular technique, such as eXtreme Programming (XP), because hot topics have a habit of cooling quickly. I agree and am not addressing agile development *per se,* but I do want to mention some of the techniques advocated by XP, which is the most prominent form of agile development.

In *eXtreme Programming eXplained* [2], Kent Beck claims that XP changes code so fast and economically that it obviates the fixing-defects-late multiplier. In fact, a major XP premise is that it's better not to add code now in anticipation of future needs, because many of those uncoded capabilities may turn out not to be needed or to be different from the way they seemed initially.

I certainly second XP's admonitions against overengineering systems and building things that hindsight shows never needed to be built. As I said in the Introduction, my purpose is to provide value for practitioners, not to engage in intellectual arguments regarding what other authors have written. That said, I think XP mostly is addressing much different parts of the story than this book is. XP focuses mainly on what can be coded in a few hours. Business needs start larger. Also, one codes from design, not requirements.

Moreover, I think even XP aficionados would acknowledge that no matter how fast one does something, and no matter how small the piece is, it still takes longer to do it twice than to do it once. Not having to do it twice provides differential time to do it right the first time. (I contend throughout this book that getting more of the requirements right before coding not only takes less time than coding but also does not necessarily take longer than traditional less effective ways to define requirements.) Unfortunately, very few organizations have suitable measures to determine the true magnitude of these effects. By virtue of their emphasis against paperwork, I'd expect that agile and XP organizations would be least likely to have any such measures.

Two other fundamental XP practices need to be mentioned which I suspect contribute more to XP's reported successes than merely making coding changes fast. These two practices involve working intimately with business people and writing tests before coding. While the amount of time spent with users does not by itself determine the adequacy of requirements, some time certainly is needed, and traditional programming development often spends far less time with users than is needed to define requirements adequately. XP's "user stories" requirements usually tie directly to pieces of code, making them more likely design than business requirements. Writing tests first is a valuable programming activity that helps clarify how the design is intended to work. This book goes further though and also emphasizes testing as a powerful requirements discovery technique.

Tying these concepts together, I'd say the agile/XP underlying rationale actually is largely consistent with the main concepts of this book. I think agile/XP advocates would find true agility is enhanced by becoming more aware of the business requirements before diving into coding, even when the coding appears to take almost no time.

Mind traps that hinder improvement

Regardless of development methodology, competent responsible management needs meaningful measures of what we're spending to do work, what we're spending to find problems, what we're spending to fix them, and how much of our original work needs to be replaced. Systems/software is essentially the only industry that doesn't routinely use such fundamental measures of what it's in business to do.

Organizations without such measures persist in such wasteful practices. They repeatedly provide inadequate time, resources, training, support, and rewards for defining requirements well. In its widely cited *CHAOS Report* [3], The Standish Group identifies insufficient user involvement as the most important factor in causing up to 84 percent of information technology (IT) projects to fail—either by being abandoned or being completed late, over budget, and/or with less than promised functionality. Let me reemphasize an important distinction that often is glossed over. *How much* time spent with users is *not* the critical element; it's *how well* the time is spent. This book concentrates on how to spend the time well.

For most organizations, suitable measures would make abundantly obvious the financial foolishness of proceeding with inadequate understanding of the business requirements. Not only do systems organizations (including those involved with both hardware and software for internal and/or external use) lack these necessary measures, but the industry has institutionalized several practices that assure we keep repeating our poor performance rather than improve it.

One example of such practices relates to enhancements. Someone makes a request for a change to a system. The request is categorized as either a fix or an enhancement. Systems professionals I encounter almost unanimously say a fix means that the technical organization has messed up, whereas enhancements generally are interpreted as a failing of the user. Who gets to categorize the requests? The technical organization does, of course, so most requests are labeled enhancements. It's only human nature for me to categorize in a way that says somebody else messed up versus a way that blames me.

Rather than the users' not knowing what they want, most of these enhancements represent our own failure to understand the requirements adequately. However, so long as calling the requests enhancements enables the technical side to avoid recognizing, let alone accepting, responsibility for knowing the requirements, the situation won't improve.

Jolting awareness

I've found a major obstacle to improvement is the common overestimation of one's own ability to identify requirements. Sometimes, though, requirements definers *are* willing to have those requirements *tested* for accuracy and completeness. They may be willing because they're confident that testing won't find any problems in their requirements. My experience is that such testing can be eye-opening about how many problems do exist.

Throughout this book, we're going to intermix requirements *discovery* methods with techniques for *testing* the adequacy of the requirements. These requirements testing techniques should be applied up-front, in conjunction with requirements definition activities. We want to find any problems with the requirements as soon as possible, when we have the greatest opportunity to correct them most quickly, economically, and easily.

Proactive Testing

The approach of intertwining testing with the various development activities is integral to the powerful methodology I call Proactive Testing™ [4, 5]. This book is not specifically about Proactive Testing, but we apply some of its concepts, so I believe a brief explanation of it will be helpful. Figure 1.3 shows the Proactive Testing Life Cycle, which depicts the various types of testing that are most appropriately performed with each of the development phases. As can be seen from the diagonally shaded testing activities, not only should we perform traditional technical testing of the developed code; but we also should test the other intermediate deliverables (such as feasibility report, business requirements, and high- and low-level system design specifications) of the development process at the times they are developed. *This book describes more than 21 ways to test that business requirements are accurate and complete before designs are based on them.*

Note that the Proactive Testing Life Cycle anticipates iteration and is in fact quite consistent with light-weight development. No particular sized piece of software is prescribed; documentation for documentation's sake is not intended and in fact is actively discouraged; and the phases don't refer to hard and fast events that should each be completed lockstep before the next starts. Rather, the phases refer to the logically different types of activities that should be performed with respect to whatever size piece of software is coded.

That is, any piece of code first should have been designed; and the design should be in service of suitable business requirements. Both requirements and designs should be tested by appropriate means to get them as correct and complete as practical, and both acceptance and technical tests of the developed code should be planned in conjunction with design. For sake of integrity and understandability, each of these artifacts should be written, but they should be written in the minimal form that supports their purpose. This book is primarily concerned with the activities involved with defining and testing the adequacy of the business requirements.

CAT-Scan Approach

In Chapter 2, we'll examine some of the more common, regular ways to test a requirements definition. Before we do, though, I want to explain the CAT-Scan Approach™, which is an important Proactive Testing concept that we'll be applying throughout this book. A CAT scan is a medical technique like an X-ray for observing things inside a person's body. Whereas an X-ray displays in two-dimensions, a CAT scan can reveal more because it essentially depicts three dimensions. Let's consider an example that highlights the important concepts.

Pretend that your shoulder hurts. You go to the doctor, who sends you to the hospital, which in turn directs you to the Radiology Department. Let's say they take an X-ray, which the radiologist examines but can find no

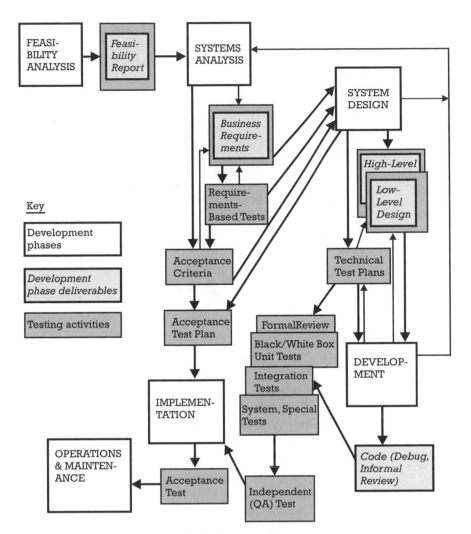

Figure 1.3 Proactive Testing Life Cycle.

reason for your shoulder pain. If they retake the X-ray, nothing will change unless there had been some mistake with the first X-ray. If they try harder, say by turning up the level of radiation, it still would not produce different results unless the first X-ray failed because the initial level was inadequate.

Two of American management's most common responses to difficulties are: "Do it again" and "Try harder." As you can tell from the example, neither of these is likely to reveal more information about your shoulder. We need a different approach to find more.

You may decide to get a CAT scan instead. A CAT scan works by taking many two-dimensional images, each from a somewhat different perspective. It can find more because each individual CAT scan image has the potential to reveal things that weren't observable from other CAT scan image angles. We use this same CAT-Scan Approach principle to improve the thoroughness of testing. That is, instead of doing the same test over and over, or just trying harder, we test from different angles. Each different test angle (which we refer to as a different testing CAT scan) offers the opportunity to reveal things that other testing CAT scan angles miss. Together, multiple CAT scans find more.

In the remainder of this book, we'll describe more than 21 ways to test that requirements are accurate and complete. You'll see that each of the 21+ ways is like a different CAT scan angle and reveals requirements problems that the other ways don't detect. The more testing CAT scan angles you use, the more problems you'll find. That's true whether we're testing developed code or requirements.

In this book, we'll highlight each different requirements-testing CAT-Scan technique with the following star symbol: ✪. While the Appendix does contain a summary list of all these testing techniques, I also encourage you to keep your own summary of the various techniques on a separate sheet of paper. In that way, you can have a convenient reminder to take with you of the 21+ ways to test requirements. I've found that such cheatsheets tend to be more useful and used when you've written them yourself, and you can include any personal notes you find helpful with regard to them.

Like trying to make a silk purse from a sow's ear, projects go awry at the start by inadequately defining requirements—*what must be delivered to provide value*. Largely due to lack of awareness and lack of appropriate measures, coupled with conventional wisdom that inadvertently can prevent awareness, organizations repeatedly underestimate the extent and impact of inadequately defined requirements. In turn, organizations don't provide suitable resources or develop necessary skills to define requirements well.

It's also our *awareness* of the requirements—rather than the requirements themselves—that mainly changes and causes creep. How we spend our time, not just the amount of time users are involved, determines how effectively requirements are defined. Proactive Testing identifies more than 21 ways to test requirements, each way being like a CAT scan angle revealing additional issues, that complement discovery methods. Chapter 2 describes the regular ways most commonly used to test requirements.

References

[1]   Boehm, B., *Software Engineering Economics*, New York: Prentice-Hall, 1981.

[2]   Beck, K., *eXtreme Programming eXplained*, Boston, MA: Addison-Wesley, 2000.

[3]   The Standish Group, "CHAOS Report," http://www.standishgroup.com/sample_research/chaos_1994_1.php, July 2003.

[4]   Goldsmith, R. F. and D. Graham, "Proactive Testing," *Software Development*, September 2002, pp. 42–45.

[5]   Goldsmith, R. F. and D. Graham, "Test-Driven Development," *Software Development*, October 2002, pp. 52–53.

CHAPTER 2

Contents

The "regular way"

Moe: I know 20 ways to test business requirements.
Joe: Well, there's the regular way...
Moe: 21 ways!

As mentioned previously, we're going to intermix requirements *discovery* and requirements *testing* techniques. We do this partly because testing often makes it easier to see more clearly requirements issues that discovery misses, and partly because I think you'll find that the tests we use also can serve as discovery methods.

That's why we're going to start by looking at the "regular way" organizations ordinarily test requirements that already have been defined and the reasons why it's frequently so difficult to test that the requirements are right. In subsequent chapters, we'll address both methods to discover the requirements and also additional (for a total of more than 21) ways to test that the requirements are accurate and complete.

Some organizations, perhaps many, essentially do not use any methods to assure that their requirements are accurate or adequate. Organizations that do not have requirements (which unfortunately seems to describe a lot of organizations), by definition do nothing to test their requirements. Others don't test their requirements for reasons such as they:

▸ Don't realize that requirements can be tested;
▸ Don't know how to test requirements;
▸ Don't feel their requirements need to be tested;
▸ Don't have time or resources to test the requirements;
▸ Thought someone else already had tested the requirements;

> ▸ Don't want to slow down the process by finding "too many problems" (I've taken a reviewer's word on this, for I've never seen such insightful candor);

> ▸ Forgot.

Organizations that do test their requirements ordinarily use one or more of the five regular ways that follow.

✪User review (test method #1)

Overwhelmingly, review by the user is the technique that organizations rely on most to test whether the requirements are right. For many, probably most, organizations, user review is the only method they use to test the requirements. Since the requirements are the user's (recognizing that we've used the term "user" broadly and collectively and may refer to more than one individual in one or more roles, any of whom may or may not physically use the system), it's pretty obvious why one would want the user to check the requirements to make sure they were right.

What's amazing is that not every project actually has its users review the requirements. For example, I once had two seminar participants who assured me that they had no users. They worked for a computer manufacturer and produced utilities, programs that performed various standard functions such as file maintenance, sorting, and reporting. Since their utility programs were included with the computer when it was sold to customers, these two developers never had any personal contact with the people who would use their software. Consequently, they didn't think they had users. By the way, their company has been sold several times since then, and the products they worked on long since have disappeared from the marketplace. Perhaps there's a connection.

Many companies that produce software for sale truly do not have contact for requirements purposes with the individuals who will be using their software. Instead, product or marketing staff presumably provide the requirements on behalf of the true end users. In such instances, the product or marketing staff typically would be the ones who perform user review of the requirements.

Ironically, even in many organizations that develop software for internal use, developers may have no familiarity with or access to the people for whom the software is being created. Forcing person-to-person interaction between developers and business people is clearly a strength of methods such as XP.

✪Management review (test method #2)

Probably the second most common regular way of testing requirements is for members of management to review the requirements. Management seems to feel entitled to approve things that are likely to require expenditures, such as a system to meet the requirements. Management may know about the affected business function and thus be able to make meaningful judgments about the requirements. Even when management is not conversant with the subject domain, it still is expected to make sure the requirements fit within the organization's strategy and plans, especially since business-area users may not be familiar with or empowered to address strategy. Similarly, management may be aware of other potentially affected parts of the organization that the system's users may not know about.

✪Supervisory review (test method #3)

Many organizations rely on analysts, or other similarly skilled professionals, to carry out the physical work of identifying requirements. These analysts typically report to a supervisor (or some such title) who is responsible for overseeing the analyst's work. Thus, the supervisor checks the requirements as a way of checking the analyst's performance. Like management, the supervisor may be familiar with the business domain and may also be aware of other affected functions. However, a supervisor may have no relevant knowledge of the specific business area. In such instances, the supervisor mainly would be in a position to review only the more general aspects of the requirements definition and the methods the analyst employed.

✪Peer review (test method #4)

Many analysts find it very helpful to get feedback on requirements from other analysts—their peers. Like their supervisor, who probably was an experienced skilled analyst himself, other analysts can offer insights regarding requirements identification techniques, and often they are familiar with the business situation under study or related business situations. A further advantage of feedback from peers is that it may be less threatening than from a supervisor.

✪QA review (test method #5)

Some organizations have an independent quality assurance (QA) function. Some of those functions include review of requirements among their responsibilities. For those functions that do, reviewing may be a major part of the job; and QA staff therefore may develop considerable specialized proficiency as reviewers. As with the other reviewer categories, QA reviewers may not have specific knowledge of the particular business area whose requirements are the subject of review, but the QA role often provides broader access to and awareness of related business areas. Often too, the QA reviews are the organization's means for enforcing standards regarding requirements, such as topics to be covered and formats to be used.

Furthermore, in contrast to the technical people whose work QA tends to review, QA ordinarily is expected to have a greater responsibility for representing the interests of the business and users.

As you can see, I'm indicating with a star ✪ and numbering each of the ways for testing whether the requirements are accurate and complete. There will be more than 21 ways. I'll encourage you to keep a separate cheatsheet list for yourself to help remember all the ways when you don't have this book with you. You should have the five regular ways on your list so far: user review, management review, supervisory review, peer review, and QA review.

✍ Exercise: Review requirements

Read the following business requirements and review them quickly. *Do not skip this. You'll need to understand this business case. We'll use its fact situation throughout the book to demonstrate the various methods for discovering and testing business requirements. You'll learn a lot more by doing the exercises with the case before reading further.*

Business Requirements

ElecTech manufactures electronic devices. The IS director recently completed a million dollar replacement of the customer information system and now has assigned Ann Analyst to identify the requirements for replacing the order entry system. Ann investigates and finds the following requirements.

ElecTech has five major product groups consisting of about 45 product lines. Each product line is based upon a separate base product, each of which has numerous options. Each base product and each option has a unique product number. The salesperson lists on the sales order the product numbers of all products in the configuration the customer is to receive.

For example, a salesperson would write an order for two *Base Product X*s and one *Product X2* (a configuration of *Base Product X* which is so common it has been assigned its own product number) in the following format (also on confirm):

Qty	Product	Description
2	#9240	*Base Product X*
2	#9241	*Base Product X*'s A/C power cord
2	#9706	*Base Product X*'s high-frequency adapter
1	#8301	Rack mount (holds up to 2 Base Products)
4	#5001	15-foot cable
1	#9250	*Base Product X2*

> 2   #5002   6-foot cable
> 1   #8301   Rack mount
>
> Salespersons submit orders to HQ order processing (O/P) either on multipart ElecTech order forms or by entering them into a PC at their district sales office. The PC performs basic editing and each night transmits the new orders to a printer in O/P. The PCs in the district offices can be switched to serve as remote terminals able to query customer information and order status in the mainframe.
>
> At HQ, an O/P customer number specialist checks, assigns, and corrects customer numbers. An O/P pricing specialist confirms prices, getting written management approvals as needed, especially for special prices pursuant to a contract with the customer or deals offered by the salesperson.
>
> After other O/P specialists have reviewed the order, an order entry (O/E) specialist enters the order into the computer. All subsequent questions and changes go through this specialist.
>
> In manufacturing, the product's manufacturing planner assigns a shipping date to the order in the computer. This triggers printing of an order confirmation for the customer. The confirmation lists all the product numbers and quantities plus the shipping date. If the order is later changed for any reason, another confirmation is printed and sent to the customer.

Analysis of the regular way

Before we examine the findings of your review of Ann Analyst's definition of requirements (in Chapter 3), let's see whether we can learn anything about how the review itself was carried out. To help us, I'm going to draw upon experiences and feedback of many business and systems professionals who have performed this review exercise in my seminars. I think you'll find a lot of similarities between their perceptions and your own. Let's start with a few key questions:

Did you know:

▸ *What to do?*

▸ *How to do it?*

▸ *How to tell if you'd done it well?*

How confident were you that you had done it well?

When seminar participants perform this exercise, they routinely acknowledge that they didn't have much idea what to do, how to do it, or how to tell whether they'd done it well. After a few minutes into the exercise, they often ask what I mean by "review." Many spend their time trying to rewrite Ann's requirements. Participants also generally report that they are not very confident that they had performed the review well, largely because of not being sure of what they were supposed to do or how to do the review.

I suspect you had similar issues. You are not alone, and I'm not just referring to carrying out this same exercise. In fact, *you have just performed a review very much in the regular way that most requirements actually are reviewed.* Users and the others who are responsible for regular way reviews generally are given the requirements to review without any idea what the review is for, what to review, or how to do the review.

By performing the exercise so you experience the regular way yourself, you may find it's more meaningful and easier to understand why this way usually is not very effective. Perhaps you also can appreciate, though, that users and others who are actually engaged in reviewing requirements the regular way seldom realize how limited in effectiveness their reviews really are. By carrying out this exercise in the manner we did, you were positioned as both a reviewer and also as an observer of the review process. Such a dual perspective enables you far more than actual users, who can see the review only from the narrow perspective of a reviewer, to become aware of some of the inadequacies of the regular way.

Why requirements are hard to test

Some of the weaknesses of the regular way are inherent to all methods of testing requirements. We've already mentioned that people often simply are not aware that requirements can be tested, or need to be tested. There's another fundamental requirements testing limitation that we also need to appreciate. To understand this weakness, first we need to understand a few basic principles of testing. Executing a test involves running the test, getting actual results, and comparing the actual results to the expected results. For the test to be useful, it is essential to define the expected results independently of actual results.

If we simply run a test and get actual results, but we have not defined expected results, we may assume that the actual results represent the correct results. That's not testing. People do it all the time, especially when they are reviewing requirements definitions (the thing being reviewed is the "actual results"); they have no way to detect problems.

What if we run the test, get actual results, and *then* figure out what the expected results are supposed to be? We are likely to fool ourselves into the same situation, except that we actually do appear to define "expected results." However, because we already know the actual results, our minds lead us to expect only results that match our actual results. People do this all the time too and fail to detect problems.

To provide a meaningful comparison, the expected results must be defined objectively, without being influenced by the actual results.

Typically, therefore, it's desirable to define the expected results before running the test. It's also very important to define the expected results correctly. *We need to know the right answer and check to determine whether the actual results in fact match the right answer.*

While these fundamental testing principles now seem obvious, it should be equally obvious that software development and especially the regular way of reviewing requirements definitions often seem oblivious to these basics of effective testing. Moreover, these principles raise a very critical difficulty that is uniquely special to the testing of requirements.

Requirements are the starting point. There is no right answer to compare actual results to. How then can we possibly define the expected right answer independent of the actual answer?

You'll see that our more than 21 ways to test requirements adopt a variety of methods for overcoming this fundamental difficulty. Many of the approaches at best have sort of an *unconscious* attention to making up for not knowing the right answer, and I'd maintain these methods generally are far less effective than their advocates often assume. We'll also describe a number of additional *more powerful methods for consciously approximating the right answer*. However, I'm the first to acknowledge that no method by itself is able to determine independently with certainty what the requirements' expected "right answer" is. The power of requirements-testing methods stems largely from our degree of confidence that the method enables us *independently to define expected results that reasonably approximate the right answer*—the real requirements.

Other weaknesses of the regular way

All things considered, the regular way usually represents a weak passive review. The review is weakened by lack of understanding about how to do the review and by its passive nature. The review is passive because ordinarily the reviewers simply respond to whatever is placed in front of them as requirements without independently ascertaining what results they expect. Although reviewers are implicitly assumed to know what the business actually does and needs, the passive review format tends to lull them into thinking that may be shaped largely by whatever is in the actual requirements they are reviewing.

While it is reasonable to expect the users to know the business, often the people doing the review don't have sufficient knowledge of the business subject-area domain. Such lack of knowledge is exceedingly likely in reviews by management, analysts and their supervisors, and QA. Without necessary knowledge of the requirements subject area, the reviewers may mainly be limited to addressing superficialities.

✖ Warning

This can be a big hidden trap for QA/testing people. Although some QA groups have classic explicit responsibility for assuring the quality of precoding deliverables such as requirements and designs, in actuality many QA groups only do testing and may only become involved late in projects, after the code has been written. For such groups, requirements often are a constant frustration. It's common for the QA/testing people not even to know the requirements, which obviously considerably diminishes the effectiveness of the testing. Additionally, these people often are frustrated by realizing how little ability they've had to help make the requirements more accurate, complete, and useful.

Consequently, those who primarily test code are usually very receptive to suggestions that they need to get involved up-front, starting with participating in requirements reviews. Such messages are exceedingly common at QA/testing training or conferences. Encouraged by such exhortations from the gurus, testers often return to work demanding greater up-front involvement.

That in itself is not bad. However, it's equally common for these people to finally get invited to requirements reviews without realizing they also need to bring along sufficient subject-area knowledge. Without such domain knowledge, they often will be restricted to dwelling on superficial issues that others don't find important. By tying up reviews with trivia, QA's presence can be perceived as nonproductive or even counterproductive. In turn, this may confirm common prior perceptions that previously had caused QA not to be involved. Thus, by demanding participation they are not prepared for, QA may lose its one bite at the apple and may not get invited back to other requirements reviews.

People from areas such as QA/testing, training, and support can contribute productively to requirements reviews, but they have to bring more to the table than just being from their respective areas. Each perspective, especially the questioning skills associated with QA/testing, can be valuable CAT scan angles for discovering requirements issues that others miss. However, without suitable subject-area expertise, contributions can be compromised and can cause early participation to backfire.

Testing one's own work

Most organizations rely primarily on users to review requirements because the users *do know* the subject area domain. In fact, in most instances, the users doing the review were the source of the requirements being reviewed. Who could be better qualified to do the review than the source of what's being reviewed? Watch out, that's a trick question that fools most organizations.

Consider the typical scenario. The analysts collect the requirements from the user and then ask the user to review the requirements. Will the user be reviewing the accuracy and completeness of the requirements? Or will the user actually be reviewing the accuracy and completeness of the analyst's ability to take dictation? It's the dictation; and such a review generally finds only trivial problems.

If the user didn't know a requirement or was mistaken about a requirement, the user's review will not be likely to identify his or her own oversight or misunderstanding. Mainly the user review will only assure that the analyst's documentation is faithful to what the user said, not that the user knew or said what really needed to be said.

Another important QA/testing principle is that people are not very effective at testing their own work. Even though they may have considerable subject-area knowledge, which is essential to effective requirements reviews, users don't know what they don't know, and their minds fill in gaps that would be readily apparent to someone else.

Consequently, the user reviews upon which most organizations primarily rely turn out often to be very weak tests of the requirements. The weakness is exacerbated because few organizations have any inkling that their reviews indeed are so weak.

Many organizations have someone independent test the developed software after the developer thinks it's right. Such independent testers routinely find problems the developer missed. The independent tester's value increases as a function of the tester's knowledge of both testing techniques and the subject area under test. In general, testing techniques that are explicit and systematic will be more effective and efficient than those that are not. The value of having a knowledgeable independent tester and systematic test guidelines/procedures is just as great when it comes to the testing of requirements.

Strengthening the review

To recap, three factors influence the effectiveness of requirements testing: (1) independence, (2) subject-area knowledge, and (3) knowing what to do and how to do it efficiently and effectively. All three are important. In fact, I'd suggest their joint value is somewhat multiplicative. That is, good procedures can dramatically enhance an independent knowledgeable reviewer's ability to detect requirements problems.

To some extent each factor can help make up for shortcomings in one of the other factors. Of the three factors, though, the most benefit would seem to come from guidelines and procedures that promote more thorough and productive problem detection. For instance, suitable review guidelines and procedures can help nonindependent users (i.e., those who were the source of requirements) find some requirements problems they otherwise would not have picked up on. Similarly, guidelines and procedures can help those with less subject-area knowledge become more productive reviewers of requirements.

Besides, it's much more likely that we can introduce such procedural aids. In contrast, we cannot really change a user who was a source of the requirements so they are able to view the requirements totally independently, and we seldom have the time and resources for all reviewers to gain sufficient relevant subject-area knowledge. Therefore, from this point on, we'll concentrate primarily on procedural guidelines and techniques that can enhance the effectiveness of any reviewer, realizing that the enhancement increases with the reviewer's relevant knowledge and independence.

We'll start with two *foundation techniques* that essentially *apply to* and enhance the effectiveness of *all the other subsequent testing techniques* we'll be describing.

✪Use formal technical review (test method #6)

A formal technical review is conducted in a systematic defined manner. Not only does the structure help prevent overlooking things, it also increases the likelihood of using methods that have been found to be more effective. Perhaps most importantly, formal technical reviews have a clear purpose: *Find as many potential problems as possible.* It's amazing how much difference simply having this clear purpose makes. Note, the reviewer's job is to find the things that could become problems. The purpose is not to make sure there will be problems, although some degree of prioritization is necessary in order to keep focused on issues that provide the greatest value.

The reviewer's purpose also is not to solve the problems. A reviewer's ability to spot the author's problems becomes compromised as soon as the reviewer becomes an author too, which is essentially what happens as soon as the reviewer decides how something should be instead. The author is responsible for deciding how to fix the problem, including deciding not to fix it; the reviewer is entitled to accept or not accept the author's solution upon rereview.

A formal technical review recognizes that reviewers must have adequate *preparation* in order to participate effectively. The reviewer must know enough about the subject area and the review procedure to spend the review time reviewing productively. The reviewer must know enough to be able to judge reliably what seems right and what seems wrong. Anything that is not understandable should be identified as a source of potential problems.

Without adequate preparation, the reviewer's efforts will be off-track and overly devoted to trying to understand the material being reviewed, rather than making informed judgments about the material. Once prepared, the reviewer should *participate* actively. Formal reviews are performed by a group, and it can be easy for a reviewer to just come along for the ride. The power of the group is a CAT scan, getting the benefit of each reviewer's separate angle of view. A reviewer who doesn't actively participate not only fails to contribute but also can give a false sense of security about how thorough the review actually was.

Furthermore, each reviewer should be held *accountable* for the quality of his or her review. When the reviewers determine that the requirements are adequate, they too, along with the author, become owners of the requirements. If problems later are detected, it is fair and reasonable to point back to the reviewers as well as to the author. Such accountability increases people's attention and provides a basis for continuously improving the reviews.

Formal technical reviews also define what to do in terms of reviewer roles. Four roles are especially important. The *moderator* is responsible for making sure the review is performed. Moderator duties include scheduling the review meetings, enlisting reviewers, providing access to preparation materials, and assuring that reports are prepared and disseminated appropriately.

The moderator may or may not be the *presenter*, the individual who physically leads the group through the materials being reviewed. Authorities on formal reviews generally agree that the author of the materials being reviewed should not be the presenter. In contrast to informal reviews, which often are presented by the author, having someone else do the presenting forces the materials to stand more on their own, without having the author's explanations to shore up weak points. Furthermore, having an independent presenter also can dramatically reduce emotionally charged arguments, hurt (review comments are a way of saying the author's "baby is ugly"), and defensiveness.

The *recorder* (or *scribe*) is responsible for capturing the review findings so they don't get forgotten. It's amazing how frequently the findings of informal reviews are lost or mistaken because nobody wrote them down in a clear reviewable manner. In order for the recorder to pay adequate attention to keeping notes, it's unwise for the recorder also to be the moderator or presenter.

The individuals in each of these roles, as well as any other participants, also all serve as *reviewers*. Organizations differ as to whether or not the author is allowed to be present. Some find that keeping the author out of the review cuts down on interpersonal problems during the review. Others find that authors make some of the best reviewers of their own work, once they are able to switch their author hat for a reviewer one.

One of the moderator's key responsibilities is ensuring that suitable reports are prepared documenting the review finding. Two reports are especially important. One report is a summary of the review and goes to management. This management report identifies what was reviewed, who reviewed it, and what the decision of the review team was. Commonly, the review team will deem the requirements as either:

› Acceptable as is;
› Acceptable provided minor corrections are made, either:
    › Relying on the author to make the changes suitably, or
    › To be approved by a subset of the review team.
› Unacceptable and requiring rereview by the full review team when fixed.

Because a review should focus on enabling the author to get the requirements right, finding a lot of potential problems is desirable. Unfortunately, such information is prone to misinterpretation. For instance, a review that finds a lot of problems can give an impression that the author did very poor work. Such misuse of review data can be extremely damaging, not just to the review but also to the author and the entire organization. Therefore, formal reviews include procedures to help prevent erroneous interpretations. Foremost among these procedures are excluding people from the review who are in supervisory capacities over the author and reporting the specific identified issues only to the author (and not including them in the management report).

Some key additional points about reviews

Formal technical reviews are by their very nature group activities. Having multiple participants interacting adds to the power. The power is increased even more when the participants represent diverse roles and experience in areas relating to and affected by the requirements' subject domain. Besides QA/testing, training, and support functions, other potential participants include auditing, operations, security, up- and downstream users of interfaced systems, suppliers, and end-customers. Not only does each participant provide a separate CAT scan angle which may detect issues that other participants' own CAT scan angles may miss, but the group develops synergies which generally cause them to find more problems together than the sum of problems they would find by themselves.

Nonetheless, *the power of formal review techniques is not limited to use by groups.* An individual's review will be strengthened considerably by having a conscious purpose to find all the potential problems, writing down the findings, concentrating on making the requirements right rather than on personalities, and accepting accountability for the quality of one's review.

Having a defined, systematic procedure for conducting the review also adds strength regardless of whether the review is carried out by a group or an individual. The two most common procedural formats for formal reviews are *walkthroughs* and *inspections.* As with so many terms, many authors use these same terms with a wide variety of different meanings. This is one of those arguments that this book doesn't need to get into. The distinction I make is that *walkthroughs are guided by the flow of what is being reviewed, whereas inspections are guided by a list of guidelines/topics to be examined.* Each approach provides a different CAT scan angle for finding problems. Many formal reviews employ both approaches simultaneously, thereby using two different CAT scans, which undoubtedly will increase the review's power to find problems.

What's most essential is that the review concentrate on what really matters. One of the biggest common weaknesses of formal reviews is that reviewers can get wrapped up in superficialities at the expense of content significance. Moderator training in facilitation and review skills can help keep meetings on track, but such training easily can fall prey to an unintended trap, due to some review proponents' overattention to review techniques *per se* with less concern about content and context significance.

That's why I'm not going beyond the above description of formal technical review procedures. I think these should suffice for most readers' purposes. I do want you to be aware of several well-recognized resources for further reference. Karl Wiegers' *Peer Reviews in Software* [1] provides a good summary of much of the writing on reviews, including the books *Software Inspection* [2] by Tom Gilb and Dorothy Graham and *Handbook of Walk-throughs, Inspections, and Technical Reviews* [3] by Daniel P. Freedman and Gerald M. Weinberg. All formal review techniques ultimately draw upon Michael Fagan's pioneering work at IBM [4] on software inspections.

✪Predefine topics, guidelines, and specifics to examine (test method #7)

I've heard that when one grows older, the first two faculties to deteriorate are the memory and something else—but I've forgotten what it is. We can aid our inherently weak memories by using checklists and templates to remind us what to look for when reviewing requirements. Moreover, once these issues are captured in some semipersistent manner, we have the opportunity to refine and enhance them based on our experience.

You may recognize that we've already alluded to this starred way to test requirements in conjunction with the prior starred technique, Use Formal Technical Reviews, where I distinguished inspections as being guided by a list of guidelines/topics to examine. So why then do I designate having a predefined template or (check)list of topics, guidelines, and specifics to examine as a separate starred way of testing requirements? There are three reasons for giving this way its own starred emphasis:

1. It's very important for all the subsequent starred ways and thus deserves to stand out separately.
2. Formal techniques can be used without a list to examine.
3. A list can be used without using formal techniques.

Testing can be a very useful complement to discovery. However, the five regular ways organizations commonly rely on to test requirements tend to be much weaker than ordinarily is recognized. Therefore, to enhance effectiveness of defining requirements, this book describes a number of additional ways to test requirements, each of which provides a different CAT scan angle to reveal issues that other tests don't spot.

Two of these additional ways are procedural foundations and apply to all the other ways. The first of these involves using formal structured review techniques, most notably having a clear purpose to find all potential problems and being sure to record one's findings. The second procedure is to guide one's review with predefined topics, guidelines, and specifics. *Each of the book's remaining starred ways to test requirements is essentially a checklist or template of topics, guidelines, or specifics to examine.* In addition to these ways that apply to testing requirements in general, some organizations also may have similar review guides that pertain to prescribed formats for requirements or to the functions that the business domain presumes particular requirements should address.

References

[1]   Wiegers, K. E., *Peer Reviews in Software,* Boston, MA: Addison-Wesley, 2002.

[2]   Gilb, T. and D. Graham, *Software Inspection,* Harlow, England: Addison-Wesley, 1993.

[3]   Freedman, D. P. and G. M. Weinberg, *Handbook of Walkthroughs, Inspections, and Technical Reviews,* New York: Dorset House, 1990.

[4]   Fagan, M. E., "Design and Code Inspections to Reduce Errors in Program Development," *IBM Systems Journal,* Vol. 15, No. 3, 1976, pp. 182–211.

Real requirements

You folks start coding.
I'll go find out what the requirements are.

You undoubtedly have seen the broadly circulated cartoon with this punch line. It's funny because for many of us it comes too close to reality. Later in this chapter we'll explore some aspects of how we can be tricked into starting coding without knowing the requirements. In later chapters, we'll get to finding out what *the* requirements are. First, we're going to concentrate on finding out what *requirements* are, and what they are not.

I know this distinction between "the requirements" and "requirements" can sound like merely a play on words, but it's not. Misunderstanding the very nature of business requirements is one of the main reasons we have difficulty correctly and completely identifying *the* specific requirements content. Unfortunately, much of the widely accepted conventional wisdom about requirements may be leading us astray.

I'll highlight some critically important distinctions from conventional wisdom about the nature of business requirements. Not appreciating these distinctions leads to many of the "not what I expected" requirements problems. *Once you're aware of these seldom-recognized distinctions, the major cause of scope and requirements creep should become more apparent and thereby much more preventable.*

Ann Analyst's definition of requirements

Chapter 2 introduced the business case that is used throughout the book to demonstrate the various concepts and techniques for discovering and testing requirements. I think you'll find that the case examples help make these concepts and techniques more concrete and consequently more meaningful.

If you haven't read the case, or if you can't remember it well, you might want to go back and reread it now before continuing with the analysis of the case that begins in the next paragraph.

When systems professionals in my seminars review Ann Analyst's definition of the case's requirements, they commonly identify issues such as the following:

- The write-up merely describes what is going on currently.
- It is not a requirements definition.
- It only documents the current system, process, or business flow.
- It describes a process rather than requirements.
- We'd have to interpret and extract the requirements from the write-up.
- It doesn't describe the "should be."
- It doesn't identify business objectives, expected benefits, or value.
- It doesn't describe a problem that needs to be addressed.
- It doesn't say what's good and bad now.
- It doesn't explain why we need to replace the order entry system.
- It should suggest other, less manual, ways to do things more efficiently.
- The write-up is not clear and would lead to misinterpretation.
- It needs to be more detailed.
- It needs to be higher level and identify functions that are needed.
- It's not a requirements document in the format we use in our organization.
- It doesn't identify the budget, time frame, or available resources.
- The write-up does not describe *whats*.
- It does describe some *hows* that limit options.
- It's not clear how the customer information system fits in.
- It doesn't identify what software would be available for order entry.
- It doesn't adequately describe a system to implement.
- The write-up needs to be sent back so it can be redone better.

I'll assume you identified many of these same issues that seminar participants commonly raise. By examining these issues systematically, perhaps we can come to a better understanding of what we mean by a requirements definition.

Let's start with the last point, that the requirements write-up is not adequate and needs to be redone. While this may be true, and often is the type of feedback from a "regular way" review, just saying something needs to be redone doesn't give any clues as to how to redo it. Reviews should provide specific information on which to base improvements. A side benefit of this book's 21+ ways to test requirements is that they do make feedback more specific and thus help guide improvements. The most fundamental and important of the 21+ tests is whether in fact they are business requirements.

✪Are they business requirements? (test method #8)

Seminar participants generally agree that Ann has not provided a definition of requirements. There's somewhat less consensus on the changes needed to make Ann's write-up a more suitable requirements definition.

Since this single "are they business requirements?" test covers a number of issues, and recognizing that some of the identified issues overlap, we'll systematically address the specific points raised above within three key subgroupings:

> "As is" versus "should be";
> Format and contents;
> *What* versus *how*.

Then we'll extend the *what* versus *how* analysis to cover the often unrecognized key distinctions between business and system requirements that get to the heart of creep.

"As is" versus "should be"

While perhaps helpful as background, merely describing the current ("as is") situation does not state sufficiently what is required. Ordinarily the impetus for defining requirements occurs when there is a problem to solve, a challenge to meet, or an opportunity to take. Requirements then mainly represent a need for a *change*, presumably *for the better*, from what is presently happening. Thus, requirements can be characterized as what "should be" in order to achieve value by suitably addressing the problem, challenge, or opportunity.

It's helpful to understand the context of why change is needed, such as what is working well, what is not, and what may be needed in addition to what we have currently. Such information helps us understand the *purposes, objectives, and desired benefits*. Note, however, that these *are not the requirements but will be achieved if the requirements are right and delivered*.

Since Ann's write-up does not specifically indicate the need for changes, one possibility would be to infer that the current system basically defines what needs to be delivered. Although a requirement to replace a system with one that's essentially identical at first seems unlikely, such projects actually are quite common, especially to employ upgraded technology. We can't tell whether Ann's objective is simply changing technology.

Assuming a straight replacement is not the intention, where might Ann's description of the current system fit? Perhaps it's not totally off-base. After all, most people embarking on requirements definition typically start with a description of what's being done currently—the present process (or system). Understanding the process helps identify where changes are needed, as well as things that should not be changed. We often do infer needs for improvement, though be careful about automatically assuming anything done manually needs to be automated, which is not always true. We need to understand the process in order to judge reliably what to change, and what not to change.

Recognize that *requirements are not just the changes*. That is, requirements are the full set, both what has changed and what has not changed, which taken together provide value when delivered. At a minimum, requirements usually need to cover whatever already is being done, which describing the current system helps us understand and evaluate.

Ann probably made a reasonable start by identifying the current "as is" process. The biggest shortcoming of Ann's definition was in not going beyond that starting point to identify what "should be" delivered in addition to or instead of what's currently done. I agree that without a "should be," Ann's write-up is not a requirements definition.

Before judging Ann too harshly, though, let's candidly put her efforts in perspective. This book is about reality. In (pardon the expression) the "real world," I'll bet you too have seen systems whose requirements are essentially equivalent to Ann's, and many systems professionals say they wish that they had requirements as good as the ones Ann wrote.

In fact, while we're being real and candid, let me guess that if you know how to program, you're probably like me and many of my seminar participants: you've already at least half programmed in your mind a computer system to replace the present order entry system described by Ann.

Ordinarily, our industry often routinely proceeds to create systems without having adequately defined requirements—and without being aware we are doing so. The outcome inevitably will be no better than what purports to be the requirements. It's truly a sow's ear when a silk purse is needed. Yet, while we may complain, nonetheless we keep doing it over and over again—and getting the same undesirable results.

We're hurt not just by poor or nonexistent requirements, but also by *lack of awareness* that we've fallen into this trap. For some reason such issues don't seem to stand out to us in our "real" projects. When we don't sense that we're in a trap, we have no way to tell how we fell into the trap or how to spot and avoid the trap in the future. It's much easier to see a trap when it happens to Ann than when it happens to us on the job, but it's more instructive when we experience the pitfall, so long as we can analyze and learn from it. Performing the case exercises enables you to both experience and observe falling into traps.

Format and contents

Business requirements should be in the language of the business. When I ask why, the most common response is "so the users can understand the requirements." This widely accepted conventional wisdom rationale has a subtle but important misorientation. Thinking in this way suggests that we already know what the requirements are but have to phrase them in terms the business people can understand. That's wrong and backwards.

Pretend for a minute that we're defining requirements for a company in a foreign country whose native language is not the one you speak. The requirements should be in that country's language—*because the requirements are theirs and should be in their language.* Obviously the burden is on the foreigner to understand that country's language, not the other way around. Similarly, requirements also should be in the language of the business, because they are the requirements of the business. *It's the job of those of us on the development side to learn the business language.* It is *not* the business' responsibility to translate their requirements into our language. While their assistance can be greatly appreciated, very often business people's efforts to translate into the language of developers fall short and are blamed for the requirements not being clear.

Requirements need to be clear, or they will be subject to misinterpretation. To be fair, clarity is a matter of degree. Perfect requirements clarity is unlikely, because natural languages are not perfectly clear, and requirements need to be in the natural language of the business. Therefore, *clarity means reasonable likelihood of common interpretation by people with reasonable familiarity with the topic.* The more critical the application, the clearer and more precise requirements need to be.

Many organizations have prescribed formats in which requirements must be written. If your organization prescribes such a format, I'm certainly not going to tell you not to use it. On the other hand, to the best of my knowledge, there is no single divinely specified format for documenting requirements. In other words, the format does not in and of itself determine whether something really is a requirement.

Interestingly, Ann's write-up was criticized for not being sufficiently detailed and also for being too detailed. In fact, requirements can be defined at varying levels of detail. It's easiest to think of requirements as forming a hierarchy, like an outline. High-level requirements are rendered more specific by breaking them down into lower levels of detail. Detailed requirements can be summarized or consolidated into higher levels.

It's also common for people to think that project variables, such as budgets and deadlines, are the business requirements. Budgets are not requirements, since just spending the budgeted amount provides no value. However, a budget is a *constraint* on the requirements and therefore *needs to be captured in conjunction with the requirements.* Effective project budgets are based on the value expected from meeting the requirements. Projects frequently fail when budgets are set (typically arbitrarily) based on external factors without regard to (and often before adequately defining) the requirements and the value of meeting them.

Deadlines are a constraint too but also may be requirements, since *when* the requirements are delivered may affect their value. Unlike budgets, external factors frequently are very relevant for setting deadlines. For example, Y2K changes really did need to be completed before the new century arrived.

What versus *how*

Remember, we defined requirements as, "what must be delivered to provide value." We also emphasized that requirements are *what*, whereas designs are *how*. It's common to think the user's job is to provide "requirements that the programmer can code from." However, *programmers code from designs, not from requirements.* Over the years, users may have been "trained" that they need to speak in terms programmers can implement, if they're going to have any success communicating with the technical side. However, users seldom have either the knowledge or skill to be specifying designs, and it's not their job.

Examples of items in a design include screen and report layouts, reference to internal variables, and identification of existing software to implement. While these sometimes may be constraints, and thereby should be included with requirements, I think all requirements authorities would agree that a description which mainly consists of such items usually is depicting *how* rather than *what*. Ann's write-up did not define these types of design, which are what we characterized in Chapter 1 as the *what* versus *how* distinction's lower level of abstraction.

Business versus system requirements

The higher level of abstraction is where the *what* versus *how* distinction has the most impact, because *what most people call requirements almost always actually refers to hows; conventional thinking is essentially unaware it's happening.* Consequently, *much of the conventional well-intentioned effort to define requirements falls short because people are defining high-level design rather than the real requirements.*

The real requirements are the *whats* of the people who have some business purpose to accomplish and provide value when delivered. Since system users are a major category of people with business purposes, these often are called "user requirements." However, nonusers also can be sources, so we're going to use the somewhat more inclusive term *business requirements* to refer to these, *the real requirements.*

Note: I realize that some specific groups (such as US military contractors) tend to put great stock in using the term "system requirements" only for requirements that will be implemented at least partially in hardware, whereas the term "software requirements" denotes those requirements that will be allocated to implementation in software.

For purposes of this book, such "system" versus "software" distinctions are irrelevant. They reflect design *hows*, not business *whats*. For simplicity I'm going to use the single term "system requirements" in a broad manner to include what many people call by other terms, most commonly "software requirements" and/or "functional specifications."

In contrast, most uses of the term "requirements" actually refer to *hows*, albeit at the higher level of abstraction and unconsciously. I'll refer to this other usage as *system requirements*.

We'll focus on the really important distinction between business requirements and system requirements, which is the major reason for "requirements creep." This seldom-recognized distinction also is at the heart of why users don't always seem interested in working with technical people to identify requirements. Quite simply, *the requirements that interest technical people are not the same—literally or figuratively—as the requirements that should interest the business people.* Table 3.1 contrasts the key differences between these two important, different uses of the same term "requirements."

Business requirements state conceptually in business language *what* business results must be *delivered* to provide *value*. The requirements must be the business' (which often are identified with respect to the business needs of users and thus may be considered synonymous with user requirements). Only business requirements, when delivered, provide value by meeting business objectives. Business requirements exist already within the business environment, but may not be evident and therefore need to be captured or discovered. There could be many different ways to deliver (or meet, or satisfy) the business requirements.

System requirements describe the *high-level design of a product*, which is *one* of the possible ways presumably to deliver the business requirements (regardless of whether the business requirements have been articulated).

Table 3.1 Business Versus System Requirements

Business Requirements	System Requirements
Business/user view/language	Product/operational view/language
Conceptual	Concrete, high-level product design
What business results must be delivered to provide value by meeting business objectives (problem, opportunity, challenge)	How the product must function (from an external perspective) to work as designed and presumably deliver desired business results
Exist already within the business	Specified by someone
Many possible ways to meet them	One of the possible ways to meet the (albeit often unarticulated) business requirements

The product can work as designed but provides value only if it actually does meet business requirements. When the product consists of computer software, these often are referred to as software requirements. Because these requirements ordinarily focus upon the external view of how the product must function to work in its intended manner, they are also often called "functional requirements" or "functional specifications." (*Note:* "specification" denotes design, not requirements/need.)

It should be clear that:
- Business requirements and system requirements are not the same.
- System requirements are relevant only when they meet business requirements.
- Projects seldom are adequately aware of, let alone articulate, business requirements.
- Most projects have only (high-level product design) system requirements, and aren't aware that's all they have.
- *Projects are unsatisfactory and "requirements creep" when the system requirements don't meet the real, business requirements.*

I think you will find that most of the books and articles written on requirements refer mainly to what I am calling system requirements, which as we've said subsumes software requirements. For example, "Software Requirements" is the title of the pertinent section in the proposed *Software Engineering Body of Knowledge* (*SWEBOK*), which is close to release by the IEEE [1]. Probably the biggest selling recent book on the topic is by colleague Karl Wiegers; and its emphasis is clear from the book's title, *Software Requirements* [2]. Another prominent recent book by other colleagues, Suzanne and James Robertson, doesn't include the word "software" in its title but gives this definition: "The requirements are a complete description of the product" [3].

I cite these leading examples, not to argue, but to show that in the industry the term "requirements" commonly refers to system requirements as we're using the term, whereas *this book indeed is addressing something qualitatively different*—business requirements.

Automated teller machine example

Many requirements authorities seem to use an automated teller machine (ATM) example. Table 3.2 lists a number of functions that I've heard fellow authors and speakers describe as an ATM's business or user requirements. For this type of example, details are omitted, such as the business rules determining how much cash to issue. I think you'd agree these indeed describe an ATM's typical business or user requirements.

Then what is Table 3.3 describing?

Comparing the tables, it should become apparent that meeting the requirements in Table 3.2 will not provide value unless they in turn satisfy

Table 3.2   Typical ATM Requirements

Require customer to insert card.
Read encrypted card number and ID data from magnetic stripe.
Require customer to enter PIN (personal identification number).
Match entered PIN to calculated PIN or PIN on file.
Accept envelopes containing deposits or payments.
Dispense cash in multiples of $10.
Display selected account balances.
Transfer indicated amounts between customer's designated accounts.
Issue printed receipts.
Return customer's card.

Table 3.3   Another Set of ATM Requirements

Provide secure, confidential access to banking services at time and location convenient to customer.
Confirm identity of customer.
Enable customer to perform ordinary bank transactions himself/herself quickly and accurately.
Provide customer documented evidence of the transactions.

the Table 3.3 *business requirements—the real requirements that provide value when met*. In contrast, Table 3.2 actually is describing *system requirements* of one product, which is one of several possible products that presumably could meet the business requirements in Table 3.3. Although at a higher level of abstraction than people ordinarily think of as design, a product design such as in Table 3.2 is a *how* to deliver the Table 3.3 *whats*.

It may be hard to see the difference. After all, if users say they need the ATM described in Table 3.2, then those would seem to be the user's or business requirements. Yet, many of us have had the common frustrating experience of delivering a product that functions exactly as the user has described, such as in Table 3.2, only to have the user then declare the delivered product "is not right" or is "not what I expected."

Many authors attribute the discrepancy to lack of clarity. Consequently, they tend to concentrate on making sure the requirements are written, reviewed for clarity, and then signed off by the users. Such efforts do reduce the chances for misunderstanding, and I encourage them. Chapter 4 describes a number of ways to check clarity. While necessary, though, clarity alone is not sufficient to prevent the "not what I expected" response.

A product can function exactly as described in perfectly clear and reasonable-sounding system requirements, like those in Table 3.2, yet still not provide value because it does not meet the real, business requirements, such as in Table 3.3. *Almost always the mismatch occurs, not because the system requirements were unclear, but because the business requirements were not defined adequately, or usually not at all.* At best, the business requirements may have been assumed, which can easily lead to problems when different people's assumptions don't really coincide.

Both types of requirements are important, but *the business requirements are more important, and we need them explicitly and first.* The business requirements are the measure of whether the product's system requirements are on target to deliver value. When business requirements have not been defined explicitly, it's worse than trying to hit a moving target. It's more like trying to hit an imaginary target. Unfortunately, neither business nor technical people tend to be sufficiently aware that they need both types.

Since it still may be difficult to comprehend this important distinction, let's consider some ATM examples that highlight it. Suppose after signing off on the ATM described in Table 3.2, the user then decided to use biometrics to identify the account holder. If I can be identified positively by an eye scan, I don't need to have a PIN or even a plastic card with a magnetic stripe or smart chip on it. Supporting biometrics identification would necessitate changing the requirements in Table 3.2.

To many people, this typical example would be considered clear evidence of requirements creep. They might attribute the change to "users not knowing what they want" and probably would further contend that such requirements changes are inevitable.

I'd say instead that this example demonstrates that the *real requirements don't change nearly so frequently as our awareness of them changes.* Biometrics don't change the business requirements described in Table 3.3. Most of the time, we become more aware of real requirements only when system requirements turn out to be inadequate. *By learning to better identify the real, business requirements, we can dramatically reduce the requirements creep that many people think is inevitable.*

Let's take another example. Suppose after we've implemented the ATM the users decide the system also should allow customers to submit loan applications. That certainly seems like a change of requirements. Again, though, this apparent requirements change is already covered in the Table 3.3 business requirements, even though the Table 3.2 product system requirements would indeed need to change in order to address loans.

Level of detail

Widely held (but mistaken) systems industry definition:
Business requirements are high-level and lacking in specificity. They decompose into system requirements, which are where the detail is.

Several common myths help to perpetuate creep by contributing to misunderstanding the business versus system requirements distinction. One of the most prevalent conventional wisdom myths is stated above and is shown graphically in Figure 3.1. This widely accepted definition is especially troublesome because it provides well-intentioned people with false assurance that they *have defined* business requirements.

The view that level of detail distinguishes business requirements from system requirements is easy to understand and fits comfortably within a mindset that concentrates on the product to build. While certainly typical of those who do the building, all humans seem naturally to gravitate to the implementable solution details.

By the way, some people in the industry describe similar distinctions based on level of detail but call the pieces by different names. For example, the IEEE's proposed Software Engineering Body of Knowledge and its related standards generally don't use the term "business requirements." Instead, SWEBOK refers to a "problem of the real world" [4], and then only briefly in passing. Mainly, though, it embraces IEEE Std. 1362-1998 [5], which concentrates on high-level "system requirements" in a Concept of Operations document, which is clearly describing a product-type solution, from the external perspective of a user. In turn, IEEE Std. 830-1998 [6] describes allocation of the high-level "system requirements" to a detailed software requirements specification.

Quite simply, *the difference between business and system requirements is not a matter of detail*. The difference is qualitative: *what* versus *how*. That is not equivalent to high-level versus detailed, which is more of a quantitative difference. When people act as if it were only a matter of detail, they are going to end up with detailed system requirements that are wrong and incomplete. The difficulty is that at a high-level view, it's less apparent that *product system requirements actually are a design how*.

Moreover, *product design is not simply the decomposition of business requirements*. It involves describing something separate, not the business requirements but something able to satisfy them. The only possible way to go directly from high-level business requirements to detailed product design

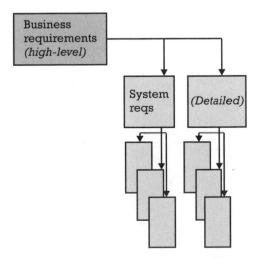

Figure 3.1 Common view of business-system requirements relationship.

system requirements is to guess and inevitably to leave things out. That's why we get so much requirements creep, and it's not necessary.

The key to avoiding creep is to define the real, business requirements in detail too, as shown in Figure 3.2. When defined in detail, business requirements usually map very straightforwardly to system requirements for a product that meets the business requirements. When such mapping occurs at both high and detailed levels, it dramatically reduces chances for systems requirements that don't meet the real requirements.

I strongly suspect that skilled requirements definers, such as many speakers and authors on the subject, actually already do break business requirements into detail and then map them to detailed product system requirements, but they do it unconsciously and implicitly. When such experts try to describe their techniques to others, they tend to leave out this essential intermediate thought process, because they're not consciously aware of it. In this book, we're making those thought process steps explicit and conscious, which in turn makes them more reliable, repeatable, and thorough.

Here's the paradox. When we define detailed business requirements first, and then map them to detailed system requirements, the two sets often will appear very much alike. That overlap makes the mapping quicker and easier, truly reducing the amount of extra effort seemingly involved in defining both types of requirements. The risk is that the overlap could cause us to discount the distinction and fall into the trap of assuming the system requirements of the product we intend to build must also therefore be the business' requirements. Saving time by going directly to the system requirements is likely to turn out taking more time, because they won't meet the real business requirements. Only by keeping a conscious separation, first defining business and then system requirements, can we tell reliably when it is, and is not, appropriate for them to be the same.

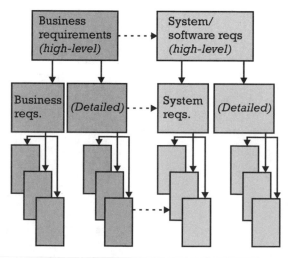

Figure 3.2   Key to avoiding requirements creep.

By developing proficiency at identifying the business requirements detail, we are much more likely to spot otherwise-overlooked requirements, such as for biometrics. Traditionally, we don't realize we've overlooked such requirements. Instead, when we do become aware of them, they seem like changes to the requirements. For instance, when we drive the high-level "confirm identity of customer" business requirement down to its component business requirement detail, we are much more likely to anticipate biometrics and other business requirements that a product design focus would be likely to overlook.

A few more mythical distinctions

The mistaken premise that business requirements are only high-level also leads to the assumption that business requirements are not an issue for small changes. Perhaps you are familiar with the typical request to just "change this field" or "add a column." Many of us have made such prescribed changes only to be told it's still not what is needed. Fields and columns clearly are detailed designs, not even system requirements, and especially not business requirements. The apparently simple change turns out to be inappropriate because it was presumed to solve an inadequately identified business requirement. *Find the business value to be accomplished, and the design follows more reliably the first try.*

Similarly, there is a common assumption that managers by definition know the business and whatever a manager prescribes therefore must be a business requirement. Managers are just as likely as nonmanagers to fall into the trap of confusing system and business requirements. Many people who hear this seem to think erroneously that I'm advising you to tell your managers they don't know what they're talking about. I am *not* saying that. It may or may not be true, but it's sure not a politically savvy message to give.

Let me emphasize.

Just because a manager declares something to be a business requirement doesn't mean it really is. You need to check and confirm that it really is, rather than just accepting on face value that the source makes it a business requirement.

I suggest playing Columbo. Just as Detective Columbo essentially disarms the guilty by seeming thick-headed, you can avoid confrontation by appearing to be the stupid one who's not smart enough to understand the requirements. Ask the smart manager to help your poor feeble brain be sure you understand what the expected value is, so you will be able to deliver it. In the process, ask suitable questions to make sure it indeed is what must be delivered to provide value.

It's amazing how often the act of explaining the value to someone else helps managers recognize their real requirements, which often may be different from what they seemed initially.

One other common myth is that business requirements are not an issue when buying packaged software. When you buy a package, you actually are buying the system requirements inherent in the package's (product) design, along with implementation of that product. *The main reason software acquisitions so frequently encounter difficulties is due to the buyer's failure to identify his or her business requirements that the vendor must meet.*

Who defines the requirements?

Now that we've identified what business requirements are, we need to examine who should be involved to identify the requirements content. Conventional wisdom, as exemplified by authorities such as the Standish Group in their *CHAOS Report* [7], cite the *quantity* of user involvement as a key determinant in project success. While quantity indeed is important, the *quality* of such user involvement is more important. Of course, spending some minimum amount of time is necessary to identify requirements, but *simply spending more time applying ineffective practices is unlikely to produce appreciably better results.* It's not just employing suitable discovery techniques, but how they're carried out that also often significantly impacts the quality of user involvement.

For instance, for many projects like Ann's that will involve computers, the technical organization ordinarily is responsible for defining the requirements. This responsibility also presents some potential pitfalls. While not always, technical people's attitudes and approaches frequently interfere with defining business requirements adequately.

(By the way, I'm not attributing any behaviors to technical people that I haven't done personally in more than 35 years as a developer. The fact that these experiences are common doesn't make them any more desirable. Becoming more conscious of these ineffective requirements behaviors helps make one less prone to employing them.)

Part of the difficulty stems from problems communicating with users. Technical people can seem arrogant and intimidating, which can suppress user cooperation. Technical and business people truly do seem sometimes to speak different languages. Moreover, the technical people often are not interested in hearing about the business. Instead they want to talk about things that interest them, especially specifications that can be programmed.

Over the years, users in general have been trained that they may need to "talk techie" to be listened to at all. Of course, when the nontechnical users try to translate their information into technical terms, they often say something that's technologically unsound or even foolish, which further reinforces the stereotyped perception that the users don't know what they're talking about. (I've certainly heard many technical folks privately snicker and say that "dumb user" is redundant.) Consequently, talking with the users can seem to the technical types to be a waste of time, which indeed does diminish the value of talking.

But that's only part of the problem. Consciously or unconsciously, requirements definers often believe that they "already know what is required." Thinking they already know the requirements means (to them) that they don't even have to make a pretense of exerting additional effort to find out what the users think is required. They can just start coding. Moreover, many managers—from both the technical and business sides—assume that requirements are obvious and take only an hour or two to define anyway. Thus, even if the technical folks do talk to the users, they may not put much effort or thought into it.

These technical side rationales for skipping all that annoying involvement with the users are further reinforced by the technical world's widely accepted notion that, "Users don't know what they want." If the users don't know what they want, why bother wasting time asking them? Of course, *it does make sense not to spend time talking with people who truly don't know what they want. Ironically, users often apply the same type of reasoning in reverse by being too busy to spend time with the technical folks.*

Consider the term "user." Think of one of your key users. Let's call her Ursula. Perhaps Ursula is attending a family gathering where a great aunt asks what she does for a living. Do you think Ursula would describe her work as being a "user" of your systems; or might she more likely say she's a surgeon, shipbuilder, or salesperson?

"User" reflects a demeaning view (and only the drug industry also has "users"). It makes the technical people important, and makes secondary all the people who do whatever the organization is in business to do. Even when unconscious, this mindset can make it easier to dismiss users' views and send such messages in tone and body language without being aware of doing it. If I were Ursula, I'd be "too busy" too to subject myself to situations where technical folks say outright or between the lines that I'm inferior.

Many organizations have tried to foster suitable appreciation of the business people by mandating the term "customer" instead of "user." The premise is that customers pay the bill and "are always right." The intention is good. In practice though, I haven't seen it change much behavior. Calling someone a "customer" to their face doesn't accomplish much when one still thinks of them as a user. In fact, it can cause our more-believed and often unconscious nonverbal messages to conflict with intended display of respect.

Thus, technical people often do not sufficiently understand the business or in turn the requirements; they also seldom seem to realize they don't understand, or at least not enough to stop them from charging ahead with costly inappropriate development based on inadequate requirements. That's why the cartoon punch line sounds familiar.

Make users responsible

Recognizing the technical organization's limitations in discovering requirements, many organizations have adopted an opposite approach. Predicated on the requirements being the business' (or user's), these organizations make the business/user responsible for defining what they require. It may be reasonable, but it also has its pitfalls.

Let's say Ursula is a shipbuilder, and a very accomplished one at that. She has studied shipbuilding, practiced it extensively, refined and expanded her shipbuilding skills, and repeatedly been rewarded for excellent shipbuilding. Although Ursula may know shipbuilding, it does not mean she is equally proficient knowing how to analyze and define requirements for systems to support shipbuilding. While understanding the business subject area is necessary for defining requirements, domain knowledge alone is not sufficient for defining requirements well. Defining requirements also takes specialized skill in analyzing and organizing. User backgrounds, reward structures, and training are less likely to develop the types of analytical skills needed for defining requirements.

Requirements involve identifying problems and what would constitute improvement. It's extremely difficult for someone to identify problems in things that are very close to them. For instance, perhaps you have a child and have attended a recital or play in which the child performed. Chances are you thought your child was ready for Broadway, but the other kids seemed just dreadful. Chances are too that the parents on either side of you felt the same way—but about their little darlings. This very human limitation also affects users trying to define their requirements. It's hard for users to step back and view their situation objectively. Similarly, it's hard for them to conceive how something they are intimately familiar with could be done differently.

So, if technical people are not good at understanding the business sufficiently to define requirements by themselves, and users lack the objectivity and analytical skills to be good at it by themselves either, what's the answer? We need both. We need the business people to supply the business understanding, and we need the technical people to provide analytical skills and objectivity needed to see problems and solution alternatives.

Perhaps in recognition of this need for both roles, many organizations put responsibility for defining requirements on some sort of hybrid liaison role. The designated liaison often may be a business analyst or a product/marketing person, usually someone with greater subject area understanding than technical people and more analytical skills than users.

The trap liaisons typically get pushed into is due to an assumption that the liaison already knows the requirements. In fact, liaisons seldom do know the full story because they are one step removed from being real users. However, when a liaison is presumed to know the requirements already, they seldom are given sufficient time to find out from others what the requirements are. Liaisons still need time to draw upon sources of greater knowledge, and they may also need analytical assistance.

Three necessary elements

Thus, the first essential element for effectively defining requirements is *bringing together sufficient business knowledge with analytical skill and objectivity.*

Ordinarily this will necessitate discovery, not simply relying on a single individual to know everything already. However, while necessary, it is not sufficient merely to bring these sources of knowledge together with the requisite analytical skills. After all, business and technical people have worked together on many projects that still failed to define requirements adequately.

Two other elements have to be in the equation in order to end up appreciably better than we have been doing with regard to requirements. The next of these elements involves the attitudinal environment in which the knowledgeable interact with the analytical. *The technical people have to develop and communicate a sincere appreciation for the business and business people.* Systems are there to support the business, not the other way around. Without the business, systems aren't needed.

Constructively coupling business knowledge with analytical skill makes a giant leap beyond where many organizations currently are with requirements. It's still not enough. The leap has to be in the right direction. They have to *recognize the separate existence of and identify the real, business requirements.*

How much is enough?

There's a trade-off between time spent defining requirements and time spent implementing systems and software. As in the legendary cartoon punch line mentioned at the beginning of this chapter, many technical people, and many managers, are very impatient to get to the "real work," the coding. In most instances, that's a false economy based upon the absence of necessary measures that reveal what's really happening, and its full costs.

The story of course has other sides as well. "Analysis paralysis" can take hold where the project never moves from requirements definition to implementation. Remember, requirements provide value only when delivered. With analysis paralysis, nothing is delivered. Our focus in this book is on moving quickly to delivery, but we need to do so in a manner that is based upon the real requirements.

The emphasis on moving quickly creates a middle ground where most projects probably are. It's also a place with a few traps which suitable understanding can help us avoid. This middle ground is influenced by the realization that it's hard to get requirements right and that requirements changes are very prevalent.

Many developers simply accept as a given that it's impossible to know requirements up-front and embrace methodologies that incorporate this assumption. This line of reasoning says that *surely it's a waste of time to spend time defining requirements that just end up changing.* I would suggest such logic cannot help but become *a self-fulfilling prophecy.*

While developers readily recognize the leap-into-code foolishness of the old cartoon, that's essentially what the don't-waste-time-defining-requirements methods as usually practiced often rationalize. Developers mainly start by coding what they think is needed, albeit in abbreviated form, and then back their way into the requirements by repeatedly reviewing and revising their code. When called "iterative development" or some similar term, it's conventionally considered a brilliant strategy, rather than merely a way to get coding before knowing what is required.

Always charging off into coding on the assumption that it's impossible to define requirements well merely assures that project teams don't define requirements well—and never learn how to. Such methods actually continually prove that *they* don't know how to define the real requirements, not that the real requirements can't be known.

In my experience, iterative development is far more productive and satisfying when it begins with identifying the real requirements. I've found that *defining real requirements well not only takes no longer overall to create systems, it actually takes much less time than the illusory iterating based on system requirements alone*. The key is a different form of iteration, starting with more complete understanding of the real business requirements at a high level to set direction reliably. Then, drive the business requirements selectively down to detail and map them to product system requirements.

Approaches which bypass such fundamental stage-setting are destined to run into trouble. While he doesn't speak specifically of the real requirements we're describing, widely recognized iterative development advocate Steve McConnell in his classic book *Rapid Development* comes down strongly on the side of getting clear on overall project direction. This I would maintain depends mainly on understanding the real, business requirements "should be" *whats*, before becoming absorbed in iterating product system requirements *hows* [8].

In subsequent chapters, we identify additional ways to discover and test that the real business requirements are accurate and complete. We'll see how to do this to a far greater degree than most projects are accustomed to—iterating appropriately so we deliver value quickly and don't fall prey to analysis paralysis.

References

[1]   IEEE, "Chapter 2: Software Requirements" in *SWEBOK* (Software Engineering Body of Knowledge), Trial Version 1.00 (http://www.swebok.org, under "Reviewer Working Area Trial Version 1.0)," May 2001.

[2]   Wiegers, K., *Software Requirements*, Redmond, WA: Microsoft Press, 1999.

[3]   Robertson, S. and J. Robertson, *Mastering the Requirements Process*, Harlow, England: Addison-Wesley, 1999, p. 2.

[4]   IEEE, "Chapter 2: Software Requirements" in *SWEBOK* (Software Engineering Body of Knowledge), Trial Version 1.00 (http://www.swebok.org under "Reviewer Working Area Trial Version 1.0)," May 2001, p. 10.

[5]   IEEE, *Guide for Information Technology—System Definition—Concept of Operations Document*, IEEE Std. 1632–1998, March 1998.

[6]   IEEE, *IEEE Recommended Practice for Software Requirements Specifications*, IEEE Std. 830-1998, June 1998.

[7]   Standish Group, The, *CHAOS Report*, http://www.standishgroup.com/sample_ research/chaos_1994_1.php, July 2003.

[8]   McConnell, S., *Rapid Development*, Redmond, WA: Microsoft Press, 1996.

Evaluating requirements form

If it looks like a duck, walks like a duck, and quacks like a duck, it's probably a duck.

By far, issues of *form* ordinarily garner the greatest amount of attention with regard to evaluating the adequacy of requirements. Just as we'd identify a duck based on the presence of key distinctive externally observable aquatic fowl features, so too do we check that the form of requirements consists of an appropriate set of characteristics. Some features of requirements indeed are as externally evident as feathers, a bill, and webbed feet, but most take greater effort to ascertain.

In Chapter 2, we introduced two procedural techniques that apply to all subsequent ways to test requirements:

▸ Use a formal or structured review with a clear purpose to find all potential errors.

▸ Follow predefined topics, guidelines, and checklists of specific issues to look for.

This chapter describes a number of matters related to requirements form that can serve as topics, guidelines, and specifics to test requirements, in either formal or informal, group or individual, review contexts. We'll apply each technique to evaluate a concrete example of a typical requirements definition: Ann Analyst's description of the order entry system requirements.

Many experienced industry practitioners, like those who participate in my seminars, tend to focus first on the failure of Ann's document to follow a specified physical format, such as the structure or template that their organization may prescribe. We're not going to address such organization-specific conventions because there is no way to predict them, and what's true for one organization probably would be irrelevant to others. If your organization does prescribe particular formats, of course it is appropriate to check that the requirements conform to the specified format.

✪ Clarity (test method #9)

Once we get past organization-specified formats, the aspect of form which most often concerns people is whether or not the requirements are stated clearly.

A requirement that is unclear is likely to be misunderstood and therefore be addressed inappropriately. Actions based on such misunderstandings typically end up failing to provide expected value. The time and effort spent on them may necessitate significant additional time and effort for corrective rework. Moreover, misguided efforts also may exhaust the time and resources available (and possibly motivation and morale too), so that needed corrections in fact are not accomplished.

Undoubtedly the most obvious and common way to test clarity is simply asking users, managers, and colleagues whether a requirement seems clear. Merely asking is a good start, but while necessary, usually is not going to be sufficient by itself to assure clarity.

For instance, when we apply this test to Ann Analyst's definition of requirements, some reviewers might say the requirements indeed are clear, although most probably would say they are not clear. However, such a blanket judgment by itself would do little to help know how to make the requirements clearer. For meaningful identification of suitable improvements, more specific information is needed concerning the reasons for concluding that the requirements are not sufficiently clear.

Therefore, to enable going beyond a simplistic clear/not clear judgment, this chapter also delineates a number of additional more focused ways to test specific attributes that determine whether the requirements are clear. First, though, we'll explore several related issues that affect all of the ways we address the overall topic of clarity.

Form versus content

Note that we refer to these clarity-related techniques as addressing *form* because they do not assure that the requirement *content* is correct. It is quite possible that a requirement could be clear and satisfy all the tests in this chapter, yet still be incorrect. For instance, suppose our automated teller machine example had the following additional requirement, which I'd contend is both clear and yet (at least for any bank I'd want to do business with) incorrect:

> For each withdrawal, charge the customer's account a service fee equal to twice the amount of the withdrawal.

The good news is that there is wide recognition of many of the attributes of requirements form discussed in this chapter. Indeed, my perception is that much of the requirements literature deals mainly with the issues of form addressed in this chapter; although I don't recall any other sources characterizing their treatments as dealing with form rather than content. Regardless, though, many of the points may sound familiar, which I'd maintain is valuable for reinforcement. I'll also caution about a few pitfalls and present some important distinctions from the common, conventional treatments.

For instance, I've just mentioned one potential pitfall is that an incorrect requirement can pass muster with respect to form. A related pitfall is that over-relying on form can give a false sense of security about the adequacy of the requirements. At the same time, human fallibility tends to offer up a virtually limitless quantity of form issues. Consequently, checking the form of requirements can become never ending. Thus, testing form is exceedingly subject to being overdone, discounted as trivial nitpicking, and rapidly yielding diminishing returns. More importantly, an overemphasis on form often diverts from other even more important issues, such as correctness.

Two quick distinctions

Here are two distinctions between the treatment of requirements form in this book and what you may encounter in the rest of the literature. The first may appear mainly semantic but merits acknowledgment if only to remind us of the somewhat unusual way I've structured the presentation in this book. Most of the other authors describe a number of the topics in this chapter from the standpoint of *defining* requirements, whereas we're describing them as ways for *testing* the requirements.

Every one of the techniques this book depicts as ways to test requirements also can be turned around and applied during discovery, and I strongly encourage doing so. However, I've found that the techniques often stand out more and can be understood better when presented as ways to test requirements that already have been defined. I've also found that some people who don't seem interested in learning more about defining requirements sometimes are open to hearing about ways of testing them. Moreover, regardless of methods used for creating any development deliverable, double checking is vital for helping assure quality.

The second distinction from conventional treatment is very important, but I fear it easily can lead to confusion and misunderstanding. Therefore, let me spend a bit more time to explain this perhaps controversial distinction and my rationale. Here's the distinction:

I contend that most of these form issues do not *apply uniformly to* all *requirements and certainly do not apply as the black and white absolutes ordinarily depicted in much of the requirements literature.*

As they'd say in the Old West, "them's fighting words." Here's why I say these form issues don't all apply uniformly to *all* requirements:

Requirements tend to be hierarchical.

That is, a requirement can be described at a *high level*, in which case it indeed will be somewhat general and not fit some of the stricter form tests in this chapter. Thus, rather than applying the various form criteria in an often hard-and-fast attempt to make every individual requirement stand on its own with absolute clarity, I approach accomplishing clarity in a different more flexible manner—by first using a hierarchy. *With a hierarchical structure, the way to increase clarity is to drive down to lower levels.*

As we decompose a requirement into a lower level, we simply redefine the requirement in greater detail. Each lower level could be considered as describing more specifically how to tell what the higher level requirement means. The hierarchy allows reducing repetition. While the various tests of form that follow should be in accord with the tone in which the hierarchical decomposition is leading, *the more stringent and specific tests are relevant primarily at only the lowest levels of detail.*

Furthermore, we do need to keep in perspective that requirements should be and are in natural language. Consequently, *absolute and incontrovertible clarity is not practical*. Therefore, these various ways to test form need to be applied with a measure of judgment and common sense. For some high-risk requirements, such as those affecting human safety and business vitality, we need to demand stricter standards of clarity. For others, a less demanding criterion usually will suffice.

Keeping these issues in mind, the remainder of this chapter describes a number of specific additional ways to test the form of requirements in order to improve clarity and understanding. After discussing each test method, we'll apply it to Ann Analyst's definition of requirements for the order entry system.

✪Deliverable *whats* (test method #10)

Since requirements are what must be delivered to provide value, requirements therefore must be deliverable. Note, only a *what* is deliverable, whereas a *how* describes the means of delivery. Moreover, the *whats* must be deliverable in some observable and measurable manner, such that one can make a reliable binary determination—either a requirement has been delivered (or met, or satisfied), or it has not been delivered. *Regardless of the level of detail, from highest to lowest, a requirement should be deliverable.*

Thus, requirements which are subjective or qualitative in nature have to be translated into operational objective terms. Quantitative terms often can be appropriate parts of the requirement. Such quantitative terms would include volumes, frequencies, timeframes, and speeds.

A corollary of deliverability is that the requirements must be reasonably realistic and attainable. However, this aspect of deliverability is exceedingly prone to very common misinterpretation pitfalls. By realistic and attainable, we mean that the requirement conceivably could be delivered with reasonably available or foreseeable technology, resources, and skills in an inherently reasonable time frame.

Many people incorrectly assume something is not a requirement because they personally (or their organization or their group) do not have the technology, resources, or the skills to deliver the requirement. Such *project implementation issues in no way determine whether or not something is a business requirement*, although they may be constraints upon accomplishing the requirement. If the requirement could be delivered with suitable resources, it meets the realism test, regardless of whether one actually has such resources.

Consider the following examples of realism. When President John F. Kennedy announced in 1961 that the United States would land a man on the moon and return him safely to Earth before the end of the decade, he stated a requirement that clearly was not something anyone had ever done. While certainly larger and more demanding than almost any other requirement in history, the moon landing was in fact realistic; we know (a few skeptics notwithstanding) that the requirement was attained in 1969.

On the other hand, say the moon-landing requirement had a minor adjustment whereby the trip would need to be accomplished by a "Beam me up, Scotty" transfiguration of matter à la Star Trek. Such a technical capability is not reasonably or foreseeably attainable in the world at large (a few Trekkie nonskeptics notwithstanding).

Everything that Ann Analyst describes with respect to the order entry system seems deliverable. All aspects would be observable, measurable, and realistically attainable.

✪Testable (test method #11)

Although a requirement may be deliverable, it still is necessary to define how to test that the delivery has occurred. We demonstrate that a requirement is testable by writing test cases. A test case consists of an input and an expected result, plus possibly a description of procedures necessary for carrying out the test. If a requirement's delivery cannot be demonstrated reliably by a test, then the requirement cannot possibly be met.

At numerous testing conferences and in a wide variety of testing industry writings, I have heard many leading testing experts state that testability is certainly the most important, and essentially the *only*, criterion by which to judge requirements. While I agree testability is essential, it is by no means sufficient. Like all the tests of requirements form, a requirement can be perfectly testable and totally incorrect, and testability is completely irrelevant with respect to requirements that have been overlooked.

As with deliverability, testability should pertain to requirements at all levels of detail. The more detailed and specific the requirement is, the more precise and limited can be the set of test cases that would demonstrate the requirement. For higher level requirements, it would be unlikely to know all covered conditions or actual data values for them. Thus, the test cases to show testability typically would be representative of the set of test cases that could be written; but they wouldn't necessarily demonstrate specifically that all aspects of the high-level requirement had been delivered. Where data values cannot be known, use a test case specification, describing the input and expected result in words.

For example, Ann Analyst's (somewhat high-level) requirements seem testable and could be demonstrated by a test case specification alone or with hypothetical data values:

Input	*Valid customer number of an existing customer.*
Expected Result	*Confirmation of customer's name and address.*
Input	*Quantity 2 of Product Number X, where*
	list price of each Product X is $1,000.
Expected Result	*Product X description.*
	Unit Price = $1,000.
	Extended Price = $2,000.

✪ Reviewable (test method #12)

Requirements must be in a form that enables other people to review the requirements. In other words, requirements cannot just be in someone's mind. This means the requirements must be captured in some persistent reliably retrievable form. As a practical matter, written form is most likely necessary. Audio or video recording could suffice, although such media could incur certain manageability drawbacks.

Besides being physically retrievable, the form must be in understandable language in order to allow review. The issue of understandability frequently is misinterpreted, especially by technical people charged with defining requirements. Technical people, analysts, and other similar requirements gatherers, for example, often mistakenly interpret the standard to be whether *they* personally understand the requirements language.

However, *the proper standard is whether the language has commonly understood meaning by members of the applicable business, user, or customer community.* For instance, essentially everybody in the financial accounting community has basically the same understanding of the terms "debit" and "credit." Therefore, such terms usually would not need further clarification in an accounting requirement, even if the analyst or developer did not share the common understanding.

The implication, therefore, is that technical people have an obligation to learn the business language or otherwise have business language translated into language they (the technical people) can understand accurately and reliably. Conversely, although further explanation for the benefit of technical people would be gracious and valuable, business people should not feel obligated to explain their requirements beyond the point where such requirements are suitably understandable within the business community.

To be reviewable, requirements ultimately must be able to be understood when standing on their own. That is, extraneous additional information should not be necessary for achieving suitable understanding. Often a requirement is understandable only when its source provides an explanation of what is meant. When the source and supplementary explanation are no longer available, the requirement by itself may not be sufficiently understandable to be considered suitable for review.

Similarly, while a picture may be worth a thousand words, requirements need to be written in words to be appropriately reviewable. *Examples, diagrams, and software can support the written requirements, but they are not the requirements themselves.* Please note that this criterion conflicts directly with widely held beliefs that models and/or code prototypes are the appropriate form for capturing and communicating requirements. Nonlanguage forms can be less subject than natural language to misunderstanding, but only in certain limited ways which generally are more suitable for designs than for business requirements.

Ann Analyst's definition of requirements certainly is written and appears to be in a language of the order entry business and user community. Consequently, it seems to fit the criteria for being reviewable.

✪Itemized (test method #13)

One point on which all requirements authorities seem to agree is that requirements should be itemized, where each individual requirement is a separate item. Itemizing enables the form of representation to make it clear and easy to see exactly what verbiage is included in the requirement. Itemizing therefore also provides an additional way to facilitate review.

The alternative or opposite of itemizing is a narrative form. Narratives are inherently subject to confusion, especially with regard to culling out from the narrative exactly which words are intended to be in a requirement. Jumbled narrative text also increases the likelihood of failing to recognize some of the verbiage as a requirement at all.

Ann Analyst's definition of requirements very much is a narrative. Therefore, it fails to satisfy this test of form.

✪Traceable (test method #14)

Itemizing is essential for making each requirement traceable, which also is valuable for reviewing the requirements. Tracing can go backwards to identify the source of the requirement. Tracing also can go forward to map the requirement to where it is used. Note that a requirement can have multiple sources and multiple uses.

Some common uses that are frequently traced include: where the requirement is implemented in the system design and where the requirement is tested. As described in Chapter 3, tracing the business requirements to where they are addressed in the system requirements becomes especially important. Such forward tracing is valuable for making sure that each identified requirement indeed has been addressed. It's also valuable to trace the history of changes to the requirements.

Since Ann Analyst's definition of requirements is not itemized, it is not traceable. Moreover, it includes no identification of the source of the requirements information. At this point, Ann Analyst's requirements have no change history and have not yet been implemented in design, tests, or elsewhere.

As a practical matter, tracing information often is recorded in a somewhat hidden manner so that it doesn't obscure or interfere with the clarity of the requirements wording itself. For instance, addenda may be used to provide a brief synopsis tracing groups of requirements backwards to their sources. Frankly, backward tracing often is not done in a very clear organized manner. Instead, finding a requirement's source may involve some searching through discovery documents, such as interview notes. The key issue is whether the source can be identified. Ordinarily the speed with which the backward tracing can be accomplished is of lower importance, because identifying the source of a requirement generally becomes a relatively infrequent issue, usually only for (hopefully) a small subset of the requirements which seem questionable.

Forward tracing to where the requirements are used tends to be the more important type of information to have readily accessible. People tend to need to refer more frequently on an ongoing basis to such forward traces. Forward traces are essential for identifying the impact of changes. Sometimes the requirement itself changes, and sometimes we become aware a requirement has changed because a related design or test changes. Thus, it is important for the forward tracing also to include the ability to trace back from design or test to the requirement. As should be apparent, tracing can constitute an enormous administrative workload. Fortunately, automated requirements management tools are available to assist in identifying and maintaining backward and forward tracing.

✪Ambiguity (test method #15)

One of the key elements of clarity is lack of ambiguity. Requirements are ambiguous when reasonably knowledgeable people can interpret the wording of the requirement with markedly different meanings. Of all the techniques related to the form of requirements, the industry seems to devote the greatest amount of attention to various methods for formulating the wording of requirements to avoid ambiguity and vagueness.

I think it's safe to say that virtually every author describes some set of criteria for helping make requirements wording unambiguous. These authors generally describe largely overlapping sets of commonly referenced techniques. One colleague, Richard Bender, deserves special mention here for his extensive analysis and identification of a very structured Ambiguity Review methodology [1]. Bender has applied the methodology successfully not only to systems and their requirements, but also to analysis of legal contracts. I'll refer you to Bender's own work for more complete coverage. Bender's review method includes a proprietary checklist of some 30 techniques devoted exclusively to detecting and preventing ambiguity in the selection and structure of wording.

A number of Bender's checklist items are self-explanatory, such as Double Negation; several, such as Dangling Else, fit into some of the starred ways to test that we'll discuss separately. Let me describe three other items on Bender's checklist.

Bender's Ambiguity of Reference is the pronoun problem. Although I hope not, you perhaps have had some encounters with it already in this book. As a matter of fact, I've just given you an example of it; and here's another one. In this sentence and the prior sentence, what does the word "it" refer to? What does the word "one" refer to? Both are pronouns. Pronouns are a necessary and convenient way to refer to things, but sometimes what they are referring to is not clear. In this situation, "it" refers to "the pronoun problem" and "one" refers to an example of the pronoun problem. "Both" is also a pronoun which refers to "it" and "one." Is it clear? What is "it" referring to this time? Obviously pronoun references can be confusing. Concern about them also easily can be overdone, run into the ground, and annoy the daylights out of other people.

Bender's Ambiguous Logical Operators involves an area that probably nobody has analyzed more fully than Dick Bender. In Chapter 9, we'll see other applications of Bender's pioneering approach to logic analysis. Logical operators primarily come into play with regard to business rules.

Programmers are familiar with logical operators as IF statements. When business rules are defined with IF-type logic, programmers can implement the rules directly. However, humans often aren't quite so precise and disciplined as a computer is. When humans write IF-like descriptions in barely perceptibly different form from what a computer requires, the programmer adjusts to computer-acceptable form by making some assumptions about what the rules were intended to mean. Assumptions invite misinterpretation.

Consider the following rule (which is *not* from Ann Analyst's definition of requirements):

> If the customer has paid his balance in full or has no bill over 60-days old and has no current open orders, accept his order.

The rule could be translated into logic a computer would accept as either:

> If   (*either* the customer has paid his balance in full

or has no bill over 60-days old)

and also has no current open orders,

then accept his order.

or

If   the customer has paid his balance in full

or

(has no bill over 60-days old and also has no current open orders),

then accept his order.

In many cases, logical operators can be ambiguous even though the rules don't specifically use the IF construction. For example, Ann Analyst's definition of requirements describes two seemingly contradictory business rules relating to product numbers:

Each base product and each option has a unique product number.
Some configurations of a base product and its options are so common that the configuration has been assigned its own product number.

Bender's Ambiguous Statements is a topic raised by practically all authors. People commonly describe their requirements using terms such as "fast" and "easy" whose meaning is entirely subjective. Fast means something to me personally which other people have no way to know for sure. What I think of as fast may seem slow to someone else or possibly seems to them to be really fast, whatever that means.

In low-level detailed requirements, such subjective terms do need to be translated into objective terms that truly match the business people's meaning. However, I would maintain that for higher level requirements, using such imprecise qualitative terms is perfectly appropriate. In fact, the broader perspective of the higher level requirement would be compromised by including a very specific quantification. The presence of a term like "fast" or "easy" at a high-level signals that the objective meaning needs to be articulated when the requirement is driven to lower more detailed levels.

Ann Analyst's definition of requirements does not seem to include any such subjective terms.

✪Consistent, known usage of terms (test method #16)

When requirements use the same or similar terms to mean different things, or different terms to mean the same thing, one never is sure which meaning is intended for any particular usage of the term. A similar confusing effect occurs when a term is used incorrectly or in a manner that differs significantly from commonly understood meanings, such as would be found in a dictionary. Some authors consider a glossary of definitions an integral part of an adequate requirements definition. I would certainly not discourage including a glossary, but I don't think it needs to be considered an essential component of a requirements definition.

Ann Analyst's definition of requirements seems to use its terms in a consistent and commonly understood manner.

✪Identifies assumptions (test method #17)

Very often requirements make sense only within the context of assumptions made by the person providing the requirement. Frequently such assumptions have not been articulated, so it's essentially impossible for other people to know what the assumptions are. Thus, it's first necessary to raise consciousness of assumptions. Secondly, it's important to capture the assumptions so they will be available for helping other readers place the requirements in the assumed context.

Ann Analyst's definition of requirements does not seem to be based on any significant assumptions, although it would be reasonable to conclude that Ann assumes a familiarity with the ElecTech products and order entry procedures.

✪Stated in the positive (test method #18)

It's fairly common for people to state their requirements in negative terms, that is, by describing their need as the absence of something they don't want. Their reasoning is easy to appreciate: when the troublesome thing is not present, their problem seems solved. The shortcoming of this approach is that it's impossible to prove a negative.

The impossibility of proving a negative frequently is encountered with respect to testing. Unfortunately, many people misconstrue this impossibility as meaning that it's impossible to find all the defects in software. It's not impossible to find all the defects, but it is impossible to *know* for sure that you've found all the defects.

When requirements are stated in the negative, the best you can demonstrate is that the removed thing does not appear to be present, but it could still be present and just not observed, or it could be gone but return. While this may seem to be nitpicking, it gets to the heart of whether a requirement can be delivered. Instead of describing requirements in negative terms, state them in positive terms. For instance, rather than saying the requirement is "not sending customers the wrong products," perhaps phrase it, "sending customers all the right products and only the right products."

Ann Analyst's definition of requirements does not seem to state any negatives.

✪Identifies objectives (test method #19)

The issue being tested is whether the requirements include identification of reasonably understandable and reasonable objectives, as contrasted with evaluating whether the objectives are appropriate and sufficient. Thus, it's testing form rather than content. Ordinarily, a key expectation of the various regular ways to test requirements is that the reviewers are determining whether the requirements have suitable objectives.

Ann Analyst's definition of requirements fails to identify any objectives.

✪Identifies major functions and limits (test method #20)

As with identification of objectives, this issue is one of form rather than content—whether functions and limits are identified in a reasonably understandable manner and reasonably relate to the stated objectives, not whether functions and limits are correct. Limits would include matters such as volumes to be supported and constraints on the requirements.

Ann Analyst's definition of requirements does indeed describe several major business functions, which we can infer are intended requirements. The only limits identified involve the number of product groups and product lines. All seem relevant to the business and therefore probably will be relevant to the objectives at such time as they are identified.

✪Identifies business rules (test method #21)

As with identification of objectives, functions, and limits, the issue again is one of form—whether reasonably understandable business rules have been identified, not whether they are correct. Tony Morgan [2] describes business rules as "constraints: They define conditions that must hold true in specified situations…the desired logic of the business." Although generally an important part of requirements, business rules nonetheless often seem to get less attention than their importance warrants. For instance, many people think of requirements primarily in terms of use cases, but as commonly written, use cases don't address business rules comfortably, and often don't address them at all.

At the other end of the continuum, is a highly specialized community which concentrates almost exclusively on the rules aspects of business rules. A major part of their approach is oriented toward analyzing the patterns of elements which make up rules. Some of the business rules efforts are directed toward precisely describing business logic in a highly formalized and structured manner, which allows a generalized automated "business rules engine" to carry out or enforce rules for virtually any function. This book does not endeavor to address the specialized methods of the business rules community. Refer to Morgan's book for more information and references.

Ann Analyst's definition of requirements seems not to identify any business rules.

✪Alternative consequences defined (test method #22)

This test addresses basically the same business rule aspects that Bender refers to as the "dangling else." I treat it as a separate way to test rather than simply including it within ambiguity testing, because I find it tends to detect bigger and a somewhat conceptually different type of issue than mere ambiguity.

As we mentioned previously, business rules frequently take the form of an IF statement:

> If a particular condition is true,
>> then some specific action should occur.

What happens when true is only half the story. The other half involves what else is supposed to happen when the condition is *not* true. Failing to identify the alternative consequences can be quite significant and tends to be one of the most common errors in formulating requirements. Higher level requirements usually can tolerate lack of the ELSE, so long as lower level requirements are foreseeably likely to identify it.

Programming languages provide for both alternatives by having an expanded version of the IF statement which is written as IF-THEN-ELSE:

> If a particular condition is true,
>> Then some specific action should occur,
>> Else some other specific action should occur.

Since Ann Analyst's definition of requirements really did not provide any IF-statement-type business rules, there were no alternative consequence elses to omit.

✪Magic words (test method #23)

When we introduced *what must be delivered to provide value* as the definition of a requirement, we discussed briefly that some people feel "must" is one of the three most important words in the definition. In fact, a number of quite influential parties place significant importance on the specific words that are used in requirements, which is why I refer to them as magic words.

To these people, most notably the U.S. Department of Defense (DoD), which is the largest purchaser of software in the world, a requirement is not a requirement unless it includes the magic words "must" or "shall" to highlight that the requirement is mandatory. They further reason that words such as "should" or "may" are to be avoided because they indicate something is optional. To be defined (TBD) is considered especially inappropriate because it states explicitly that we do not know what the requirement is.

If you work in an organization that cares about whether or not specific magic words are used, then by all means use them in the prescribed manner. If you are not in a situation that pays formal attention to the presence of magic words, I would not encourage you to pay them undue attention. While I appreciate the purposes that motivate the magic word mandates, I think they mainly create unnecessary busywork and tend to divert attention to the superficial.

In somewhat of a related manner, a number of other authors generally prescribe that every requirement begins with the words: "The system shall" or "The product must." To my thinking that's a lot of redundancy that adds effort without adding meaning. If you find it valuable to keep repeating magic words, do it. Fortunately word processors make it relatively painless to insert the same phrase over and over and over again.

✪ Complete (test method #24)

The final test of form is whether the requirements are complete. This most often is a judgment call, which can subject us to a circular reasoning type of quandary: how do I know the requirements are complete if I don't know what the requirements are?

Also, "complete" can be interpreted in a variety of ways. Perhaps the most logical use of complete is in the sense of whether the total set of requirements tells the full story or is leaving out important parts. That is, the requirements define what is necessary and sufficient to accomplish business objectives. By definition, TBD states conclusively that the requirement is not complete because something remains to be defined. In contrast to the magic words devotees, a few authors, such as Dick Bender and I, believe it is preferable to indicate a known gap as TBD so that it will serve as a tickler reminder to provide the missing information when practical. Otherwise, a too strictly literal devotion to magic words could result in dropping the unknowns rather than noting their absence with the proscribed TBD.

Another use of "complete" pertains to whether sufficient information is included about an individual requirement to understand it adequately. For instance, if the requirement is dependent upon some other requirement, then that requirement must be present too.

Suzanne and James Robertson use "complete" in a very specialized different way, specifically that some 13 pieces of information describing an individual requirement have been provided as prescribed by their copyrighted Volere methodology [3].

I believe by any standard, Ann Analyst's definition of requirements is not complete. Without clear business objectives, there is no basis for judging whether the defined requirements would accomplish the objectives. Moreover, one could easily surmise that Ann's description omits any number of likely additional requirements.

At this point, some students (alas, I fear, especially fellow testers, who tend to be terribly literal at times) express concern that they now have more than the 21 ways to test requirements that I had promised. Perhaps some of us in the systems business are not accustomed to delivering more than is promised. You will have many more than 21 ways to test requirements on your list by the end of this book. Good for both of us!

References

[1]   Bender, R., *Writing Testable Requirements*, Herndon, VA: *PSQT/PSTT (Practical Software Quality Techniques/Practical Software Testing Techniques) 2003 East Conference*, June 9, 2003.

[2]   Morgan, T., *Business Rules and Information Systems*, Boston, MA: Addison-Wesley, 2002, p. 59.

[3]   Robertson, S. and J. Robertson, *Mastering the Requirements Process*, Harlow, England: Addison-Wesley, p. 184.

Discovering real requirements

Users never know what they want.

Of all the conventional wisdom in the IT industry, I suspect none is closer to being unanimously accepted than that users never know what they want. In some senses no doubt users don't know what they want, but I contend *the far more significant issue is that we, the side of the industry responsible for delivering what the users want, don't adequately know what the users want.*

Our job is not merely to deliver computer programs. First and foremost, our role is to enable the business to perform its functions and meet its objectives faster, cheaper, and better. If we are going to meet our responsibility in a capable, professional, and worthwhile manner, we have to know what must be delivered to provide value. In other words, *an essential part of our job is to know what the business requirements are.*

That does not mean that we have to know the requirements innately or be the source of the requirements. It does mean that before we develop systems and software, we need to acquire the knowledge of what the systems must accomplish in order to provide value. The fact that users may have some uncertainty or difficulty articulating their requirements does not in the slightest diminish our obligation to do our job competently.

To earn respect as professionals, we've got to start by appreciating that our job includes taking appropriate actions so we know what the real requirements are. The first step is recognizing that the real requirements are business requirements. The second step is to accept accountability and *stop falling back on excuses, such as blaming users for our failure to know what they want.*

Why we say users don't know what they want

I contend that users *do know* what they want, but I also agree users often appear not to know what they want. To get past the excuses, we need to understand better the possible reasons why users seem not to know what they want.

First of all, this whole human communication business is a lot trickier than most of us realize. I recently had an opportunity to participate in a well-known type of exercise that exemplified the fundamental difficulty of describing requirements. In a seminar tutorial at the *Software Measurement/Applications of Software Management 2003 Conference* [1], colleague Elisabeth Hendrickson gave pairs of participants pictures of cartoon characters from a popular children's story, which most of us old folks weren't familiar with. Only one of the partners could see the cartoon, and then described it to the other partner, who drew what he or she felt was being described.

The resulting drawings generally bore scant resemblance to the originals. The exercise impressed on us how difficult it is to convey in words what one sees visually. The same challenges would apply to describing requirements in words that everyone interprets recognizably the same.

Beyond normal human limitations, additional factors complicate communications between business and systems sides. Systems people tend to think very systematically and logically. Moreover, we get lots of practice being systematic, which is how many of us spend most of our working hours. Everyone gets uncomfortable with other people who don't think the same way we do. Many nonsystems people may have other ways of conceptualizing the world, besides step-by-step sequence; their job activities may give them lots of practice thinking in ways other than what we'd consider to be systematically. For example, some people think in terms of the big picture, while others may focus on human relationships.

Regardless of how a user's mind functions, they may not have their thoughts well organized, and they probably have not fleshed out all the details. They may overlook things and make assumptions, often without even being aware they are doing so. They may think they've addressed something, and perhaps they did, as far as they were concerned, but perhaps not in a way that someone else would recognize or understand in the same way. And, they are likely to think of new and different things when they see concrete examples.

After all, defining requirements is only a small part of how users spend their time. Most of their thinking is typically oriented toward *doing* their job, rather than defining it. We are probably asking them about their requirements because they are so good at their jobs. Realize, though, that one way we know someone has become skilled at a job is that they can do it without the need for much conscious awareness. Their very skill makes it hard for them to recognize all that goes on in what they do very well. That's one reason why sports superstars so seldom make effective coaches. The superstar just does it. He knows he is good, but he can't analyze what makes him good; therefore, he is not able to explain to others who lack his talents how to perform like a superstar.

Many of the technical people I meet acknowledge that users actually may know what they want, but "they don't know how to say it." Sometimes, alas, I fear the actual problem is that the technical people don't know how to listen. They may assume they already know what the user needs, or they may put words in the user's mouth, which the user feels helpless to challenge. I've certainly heard many users say, "I told the technical people what I want. What they said it means must be right."

However, my perception is that "they don't know how to say it" usually means the technical people expect users to provide them with a well-organized fully formed definition in language the technical person understands readily and can implement directly.

Well, first, it's not going to happen. Nobody I know spews out final-draft thoroughness, let alone in the initial pass. Second, it's not the user's job to speak the technical person's language. Requirements are the user's and need to be in the user's language. Third, developers implement designs, not business requirements. There needs to be a step in the middle, actually several steps, translating business requirements *whats* into system design *hows* that can be implemented.

In addition to all the above, a fundamental reason remains that users have difficulty describing what they want when they are expected to provide essentially the design of a *product*. Product design *is* engineering, and users are highly unlikely to be skilled at it.

Moreover, systems often involve innovating in relatively uncharted territory, where there may be no familiar products. People can't conceive of products that aren't similar to ones they already know. For example, prior to Thomas Edison's invention of the incandescent electric light bulb, nobody would have described one as a requirement. That's because the product is not their real requirements. Their real requirements are what must be accomplished—in business terms—to provide value. In Edison's time, people did *not* require a light bulb. What they needed was a safe, convenient, and powerful source of reliable illumination. Edison's invention met their real requirements.

When we ask appropriately about the business *whats*, rather than the product *hows*, and when we listen effectively, users generally turn out knowing a lot more than we'd appreciated about what they want. They also often are more willing to cooperate with us.

Requirements gathering

Although we know it's unreasonable to expect users to provide fully formed requirements, people nonetheless often act *as if* the requirements were fully formed. For example, it is exceedingly common for a technical person to ask the user, "What do you want?" and then simply record verbatim dictation of whatever the user says. Many technical people are exceedingly grateful for the user who does spout out (apparent) product solutions, as opposed to business language needs.

A related variation is when the user merely acquiesces with a solution the technical person suggests. When answers seem pat, the easy way out is simply to label them, "the user's requirements," and consider the inquiry completed. Then, when the user later complains that the delivered system is not right, we blame them for not knowing what they wanted.

Such passive techniques are the epitome of the image the term "requirements gathering" conjures up. It makes me think of going around with little green and yellow baskets picking up requirements that are lying around, perhaps neatly covered in pretty wrapping paper with a big satin bow, maybe right next to the Easter eggs. Here's a requirement, there's a requirement, tra la, tra la…. Nonsense!

Requirements are not just lying around waiting to be gathered. Rather, usually one must hunt for and *discover requirements*. In my experience, users seldom intentionally hide requirements (although it's been known to happen), but the requirements indeed are hard to spot. Fully formed solutions seem like the easy answer, but they often fool us into missing the real requirements that we need to know in order to provide value for users.

We're also prone to discarding or discounting requirements because sometimes what users say they want seems not to be what they really need. Ironically, the technical people who know the least about the business often seem to have no compunctions about deciding on behalf of the users what the users should and should not really need.

Like a detective story

To discover the real requirements, we must act like a detective. Let's use venerable popular television character Lt. Columbo as an example. The episodes all follow pretty much the same formula. There has been a murder of a guest at a posh party. Since the party usually is on a private estate, it's almost certain that the killer is still present. When Lt. Columbo arrives, he knows nothing and the guests have all the pertinent information, but Columbo is the one who identifies the killer. Why? Because he's the star of the show. Yes, but what does he do differently that makes him the star?

Most people suggest it's because Columbo knows what questions to ask. True, but much of the questioning involves the whole group of suspects, so essentially everyone hears the same information. It's not the asking so much as it's the way Columbo listens to and analyzes the answers that enables him alone to solve the mystery.

While most of us hear the words of the answers without anything registering, a detective picks up on what might be important, then analyzes further how it might be important, and eventually weaves those clues together to form a rational explanation for whodunit. Columbo doesn't try to squeeze the facts to fit his preexisting presumption. He has to keep an open mind, and he has to be careful not to leap to conclusions about plausible-sounding solutions that may be suggested along the way (such as, a guest who reports they saw another guest with the candlestick). We need to apply the same types of skills to discover the real requirements. Then we too can be stars of our own shows.

Focus on value

The single most helpful guideline for detecting the real requirements is to focus on value. This is true whether we're starting to identify the requirements for a major system or simply responding to a request for a seemingly minor change to a screen or report.

Value stems from meeting business objectives. That means in a health care organization, for example, that value mainly comes from relieving (and preferably preventing) pain and suffering. Usually directly, and at least indirectly, systems need to serve such objectives, and we need to understand the relation. If we can't find the value link, we probably don't adequately understand what the real requirements are.

Ultimately, even in organizations with noble objectives, such as health care, value needs to be translated into dollars. Although it may seem crass, someone will make a decision whether the value received warrants spending the amount of money necessary to meet the requirements. Discovering that value is key to understanding the requirements.

From a financial standpoint, value comes with respect to revenue and costs. Revenue is money we receive. We get value by enhancing or protecting revenue. A requirement will *enhance revenue* if it enables us to sell more of our products and services, to charge more for our products and services, or to collect more of what we have charged. Systems in a health care organization might enhance revenue by better scheduling patient visits so that physicians could see more patients in a day, by assuring that charges are as high as third-party reimbursers allow, or by reducing billing errors that have caused bills to go unpaid.

We *protect revenue* by keeping existing customers who otherwise might leave. Often this involves enabling us to provide products and services that our competitors also provide. For example, a system may enable a health care organization to keep its patients by offering additional types of diagnostic procedures that already are being offered by other health care providers. An even more prevalent form of revenue protection involves enabling compliance with laws, regulations, and standards. Especially in highly regulated industries, such as health care, compliance is the cost of being allowed to do business, in other words to protect the right to earn revenue. A very high percentage of a health care budget is devoted to monitoring and reporting compliance to regulators.

Costs have two similar forms of value: savings and avoidance. *Cost savings* occur when we stop spending money that we've been spending. Let's say that you work for a health care organization and are paid $10,000,000 per year. (Congratulations, lunch is on you!) If your employer wanted to save $10,000,000, how could they do it? Goodbye. (Sorry! It was nice while it lasted.) Personnel reductions unfortunately are the most common way that organizations save costs.

Suppose instead that demand is increasing for the health care service you provide. In fact, demand is rising so much that you'll need an additional person to help you provide all the anticipated services. That added person also will be paid $10,000,000 per year. However, thanks to a new system, you alone will be able to provide the full amount of increased services. The system enables us therefore to *avoid the cost* of hiring the additional worker. Most people psychologically prefer cost avoidance over cost savings. It's easier not to hire someone we've never met than to lose our own job or have friends lose theirs. Realize, though, that cost savings are a more reliably realized benefit than cost avoidance, which is easier to exaggerate since it's only an estimate.

"Should be" model

We usually become concerned about defining requirements when some need for change arises. Often the need is in the form of a problem to be solved. Alternatively, the need could be a challenge, which may not exactly be the same as a problem. Frequently, though, a challenge is also a problem, such as when the challenge comes from a competitor who has introduced capabilities that we must match. Sometimes the need relates to an opportunity, perhaps a new technology that we might exploit to advantage or some other new (or newly recognized) situation. For instance, introduction of the World Wide Web created opportunities; so too would a competitor's going out of business.

Requirements represent what we should do that reasonably will result in solving the problem, meeting the challenge, or taking the opportunity. Requirements therefore are the way things *should be*, which will be different somehow from the way things are *as is* (currently). Note, though, that requirements represent the full set needed to achieve the value, which may include things that don't change, and not just the deltas (differences) from the way things are now.

"Should be" and "as is" are terms most commonly associated with process modeling. We use these terms because understanding the *process* is essential for discovering the business requirements. We all use the term "process," but I fear usually most people use the term somewhat inappropriately. Let's examine what a process really is and what it has to do with the real requirements.

Most people, at least those in the systems industry, generally think of a process as a set of *actions or steps* that one is *supposed to perform* in order to meet a particular objective. Many systems people use the term "process" to mean a set of formally defined procedures, especially those perceived as necessary to achieve one of the higher levels of the Software Engineering Institute's Capability Maturity Model (SEI CMM[1]) [2].

We're going to use the term "process" in a much more fundamental, and frankly more accurate, way.

A process is a set of actions that together produce a particular result.

A result is the outcome of a process. If there is a result, a process exists regardless of whether or not the process is:

> Recognized;

> Intended;

> Desired.

Real and presumed processes

As we point out in Figure 5.1, there are two types of processes: presumed and real. The *presumed process* is what people think is happening. In many instances, the presumed process is simply an informal recognition of "the way we do things around here." Often the presumed process is a *defined process*, that is, it describes the actions people intend, or are supposed, to take to achieve a specific objective. Sometimes, the presumed process is *documented*; but many presumed processes have not been reduced to writing.

The other type of process is the *real process*, which is the set of actions or steps that taken together really produce the results. The real process frequently *differs from the presumed process* and often *is not recognized*.

We already have described a number of situations where real and presumed processes differ. For example, system developers often presume they know the requirements, but not only do they not know the real requirements, they don't have measures which reliably alert them to the presence and magnitude of their real requirements problem.

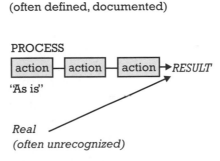

Figure 5.1   Real and presumed processes.

---

1. CMM and Capability Maturity Model are registered in the U.S. Patent and Trademark Office by Carnegie Mellon University.

Similarly, organizations presume they plan a system, code and test it, and implement it correctly by the deadline. Practically every system organization has a procedures manual, which describes the process this way. In reality, the coding almost always takes longer than expected, which means correspondingly more time therefore should also be devoted to testing. However, the testing doesn't increase. Instead, testing gets squeezed and shortchanged so that by the deadline (or more probably, late) a system is delivered which is incomplete and still full of errors. That's the real system development process that happens over and over again in organizations, yet no organization I know ever would describe their system development process that way.

Failure to recognize the real process is a major reason why process improvement efforts often fail to provide expected benefits. In fact, as we can see in Figure 5.2, changing one's results can be achieved only by changing one's real process. (Remember the definition of insanity is continuing to do the same thing and expecting different results.)

To improve, we change from the "as is" process (which produces our current results) to the "should be" process that is expected to produce the desired different results. Which process will most people try to change, the presumed process that they think is happening or the real process of which they probably are unaware?

Of course, people usually change the presumed process. If, as so often happens, the presumed process is not the real process that really produces the results, then *changing the presumed process will not have the intended effect on the results*. In fact, changing the presumed process frequently turns counterproductive, because the problem gets worse during the period when time and resources are diverted to the presumed process; and then too there no longer may be time, resources, or energy to change the real process.

For example, the way many systems organizations attempt to improve their development process is to promulgate new or changed procedures in their procedures manual. Since part of their real process usually is that people don't actually read or follow the procedures manual, and since the procedures that the manual *does* describe often are not what people actually do, publishing new or changed procedures in the manual generally fails to achieve any meaningful change in systems development results.

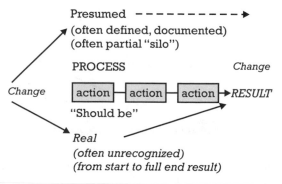

Figure 5.2   Change the real process to change the results.

Interestingly, when that set of procedures fails, it's common to publish a different set of new or changed procedures in the manual, and those fare no better. Organizations may do it again and again, and they never seem to learn that their improvement process doesn't work.

Thus, in order to change results in the desired manner, it is essential to *first recognize the real "as is" process* that really is producing the current results, and *then change it*. Only changing the real process will be reasonably likely to achieve the desired changed results.

The real requirements are the "should be" version of the real business process.

Some process pitfalls

Very often people indeed recognize the real process, but only a part of it. When they view this part of the real process out of context, it can be equivalent to presuming a process that differs from the real process. This effect is generally likened to being in a silo. Since especially some city folks may not be familiar with silos, let me explain that a silo is a tall, narrow, cylindrically shaped structure used for storing fodder to feed farm animals (such as sows). If the silo image isn't meaningful, think about being inside an elevator shaft or some other structure that constricts the breadth of your view.

Individual departments and groups within organizations have a tendency to act as if they are inside silos. That is, each group's perspective is narrowly constricted, and each group tends to be unaware of groups in adjacent silos. Consequently, each group is likely to suboptimize its own processes, which means making things work well for that group without realizing that by doing so they inadvertently may be negatively impacting other parts of the organization. Not only does *silo thinking* harm the enterprise's overall effectiveness and efficiency, more importantly it *invariably harms their customers' results*. Therefore, the keys to avoiding the silo effect are:

▸ Identify the real process from the customer's perspective.

▸ Identify the real process in its entirety, from start to full end result.

Figure 5.3 shows a systems development example of the difference between a commonly presumed process end point and the more appropriate, full end result. From the customer's perspective, the full end result is when the system works right, not merely when the developers implement it.

Without being aware they are doing it, developers routinely view their process in a silo which ends at the point of implementation. *Anyone can deliver by a deadline if it doesn't matter what they deliver.* Customers don't feel the system is done until it works right from their perspective. Almost every system needs more work after implementation to finish and fix things before they indeed do work right. The true measure of development practices must be in the full context, from the start to when the system works right, not merely in the developers' silo, which ends at implementation.

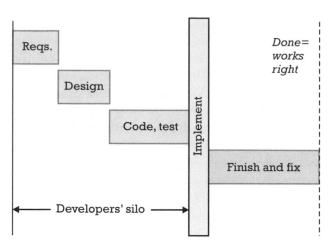

Figure 5.3 System development presumed process silo.

Judgments about development practices are likely to be erroneous if they don't take into account how those practices affect the need for postimplementation work. The same is true for any process whose requirements we are trying to discover.

Improving the process

The "should be" process ordinarily represents intended improvement over the current "as is" process. To improve a process, we need to understand its actions, sequences, and players. We diagnose points of trouble or inefficiency and then streamline the process by eliminating and/or revising actions.

Handoffs, passing information and things from one player (typically a person, group, or organizational entity such as a department) to another, are a common source of trouble. Think of a relay race in a track meet. It's not the fastest runners who win, it's the team that hands off the baton most smoothly from fast runner to fast runner. With business, capturing information about delays and errors associated with each handoff can target those process steps that are often the best candidates for improvement. Processes improve by eliminating the handoffs or changing action steps in ways that reduce the likelihood of mistakes and delays.

An action step's time and cost also can signal improvement opportunities by determining whether the action produces sufficient *value-added*. An action adds value to the extent the *customer* would be willing to pay for the action if the customer knew about it. For instance, it's highly unlikely that a customer would pay extra for system developers to perform practices that routinely lead to mistakes necessitating expensive rework. Action steps which don't provide sufficient value-added are good candidates for improvement or elimination.

To recap, we discover the real, business requirements by:

- Identifying the real "as is" process which actually produces the current business results.

- Analyzing its action steps' efficiency, effectiveness, and value-added.

- Defining the requirements, which are a streamlined "should be" process, by eliminating and/or revising action steps in the real process.

References

[1]   Hendrickson, E., "Gathering Requirements in a Low-Process Environment," *Software Measurement/Applications of Software Management 2003 Conference*, San Jose, CA, June 2, 2003.

[2]   Paulk, M. C., et al., *Capability Maturity Model for Software, Version 1.1*, Pittsburgh, PA: Software Engineering Institute of Carnegie Mellon University, 1993.

Problem Pyramid

It isn't what we don't know, it's what we know that just ain't so.

—Will Rogers

The challenge

In Chapter 5, we said the key to discovering the real requirements is to identify and then improve the real business process. The context for identifying the real business process is accurately ascertaining the real problem. This is hard to do. People often have great difficulty recognizing the real problem, partly because of focusing on presumed processes and presumed product solutions.

It's also hard because people are not accustomed to thinking in the disciplined insightful manner needed to identify and then suitably solve their real problems. Consequently, many people are certain they know what the problem is, when in fact it "just ain't so." Their illusion causes them to spend much of their time solving the wrong problem or not solving the problem right.

This chapter describes a powerful disciplined Problem Pyramid tool that helps find the real problem and identify the real requirements that address it appropriately.

Requirements arise in response to a problem (or challenge or opportunity). Therefore, *the time to use a Problem Pyramid is when we become aware of a problem, challenge, or opportunity to be addressed.*

✖ Warning

All manner of smokescreens tend to distract us away from paying adequate attention to understanding the real problem. None of these (or similar) distinctions that people get so hung up on change a whit the need to understand the real, business problem:

‣ Whether we are expecting to implement "systems" (i.e., hardware, with or, with or without software), software alone, or nonautomated procedural solutions;

‣ Whether we are using mainframe or personal computer, desktop or portable, fully configured or handheld, stand-alone or networked, local area or Web, intranet or extranet;

‣ Whether software is accessed by humans or is embedded in other products and accessed only internally;

‣ Whether the application is new or evolving, big or little, for mundane or life-critical uses, for back-office management information, such as medical billing, or intimately connected with providing services to customers, such as clinical diagnosis or telecommunications control;

‣ Whether the application is for internal use or sale to unspecified external customers;

‣ Whether development follows object-oriented, eXtreme Programming, waterfall, or any other particular methodology;

‣ Whether we are directed to find out the requirements or have the "requirements" presented to us.

Many organizations use some kind of formal "problem statement," which I find often is mainly capturing complaints. Merely delineating complaints, or listing hundreds of prescribed requirements from some authority, does not mean by itself that we truly understand the real problem. In fact, it can add to the problem by creating an illusion that the real problem is being solved.

In contrast, the Problem Pyramid in Figure 6.1 helps us reliably and accurately identify the real problem and then the real requirements for solving the problem. In my experience, the only time the Problem Pyramid doesn't work is when it's not used well, which unfortunately is common because people have difficulty conceptualizing complex situations in the orderly, disciplined manner the Problem Pyramid applies.

Problem Pyramid structure

The Problem Pyramid consists of six blocks that need to be filled out in the specified numerical sequence. At the peak of the pyramid, Block 1 describes the problem (or challenge or opportunity), which we define as the thing that will provide value when it is solved or otherwise suitably addressed. As we'll see shortly in examples, it's easy to think something is the problem when it's not.

One reason people get confused about the problem is that they're not accustomed to applying measures. Measures are key to the disciplined thinking needed to identify the problem correctly. Going down the right side of the Problem Pyramid we identify two important measures of the problem. Block 2 contains measures of the way things are now that indicate we've got a problem.

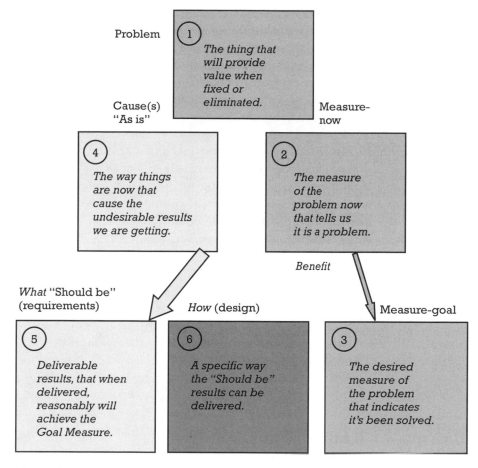

Problem

1 *The thing that will provide value when fixed or eliminated.*

Cause(s) "As is"

Measure-now

4 *The way things are now that cause the undesirable results we are getting.*

2 *The measure of the problem now that tells us it is a problem.*

Benefit

What "Should be" (requirements)

How (design)

Measure-goal

5 *Deliverable results, that when delivered, reasonably will achieve the Goal Measure.*

6 *A specific way the "Should be" results can be delivered.*

3 *The desired measure of the problem that indicates it's been solved.*

Figure 6.1   Problem Pyramid, explanation of the blocks.

For instance, let's say that I've decided my problem is that I'm out of shape physically. Defining the current measures in Block 2 forces me to get clear and objective about how I can tell that I'm out of shape. I might use as a measure of being out of shape that it takes me an hour to walk a mile. If I can't meaningfully measure my problem, I've probably not defined it appropriately.

Block 3 lists the goal measures that when achieved would lead the problem's owner to say the problem has been solved. For instance, I might decide that being in the desired physical condition means I am able to walk a mile in 15 minutes. If I can't define the goal in objectively measurable terms, I really have no reliable way to tell whether the problem has been solved.

The difference between the current and goal measures is the benefit, or value, we'll obtain from solving the problem. Remember, a requirement provides value when delivered, so it's important to be clear on what that value is. Being in better physical shape provides me the value of living longer and more comfortably, and of course, I can walk faster.

Once we've identified the problem and how to tell it's been solved, it's time to go down the left side of the Problem Pyramid and determine how we're going to achieve the goal measure. We don't solve problems directly. Rather, we solve problems by identifying the causes of the problem and what will reduce or eliminate those causes. Thus, in Block 4 we describe the real "as is" process that is causing the results which the current measures make us say is a problem.

Block 5 describes the "should be" process, that when it occurs will reasonably lead to achieving the goal measures and thus would enable us to say the problem has been solved. *This "should be" block contains the business requirements*. It is describing in business terms *what* we should be doing instead of what we're currently doing (that's causing our problem). Before getting to an example that should make this clearer, we need to point out what hasn't been mentioned yet.

Block 6 describes the high-level design of *how* the Block 5 *whats* will be accomplished. Ordinarily in our world this will be some sort of system or software, and *Block 6 is depicting major system requirements* (using the term "system" to include hardware, software, and manual procedures). Note that it makes absolutely no sense to try figuring out *how* a design will work until we know *what* business requirements the design must accomplish. Without a Problem Pyramid to guide us, though, it's easy to skip Block 5 *whats* and go directly to the Block 6 *hows* that we technical folks enjoy implementing.

Example: Reuse repository

When we subject people's typical requirements definitions to the Problem Pyramid discipline, it's easy to see why the real requirements so often are missed. The tool enables us to detect and thereby avoid common logic mistakes that ordinarily afflict requirements definitions. The Problem Pyramid is not a panacea. It actually can make the process seem harder because it reveals difficulties that we previously were not conscious of. Proficiency improves with guided practice and analyzing examples of the tool in action.

Figure 6.2 shows an actual Problem Pyramid prepared by a seminar participant who was responsible for her global organization's reuse repository. She defined as a problem that reuse data were not globally accessible, as measured by the number of people who currently lacked access, and her goal measure was for all people to have access. (The actual numbers in this example were not available, but back on the job real figures are essential.) She listed two causes of the problem. People using stand-alone PCs by definition did not have access to the repository, and the company had given low priority to implementing an intranet that would provide employees access. Her "should be" requirements were to give everyone access via the Web and intranet.

This sure sounds like a problem. You may even be familiar with similar problems. Perhaps already it's becoming clearer how organizing with the Problem Pyramid can help, but we're not done. The Problem Pyramid tool

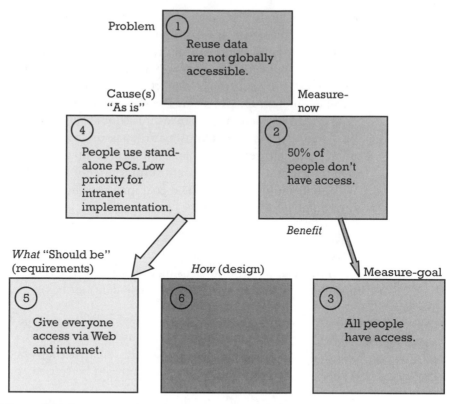

Figure 6.2   Reuse repository initial problem pyramid.

includes a set of guideline questions to systematically evaluate whether the real problem and requirements have been defined appropriately.

Guidelines for evaluating the problem definition

Is the problem really the problem?   Unfortunately, just asking this generic question by itself seldom causes a person to realize they've misdefined their problem, which is why we ask the following additional questions.

Do the measures fit the problem?   They often don't, which means either the measures, or the problem, or both are wrong. In Figure 6.2, the number of people with access indeed seems a measure of the stated problem.

Will real significant value result from meeting the goal measure? What if we take the measure to the extreme?   If everyone has access to the reuse repository, will there necessarily be any added benefit? No. Access alone is not the full story.

Why are we doing it at all? What if we just didn't do it?   Applying the guideline to the example, we ask what difference it would make if we didn't have a repository at all. The purpose of the repository is for people to reuse things rather than recreating them. By so doing, they can spend less time and effort developing systems and can improve quality by using proven components. That's the value to be obtained: when people actually use their repository access and then reuse artifacts in ways that produce systems quicker, cheaper, and better. However, the measures don't relate to this value.

The real problem and its measures should reflect these issues and would be stated better as, "Not reusing artifacts to advantage." More appropriate measures might refer to the amount or percentage of artifacts that are actually reused and to the time, effort, and quality needed to develop systems with that amount of reuse. The goal measures in this instance would represent improvements in each.

Do the causes reasonably cause the problem? If "Not reusing artifacts to advantage" is the real problem, then "Reuse data are not globally accessible" sounds like a cause of not reusing the artifacts. The stand-alone PCs and low intranet priority are subcauses of reuse data not being globally accessible.

Have we identified all the likely key causes? Why else might people not reuse things? They might not know what is available or how to reuse it. There may not be things available that they could reuse, perhaps because people may not know how to build artifacts so they can be reused.

Does the "should be" solve the problem? Is it whats in business language that when delivered reasonably will lead to accomplishing the goal measure? Does the "should be" address all key "as is" causes in ways that reasonably are likely to reduce or eliminate them? When we examine "Give everyone access via the Web and intranet," we can tell it is simply restating the original goal measure and is a *how* rather than a *what*; and it doesn't address the additional key causes we've just identified.

What else should be addressed that this affects or is affected by? For instance, people often want to do things their own way rather than use what someone else did. Moreover, it generally takes more effort to make something that can be reused than to make it for a single use, and often, necessary additional time and resources are not provided. This needs to be added to the "as is" causes and addressed in the "should be."

Effects of applying the guidelines

Figure 6.3 shows the Problem Pyramid as revised in accordance with the issues the guidelines revealed. Please note that precise measures were not available in class but would be needed to guide implementation of this Problem Pyramid on the job. It would have been easy to proceed with implementing a system to "give everyone access" as originally defined in Figure 6.2, but I think applying the evaluation guidelines shows why such a system probably would have failed to provide meaningful value. It seems likely that the additional causes identified in Figure 6.3 would have appeared one at a time in ways that we'd traditionally call "requirements creep." Costs would rise and the users would be blamed for not knowing what they wanted.

In contrast, I think it's readily apparent that Block 5 of the revised Problem Pyramid in Figure 6.3 indeed is describing business requirements *whats* that when delivered reasonably will provide significant value by achieving the goal measures in Block 3.

In my experience, developers frequently start with Block 6, the system requirements *hows* of the product they expect to build. Unless Blocks 1 through 5 are defined first, and unless the guidelines are applied to make sure the real problem and requirements are identified adequately, efforts spent on Block 6 can't help getting into trouble. Thus, using the Problem Pyramid means, "It's not right" doesn't have to be inevitable.

✍ Exercise: Prepare your own Problem Pyramid

Fill out a Problem Pyramid to describe a problem that you are encountering, preferably with a project at work, since work problems tend to be easier to

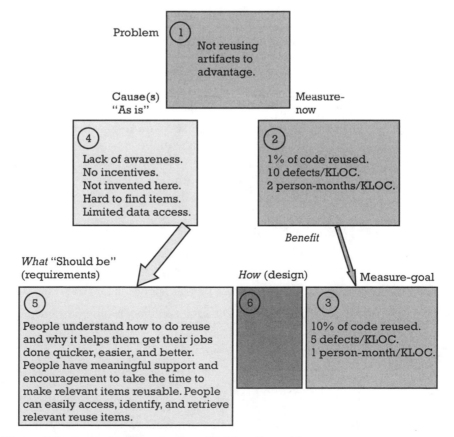

Figure 6.3 Revised reuse repository Problem Pyramid.

analyze when initially learning this technique. One further guideline: don't define your problem in terms of individuals (i.e., don't say your problem is Sara).

Try it. Using the tool, and probably struggling with it a bit, is key to learning how to apply it effectively.

Example: Social service software

The Problem Pyramid is enormously powerful, but it's also hard to get right. In seminars, I find the most effective way for participants to learn the technique is to draft a Problem Pyramid of their own and then have the group apply the guideline questions to evaluate it. Since such feedback is not possible in a book, the next best learning method is for me to share with you some of the examples from business and systems professionals in my seminars.

Following the analysis of other people's efforts still can be a very instructive way to learn better how to formulate an effective Problem Pyramid. To facilitate readability, I'll lay out the content in linear text rather than in the pyramid format.

This example comes from a seminar participant, whom I'll call Mary, who is the technology director for a private social service agency. The agency manages more than 60 separately funded service programs. Each service program is responsible for managing its own budget and providing information reports to the agency for oversight and consolidation.

The agency also has a for-profit subsidiary, which has written a software package to perform the agency's, and its own, service programs' record keeping and reporting. Each service program must pay to use the software, but has the option of whether or not to use it. In addition the software is sold to similar organizations outside of the agency. Here is Mary's initial Problem Pyramid. Note: It's the *content* that is important, not grammar or complete sentences; specific details can be filled in later.

Problem: The software package is supposed to be used by the various internal service programs but they have not chosen to use it.

Current measures: 10% of service program clients' outcomes are reported. Close to 0% of service programs are using the software.

Goal *measures*: 90% of service program clients' outcomes are reported with software.
70% of service programs use it.

Causes: Software was written for commercial use (sale to others) versus internal use.
The internal service programs have a mindset against the software now.
There's a difference between what was developed and what the internal service program staff members think is usable.

The training is poor quality.

Modules are too generic for internal needs.

Should be: A project to redefine user requirements and fit them with the existing software; and maybe also make software modifications.

Fellow systems professionals generally felt that Mary had a real problem and described it well. Now, let's apply the guideline questions to analyze and improve Mary's Problem Pyramid. The measures do relate to usage of the software. However, it was not clear what value would be gained if the service programs actually used the software. This suggests either the measures are wrong or the problem is not the real problem.

Mary explained that the agency was counting on the software usage fees to provide significantly more revenue for the agency than fees currently were generating. Ironically, the software has been sold successfully a number of times to outside organizations, although revenues from outside also are lower than desired. Upon reflection, Mary further realized that failure of the service programs to participate in using the software greatly affected the agency's ability to achieve its social service objectives.

After further discussion, Mary realized there were several additional key causes of the problems that had not been mentioned. Moreover, the guideline questions revealed that the "should be" was describing tasks rather than deliverable *whats*. Merely redefining the requirements so they fit what the software already does seems highly unlikely to achieve desired objectives; and it's the opposite of addressing the causes of the problem.

Based on the evaluation feedback, Mary's Problem Pyramid was revised as follows. Please note that precise measures were not available for the exercise in the seminar but would be needed when used for real back on the job.

Problem: The agency can't adjust programs/services adequately and can't evaluate effectiveness of programs or create strategies for exiting from ones that aren't worthwhile.

Revenue and endowment are lower than expected from sales of software.

Current measures: Low ($___) revenues, from both internal and external sources.

Low effectiveness of programs in serving clientele, as identified by satisfaction ratings and program outcome indicators (such as number of clients served who no longer need the services).

Goal measures: X% and/or $Y higher revenues, from both internal and external sources.

Z% higher effectiveness of programs in serving clientele.

Causes: Reporting is not consistent or verifiable.

Reports of the 60 service programs don't roll up to the agency level, so the agency cannot see the impact of programs on the community.

Unwillingness of internal service programs to use the software makes it difficult to sell the software to outsiders.

The agency doesn't know its clients' demographics, so it can't learn enough about its own business to guide it properly.

Services cross programs.

Software was written for commercial use (sale to others) versus internal use.

The internal service programs have a mindset against the software now.

There's a difference between what was developed and what the internal service program staff members think is usable.

Poor training.

Modules are too generic for internal needs.

Should be: Provide consistent, verifiable reporting that rolls up to the agency level.

Facilitate actual work of the service programs' staff members in a manner which easily adjusts to the unique operational styles of both internal and external service programs.

Capture client demographics and outcomes in a simple, reliable manner that is consistent across service programs and applicable to outside organizations.

Provide support and guidance that enable effective use of the software.

Mary and her fellow seminar participants agreed that the revised Problem Pyramid identified the agency's real problem (actually two highly interrelated problems) and that the revised "should be" requirements would be reasonably likely to lead to significant value by meeting the goal measures.

Example: Web Site

One of Jerry's responsibilities is updating the company's Web site. He offered this Problem Pyramid.

Problem: Web site takes too long to update.

Current measure: 15 hours of my time a month.

Goal measure: Less than 10 hours of my time a month.

Causes: Changes are e-mailed to me to update manually.
Different content formats, static page content.
Content conversion (e.g., MS-Word to HTML).

Should be: Template-driven.

Again, the initial Problem Pyramid seems reasonable, doesn't it? Many of us can identify with being pulled in multiple directions and not really having 15 hours a month for some additional responsibility like updating a Web site. Still, we need to apply our guidelines to evaluate the adequacy of Jerry's Problem Pyramid. One seminar participant felt the problem should be restated as:

Problem: Inefficient, inconsistent manual process that needs automating.

Again, this suggestion seems initially like a reasonable problem and is probably similar to many of the problem statements that traditionally drive systems projects. Evaluating this suggested revision, though, first reveals that Jerry has given us no reason to believe his Web updating process is inefficient or inconsistent. Technical people often simply assume that anything done manually would be better automated. Such assumptions frequently are not justified. Moreover, this problem is stated in terms of a presumed solution, which by definition is not the real problem. The purpose of the Problem Pyramid is to lead us logically to identify suitable "should be" requirements, not to start with them as a given.

Looking further at Jerry's initial version, we spot a red flag. Saving 5 hours a month is a pretty small benefit; and the benefit is entirely to Jerry, with no real benefit to the company or their customers. Taking this to the extreme, Jerry could save 15 hours a month of his own time if he didn't update the Web site at all. That probably would have a significant impact on the company and possibly on its customers too. The Problem Pyramid measures may need to reflect the costs that would result from an inadequate Web site, were Jerry to spend less time updating it.

To gauge the financial effects of Web site adequacy, we need to know a bit more about the purpose/value of the site and its updating. We need to know how the company uses the Web site and what role updates play. Jerry tells us that his company is in the business of creating and hosting Internet sites. Their own site is a sales tool, showcasing their ability to do more attractive content. A customer's ability to update his/her own Web site could be an additional selling point.

Now we've found significant value. In reviewing further, Jerry realized that his "should be" about templates did not relate back to any causes. Here's Jerry's revised Problem Pyramid.

Problem: Web site is not providing sufficiently effective marketing examples economically.

Current measures: Number of Web site projects and services (e.g., upgrades) sold to customers.

Goal measures: Increased number of Web site projects and services sales to customers. (Again, Jerry needs to get real numbers to apply this at work.)

Causes: Limited customers' access to their Web sites.
Inconsistent formats requiring interpretation and content conversion (e.g., MS-Word to HTML), which is subject to errors and rework.
Delays and duplicating customers' effort when changes are e-mailed to me to update manually.
No templates.

Should Be: Customers are able to do their updating easily and reliably.
Web-based;
Template-driven.

Example: Opportunity

Another seminar participant, Terry, said he was having difficulty formulating his Problem Pyramid because he had an opportunity, rather than a problem. I explained that opportunities work the same way. The value comes from achieving a goal measure when the opportunity is taken, and the causes relate to whatever one is not able to do that the opportunity will enable. Here's what Terry described.

> *Opportunity*: Use a big multimillion-dollar manufacturing enterprise system software package.

Quickly evaluating this opportunity, it should be clear first of all that Terry is describing a Block 6 system design *how*, not a Block 1 problem/opportunity. It also should be obvious that the opportunity is for the software package vendor to make a big sale, not for Terry's company.

✍ Exercise: Review your Problem Pyramid

Rereview the Problem Pyramid that you wrote for your own project at work. Apply the guidelines to make sure it's on track. Don't be surprised if you then change it from its original version. If you're like most people who try this, you'll find that initial impressions may very likely have led you astray, but now you're on more solid footing with a better understanding of the real problem and real requirements to achieve value.

The Problem Pyramid can be an invaluable tool for getting off on the right track. The tool is hard to use, mainly because most of us are not accustomed to thinking in the disciplined manner the tool applies. Practicing with the tool, and especially applying the guidelines to evaluate use of the tool, are essential to developing proficiency. Whenever you are presented with a problem, use the Problem Pyramid. Even if the problem is presented as a no brainer, such as "change this field on the screen," at least apply the Problem Pyramid thought processes to make sure you understand what the value is that you must deliver. The following chapters describe more about using the Problem Pyramid.

Applying the techniques

Get brilliant on the basics.
　　—Vince Lombardi

Consider the differences between American football as played at the professional level compared to the high school game. The field and ball are the same size. Rules are basically the same, and teams at both levels use fundamentally the same plays. What's mainly different isn't what they do, it's how well they do it. Legendary coach Vince Lombardi led his Green Bay Packers to Super Bowl championships, not by using fancier plays, but by making sure players were excellent at executing the basics, such as running, passing, blocking, and tackling.

One develops proficiency by practicing and by analyzing one's performance, which is where a coach can be especially helpful. While superstars undoubtedly often are possessed of outstanding raw talent, many are also the first at practice in the morning and the last to leave. Just knowing techniques is no value unless the techniques actually are used, and used well.

The same is true with requirements discovery and other system development methods. I think you'd be amazed at how frequently I hear systems folks say, "I need the advanced class. I've heard all these basic techniques before." When I ask whether they use the basic techniques, invariably the answer is "No. That's why I need the advanced techniques." Truly advanced practitioners actually use the basic techniques, and they practice and analyze their performance to improve. In contrast, ineffective requirements definers haven't come close to mastering the basics.

Returning to our order entry system case, Ann Analyst indeed is trying to take feedback to heart and improve upon her original requirements definition. She has gathered more information and written an addition to her prior findings.

✍ Exercise: Review additional requirements

Read the following addition to Ann's definition of business requirements and
review her recommendation.

Business Requirements (Additional Findings)

The IS Director tells Ann Analyst that ElecTech's products are recognized widely as the highest quality in their industry, but the order entry problem causes customers to refuse to buy from ElecTech. The problem especially limits sales of new high-profit SuperProducts, that only ElecTech currently sells. They consist of complex combinations of simpler configurations, plus additional components to make them work together in the customer's unique environment.

Ann finds: Salespeople report that competitors promise delivery in 3 weeks. ElecTech can promise no quicker than manufacturing's (monthly) published lead times of 4 to 5 weeks, and often orders still are late, wrong, or incomplete.

Each of six sales regions has about 50 salespeople in the field, served by two or three O/E specialists at HQ. The IS director provided salespeople the ability to enter orders into a mainframe computer terminal at their office, so they no longer have to fax or mail orders to HQ O/P.

Now, orders contain far fewer errors but still take O/P specialists several days to review and correct. An O/E specialist for the sales region enters the marked-up order into the legacy O/E system. Orders are printed in manufacturing, which is considered ElecTech's strongest area. Planners schedule manufacture of each product component and update the computer order with the fully assembled order's ship date.

Orders identify customer name, bill-to and (sometimes as many as 200) ship-to addresses, due date (often ASAP), as well as prices, quantities, and product numbers for each of the components included in each product configuration being ordered. About a dozen common configurations have separate product numbers.

O/E specialists report that orders are constantly being changed. They feel salespeople often book phony or partially correct orders to get on the manufacturing schedule. Revisions may change ship dates, often delaying them. Each revision causes printing of a complete customer confirm. On shipment, the order is updated and an invoice is printed.

Ann Analyst has recommended that the legacy system be replaced with an XML and J2EE-compliant Web-based system incorporating Web Services and .NET. The salesperson would enter the entire order at the sales office and O/E specialists would review and update it online, rather than marking up printed documents for later entry. The salesperson also would be able to revise the order directly through their PC in the sales office.

Analysis of Ann's updated requirements

Ann Analyst certainly seems to have addressed a number of the concerns identified with regard to her original definition of requirements. She has provided much more information about the company's order entry system and its problems.

Also, Ann has made a specific recommendation, which is essentially her conclusion as to what is required: "An XML and J2EE-compliant Web-based system incorporating Web Services and .NET" to enable both sales and order processing personnel to deal with orders through the computer rather than via printed documents.

In my experience, many projects get well underway with requirements similar to Ann's. Those projects invariably encounter difficulties. Ann has fallen into a classic trap, which can be hard to realize in the midst of a project, where activity and urgency tend to be very distracting. However, by presenting Ann's situation as a case that we can observe objectively, the trap should be evident. Moreover, by learning from Ann's mistakes, we should be better able to spot—and then avoid—such pitfalls on our own real projects.

What's the classic trap Ann has fallen into? Ann's recommendation presents the organization's requirement purely in terms of technology, without any explicit identification of the real business problem, let alone any rational basis for showing how "an XML and J2EE-compliant Web-based system incorporating Web Services and .NET" has anything to do with solving the problem or providing value. Requirements phrased in such technical solution terms are very common because they are so appealing to the technical side. Business requirements may include technological constraints and preferences, but only incidentally to requirements that provide value to the business.

We favorably acknowledged Ann's efforts to improve her use of basic requirements definition skills; but she seems not to have used the fundamental key technique. If Ann had used the Problem Pyramid, it would have been obvious to her (as it is to us observers) that Ann started with the Block 6 design *hows*, without first using Blocks 1–5 to identify the real problem, measures, causes, and business requirements *whats*.

Implementing technology for its own sake almost always assures some degree of disappointment. Technology can be an enabler of improved processes but seldom provides value as an end in and of itself.

Identifying the real problem

Let's do what Ann should have done and start with Block 1 of the Problem Pyramid. I think it's very likely that you found yourself applying the tool when reading Ann's additional findings. So, what is the real problem? Here are some of the commonly suggested answers:

- Inefficient manual processing of paper-based orders;

- Too many steps involved in processing orders;
- Complicated products and product numbering scheme;
- Sales people don't understand the products adequately;
- Order entry system doesn't edit sufficiently;
- Orders that are shipped late, incomplete, or wrong;
- Lead time is too long—5 weeks versus competitors' 3 weeks;
- Phony orders;
- Order revisions;
- Low customer satisfaction;
- Customers refuse to buy;
- Lost sales.

Identifying the real problem isn't easy. Only one of the above listed common interpretations of the same fact situation can be the real problem. There's a very good chance that trouble would result from proceeding with a project to address something other than the real problem, and it is easy for that to happen.

Of the dozen choices above, some are likely to be measures. For instance, I'd suggest that low customer satisfaction and lost sales are probably measures of the real problem.

Upon reflection, it should become apparent that some of the other choices in fact are causes of the real problem. The various sources of inefficiency, extra or duplicated work, and errors all kind of cluster together, which helps tip us off that they probably are causes rather than the real problem.

Long lead time is tricky to classify because its mention of numbers (5 and 3 weeks) sort of makes it sound like a measure; but wording alone isn't the determinant of whether something is a measure. Long lead times *or* orders that are shipped late, incomplete, or wrong could be the real problem. Inefficiency, duplication, and errors could be causes of either long lead times or orders shipped late. The direct value to be obtained *just* from reducing lead times from 5 to 3 weeks mainly would be the reduced cost of carrying raw material inventory for two additional weeks. Value also certainly would result directly from reducing measures of late, incomplete, and wrong orders such as the costs of corrections, returns, and customer service.

While solving each of these potential problems would provide some value, I don't think they provide the significant value that is at issue for ElecTech. Rather, I think these two problems are examples of how problems can be hierarchical. In fact, these two problems are subproblem causes of the *real problem: Customers refuse to buy*.

Note, customers refusing to buy is much different from merely having lower sales. Low sales is a measure and could be due to having poor products, producing too few products, not advertising, or other such problems. Low sales will be improved only by solving the real problem, which is why it is essential to identify it specifically.

Customers refusing to buy is where the money is. Whatever solutions are implemented must turn around customers' present refusal to buy. Efforts to save some money on inventory or order corrections will only forestall the inevitable demise of the business if they don't also cause customers to stop refusing to buy.

ElecTech case Problem Pyramid

Figure 7.1 shows a Problem Pyramid for the ElecTech order entry case based on the analysis above. Using the Problem Pyramid as a guide, it's apparent a bit more information is needed. Therefore, Ann gathered some additional information about measures, which are stated as percentages but could be expressed in absolute dollars and units. Thus, the company knows it has a problem because total regular product sales dollars are down 33 percent compared to the prior year. The problem is even worse in that for the recently introduced SuperProducts, sales dollars are only 25 percent of the projected amount. Moreover, salespeople report that 50 percent of qualified sales prospects are rejecting proposals.

With a bit more inquiry, Ann ascertained that ElecTech management has decided that they can say the problem has been solved when customers stop

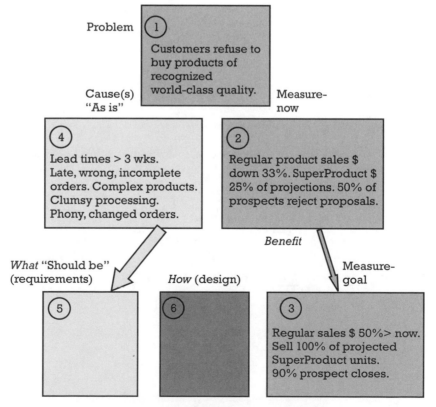

Figure 7.1 Problem Pyramid for ElecTech's order entry system.

refusing to buy, as evidenced by accomplishing the main goal measures indicated. When sales people are able to close 90 percent of qualified sales, total sales of regular products during the next year easily should increase by 50 percent over the current year (to the prior year's total); sales of Super-Products should increase by a factor of four to the original projection. Such growth is deemed reasonable considering how much sales have been suppressed.

Ann now seems to be headed in a direction where additional requirements definition efforts should be more fruitful. In Chapter 8, we'll examine ways to find out more about the requirements.

Data gathering

God gave us two ears and one mouth.
—Benjamin Disraeli

Disraeli's famous observation on physiology pretty much sums up the key to data gathering. The ears are input devices. The mouth isn't. To gather data effectively, one needs to input, not output, so listen much more than speak. Following this simple admonition alone probably would contribute more than any other single act to improving the adequacy of requirements.

Why gather data?

Defining requirements is all about data gathering, but why do we gather data? The data we gather is not the design of a product, nor is the data the specifications to direct programming. *The data are not the business requirements,* either!

Rather, we gather data to identify the real problem and its measures, understand its key "as is" causes, and suggest suitable "should be" requirements that when delivered will provide value by achieving the goal measures. In other words, *we gather data in order to prepare a Problem Pyramid.*

Note that data can come from a variety of sources, not just from actual users of the system. We'll refer to this broader collection of sources as "stakeholders," which often is what is meant by the more restrictive term "users."

The following sections discuss several techniques that have been found useful for gathering data relevant to requirements. I think it's safe to say that every book on requirements describes some of these methods, and a few books that I'll mention specifically concentrate mainly on single techniques.

This book combines both approaches. That is, we'll describe all the major data gathering techniques of which I'm aware, along with highlighting their strengths and weaknesses. All methods do have weaknesses. However, one of the biggest difficulties people have is in seeing their own techniques from a different perspective, which frequently can reveal weaknesses. People often *presume* their methods are effective when the real story may be different, but they may not recognize the possibility of any different view.

Then we'll focus in greater depth than I've seen elsewhere on the primary requirements data gathering technique, interviewing. Moreover, instead of just talking *about* interviewing, I'll endeavor within the limits of the printed page to provide you, the reader, with more of the *experience* of interviewing. I'll convey as verbatim as I can recall actual interviews that I've heard. As you get wrapped up in hearing the interview dialog in your head, you'll appreciate much more the difficult dynamics that make or break an interview's effectiveness. By experiencing and evaluating real interviews, you'll be better prepared to spot and avoid pitfalls when you go interviewing yourself.

Surveys and questionnaires

Surveys and questionnaires (which for our purposes are essentially synonymous) rely on the person being interviewed to provide information in written form, usually either on paper or directly into a computer. The advantages relate to the ability to gather data seemingly economically from a large number of people who may be spread widely in time and geography.

In my experience, the true value of these methods is largely illusory, and I find that ineffective requirements definers very often tend to overly rely on surveys and questionnaires. The fundamental risk is that these techniques tend to provide unreliable, often erroneous data. The most famous example occurred the night of the United States presidential election in 1948, when a major newspaper published the headline, "Dewey Wins!" The newspaper had relied on survey predictions rather than on actual voter tallies. In truth, President Harry Truman was reelected and defeated contender Thomas Dewey.

Surveys are notorious for very low response rates. Consequently, it can be easy to overgeneralize findings based on a sample which does not accurately represent the population. For example, it's common to send out surveys asking about system response time. Often, all the returned surveys come from people who feel response times are slow, which can make it appear there is a response time problem, when in fact perhaps the great majority of system users haven't returned the survey because they have no problem.

How interviewees interpret the questionnaire's wording also can be highly unpredictable, which means they may be answering a different question from what the interviewer thought was being asked. Being attentive to clearly wording the questions is necessary but not sufficient. At a minimum, some personal follow-up with at least some of the responders is always advisable to gauge interpretations. Organizations that specialize in conducting surveys also usually invest in significant advance testing of wording alternatives to build confidence that the responses will be meaningful. It's unlikely that most of our projects would expend such effort fine-tuning a requirements data gathering survey or questionnaire. As a compromise, consider a pilot survey of a select subset of the anticipated recipients, with very active personal follow-up to ensure consistent understanding, before circulating the questions to the full population.

Written formats generally are most effective for gathering easily discovered and verified factual data, such as how many PCs are in one's office. However, people often don't have even the types of factual data that the surveys ask about. Perhaps you too have filled out questionnaires to qualify for free subscriptions to trade magazines. They tend to ask seemingly objective questions like the annual dollar amount of computer peripherals I'm involved in purchasing, and they make it easier by providing ranges of dollar amounts. Of course, like many responders, I really don't know the dollar amount, even within the broad ranges provided, so I guess and could be way wrong.

When surveys try to solicit ideas, the responses can be hard to interpret. Sometimes the difficulty is due to the responders' inability to articulate their thoughts, but often the problem is with how they interpreted the question or conceived the response context. At a minimum, well-constructed surveys usually include some mechanism for the responders to explain their answers. Even for questionnaires that seem purely objective, it's advisable to invite free-form comments. One of the most common experiences upon receiving back completed responses is realizing what should have been asked instead.

✖ Warning

Because of the need for follow-up clarification, many surveys actually cost much more than initially appeared, and even with follow-up, few provide the expected amount of reliable information.

Literature searches

This obvious technique is too seldom employed, especially by technical people. Reading the literature in the business area may not provide immediate solutions for the presenting problem. However, becoming familiar with the literature is a valuable way to acquire a background foundation for understanding the business and the people who carry it out.

My informal surveys of participants in seminars reveal that most people employed in technical capacities consider themselves professionals. Yet, other than for formal academic programs, few read any books about the work for which they accept payment, and many don't even regularly read any technical trade periodicals. Would you keep going to a physician who had not read anything about her field since graduating from medical school? I don't think so. Being a professional includes taking personal responsibility for keeping up in one's field and honing skills, including soft skills.

Being an effective requirements identifier similarly involves taking the initiative to learn about the business domain subject area. Textbooks, journals and magazines, Web sites, white papers, industry standards, professional associations, training, conferences, and competitors' product descriptions are good sources to investigate. See what your users are reading and borrow it from them to read it too.

Reviewing documents

For many of us charged with developing systems, our only requirements are in the form of documents from somebody informing us "what is required." Such directives have a habit of turning into creep, "not what I expected," and "it's still not right." As mentioned previously, just because the source of a requirement is someone in a business management position, even at the highest levels, does not mean they are identifying the real, business requirements; nor, of course, does it mean that they aren't.

Our challenge is to make sure we know what the real requirements are, not to tell the bosses they don't know what they're doing. It's highly unlikely they know or realize the need to know the lessons of this book, but you can use a couple of the techniques without provoking political repercussions. Try reviewing a Problem Pyramid with the source to help make sure that you, the dumb Columbo, adequately understand the real requirements.

For those (hopefully frequent) occasions when we do have opportunity to gather data about requirements, various types of documents that exist for other purposes are usually good sources of data. Often we can learn specifics about the problem (or more likely the desired situation that may currently not exist) from the company's vision statements, sales and marketing reports and literature, and instructions for users of the company's products and services that are produced by the area whose requirements are being identified.

✖ Warning

These types of documents (as well as general business literature in the field) tend to describe an idealized presumed process that may bear little resemblance to the real process. However, it is important to be aware of what is presumed to be going on as well as what really is.

Effective requirements definers collect souvenirs from the business area. After all, "souvenir" means "to remember." While some such souvenirs may provide general background information, most are specific to the problem at hand and help us remember lots of details we'd otherwise forget. I always try to take *copies*, not the originals, of documents such as input forms, reports, screen prints and menu structures, current system descriptions and user instructions manuals, policies and procedures, standards, laws and regulations, and organization charts.

Perhaps the most fruitful written sources of information about the specific problem are memos, e-mails, and problem reports, including help desk logs. These documents are especially likely to provide insights into the real process.

Two practices with regard to souvenir documents tend to differentiate more effective from less effective requirements definers. First, effective requirements definers *collect forms and reports that have been filled out*, whereas ineffective requirements definers collect blank versions. A blank preprinted form shows the presumed process that can differ markedly from the real way the form is filled out. Completed forms may reveal that some fields are not used or are used differently from the presumed way, and it's very common to find additional notes and codes that the preprinted form did not anticipate.

Second, effective requirements definers *gather related transaction documents, such as for the same customer*, which allows tracking the uses of data throughout the process flow. In contrast, ineffective requirements definers tend to gather documents that don't tie together.

Prototyping

Many authors and others in the systems field consider prototypes to be a key technique for gathering requirements data. In fact, some developers consider the prototype to be *the* requirements. Let me offer some additional perspectives, because I think *prototypes can be a valuable tool, especially for guiding design, but the role of prototypes in discovering business requirements is generally overstated and is subject to turning counterproductive through inappropriate use.*

A prototype is often referred to as a model of the finished system. Typically, what this means is that the prototype is a working version of the expected computer program, but key parts of the program have been left out. While prototyping can be used to try out any type of program code, including the most complex technical details, ordinarily prototypes concentrate on the graphical user interface (GUI) that the user interacts with and omit or shortcut the "guts," the complicated behind-the-scenes processing logic that generally takes a much longer time to program. In this way, the prototype can be created relatively quickly so that it can be shown to the user for feedback.

Prototyping's three major strengths are breaking the system into small pieces, providing a proof of concept that some capability is possible, and enabling quick feedback based on concretely observable operation of the program. Prototype iterations are considerably preferable to what many development organizations used to do: program the whole system before showing any of it to users and then discovering that it all must be redone.

Not only is quicker feedback more valuable, but users can understand what the developer has in mind a lot better by seeing it in operation than by merely hearing it described in words. A prototype can spot off-base interpretations before they have tied up a lot of time; and prototypes facilitate some "what if" types of thinking. An indirect but often significant advantage of prototyping is that it gives users a sense that the developers actually are accomplishing something.

Prototyping also has a number of weaknesses. Perhaps the biggest weakness is that many people who rely on prototyping don't have an inkling that prototyping itself could have weaknesses, let alone what the weaknesses are; and frequently they treat prototyping with a sort of religious zeal which rejects out of hand even any mention of possible issues.

I'm not disputing that prototyping has value, only that prototyping is not very effective as a business requirements definition technique, for which it frequently is touted. In fact, prototypes at best are a highly inefficient and indirect way to discover business requirements. At worst, prototypes can be counterproductive because they create the illusion of having identified requirements.

Prototypes usually have very little to do with discovering business requirements. A prototype is not the requirements. It's not even the design. *A prototype is programmed code implementing a presumed design of presumed requirements.* I say "presumed" because in many instances prototyping is the epitome of the cartoon cited in Chapter 3, "You folks start coding; I'll go find out what the requirements are." Writing code is a very time consuming activity, and only a small part of that effort relates to the business requirements themselves.

Consequently, prototypes mainly channel attention away from *what* the user actually needs to the product the developer intends to deliver. The concrete working program indeed is understandable, but almost always results in feedback which is pretty much limited to tweaking *how* the code already has been written. The user almost certainly is going to end up with some version of that program code, regardless of whether it accomplishes business objectives. At the extreme, for instance, a prototype is highly unlikely to reveal a function which would best be performed manually.

What I refer to as "GUI versus guts" creates two types of problems. One is easily recognized by almost everyone who has used prototypes: The users like the prototype and ask if they can start using it in production. The developer has to decline because the prototype is only the GUI shell, and the guts that do the real processing won't be ready for some time. To avoid this result, many authors encourage use of "paper prototypes," where the screens are mocked up on paper instead of actually being programmed. Not only are paper prototypes faster, but users don't expect to be able to use them for real.

The second form of GUI versus guts is more insidious and critical, but it is seldom recognized, which makes it even more insidious and critical. *The bulk of the value in a program is provided by the guts, which prototypes generally leave out.* Thus, there is a big risk of iterating mainly with regard to GUI superficialities while paying short schrift to the guts that actually are sup-posed to be addressing the real business requirements.

Furthermore, as generally performed, prototyping presents several addi-tional concerns. Many people encounter "prototypitis," where iterations continue endlessly. Often too, even though it's supposedly just for develop-ment purposes, the prototype actually may be used for production, but because the prototype can change constantly, one never knows exactly which version caused which results, and it's seldom been subjected to suit-able testing or configuration (version) control.

In fact, for many programs, prototyping is the only testing performed. At best, prototyping usually provides no more than a general positive test proof of concept that the program can do its intended function; even then, it's seldom exercising the actual guts code. Moreover, a prototype is highly unlikely to be subjected to the negative tests that also are needed to ensure the program doesn't do what it's not supposed to do.

Focus groups

Two common techniques involve eliciting requirements from groups of stakeholders. The first, focus groups, is most familiar as a market research method. A focus group consists of stakeholders with a common, fairly nar-rowly defined interest which the group discusses in *depth*. For particularly troubling and risky areas, focus groups can help assure the requirements have been addressed more adequately. The keys to effectiveness are well-thought-out questions and skillful facilitation to assure group synergies in uncovering the important information.

In my experience, focus groups are an underutilized technique in the information systems area. I encourage you to consider them but appreciate they are unlikely to be used because conducting a focus group can be expensive, and because systems people may not feel the need for such depth on any particular topic.

Joint application development

The second group technique, joint application development (JAD), which also is called joint application design, is used fairly extensively in systems projects. JAD is a facilitated group technique developed at IBM. In contrast to a focus group's emphasis on depth, JAD assembles as many of the stake-holders as possible to achieve *breadth*.

When facilitated effectively, JAD sessions tend to produce synergies, a sense of ownership, and general good feelings. By gathering the stakehold-ers together, direct contact can overcome many of communications difficul-ties that ordinarily arise within organizations. For instance, participants may become aware for the first time how what they do affects or is affected by what someone else does. They can easily discover and smooth out rough handoffs.

Many organizations have found JAD to be *a* valuable requirements elicitation technique. Some organizations rely almost exclusively on JAD sessions, as does colleague Ellen Gottesdiener, who enlists multiple structured approaches (similar in some ways to the CAT-Scan Approach in this book) and especially emphasizes well-defined facilitation techniques to encourage participant participation [1].

JAD too has its limitations. Effectiveness is largely a function of the facilitator's skill, and I fear more facilitators are trained than skilled. Even when JAD participants may feel great camaraderie and ownership, ineffective facilitation easily can result in only superficial attention to content. My perception is that many organizations claim to use JAD but really just have some group sessions without facilitation at all.

Because of the breadth of participation, the group's interest tends to wane quickly when more than a brief time is spent on any individual's issues. Consequently, JAD is much better suited for discovering high-level rather than detailed requirements, which means that additional techniques usually are needed to discover detail. Moreover, although often called a requirements technique, most JAD sessions indeed produce designs.

Observing operations

"You can observe a lot just by watching," said the great philosopher and baseball player Yogi Berra. I'd guess many of us have been accused of just watching other people working, but it really is a powerful way to learn about requirements. When people tell us what they do, they are more prone to describe a presumed process, whereas observing what they actually do can better alert us to the real process.

I've referred to requirements as the "should be" process. The Robertsons say part of the analyst's job is "to invent a better way to do the work" [2]. Nobody I'm familiar with addresses understanding the work more than Karen Holtzblatt and Hugh Beyer, who similarly seek, "Innovative designs ... that offer new ways of working" [3].

An emphasis on the work demands observation. Beyer and Holtzblatt have attracted an enthusiastic following, especially in the human-computer-interaction community, for their contextual design methodology for getting close to the work. Their technique couples observation with having the workers describe what they are doing as they do it, and then they all follow-up together with JAD-like group activities, such as creating affinity diagrams.

I find observation, with or without the ongoing description, to be an extremely valuable addition to merely being told about what somebody does. Unfortunately, observation also is very expensive, and many managers don't appreciate the advantages enough to allocate time or budget for it.

Also, let me raise one other caution about emphasis solely on "the work." While understanding the current work is necessary, in my opinion, focusing only on how it's done now may not be sufficient for inventing the innovative better way that "should be."

Learning to do the work

Observation is much more powerful than merely hearing about the work. By at least the same degree, learning to do the work is that much more powerful than mere observation. In turn, learning takes even more time and money; and therefore learning is even less likely to be included in budgets and schedules. It's a pity. *I've found this to be the single most effective way to learn about the real requirements*; but as with observation, or any of the techniques, it is not sufficient by itself.

When just observing, one doesn't detect many of the nuances that become apparent when trying to learn how to do it oneself. For example, watching and listening to a telemarketer may reveal only a fraction of what one learns by trying to sell the pitch to a real person on the other end of the telephone.

Moreover, I've found taking the effort to learn to do the work racks up sizable additional advantages. Consider the messages that the requirements analyst usually sends to the users and other stakeholders. The quick-hit visit for an interview may not leave much of a positive impression and could send negative vibrations. Observing operations does show a certain commitment of effort, but the observer stance can come off as seeming superior to that of the person being observed. On the other hand, investing my own effort to learn what a person does sends the message that that person is important, so they trust me more. Furthermore, when the user knows that I know how to do the job, they have greater confidence in my judgments about the work.

Many organizations assign former users to the analyst role responsible for defining requirements. The former users' background certainly helps enable their understanding the business and generally garners rapport and confidence of the current users. However, *it is the learning to do the work that provides many insights into the real process*. Prior experience and expertise can cause the former user to take things for granted, especially things that might stand out as strange to someone learning.

Let me clarify that as a practical matter, the extent of learning varies with the job and is different from actually doing the job. There are many situations where the company and/or the law would not look favorably upon my performing the work for real. For example, I'd be less likely to be able to learn, let alone perform, surgery than scheduling a patient to be operated on. Nor would the company want to rely on me to close a big sales deal, but I possibly could participate more in the selling than just observing.

Interviewing

Ultimately, requirements are the requirements of people, so ultimately data about requirements needs to come from individuals. Since one-way communications, even from people with lofty titles, regularly falls short of effectively capturing the real requirements, communications with people about requirements have to be interactive.

Interviewing is interactive person-to-person communication. It's certainly the most essential, and I believe overwhelmingly the most common, way to gather data about requirements. Therefore, we'll devote the most attention to using this technique to its fullest effectiveness. To aid learning, we'll analyze some realistic interviews for the ElecTech order entry system.

One common dilemma is deciding who should be interviewed. Worker bees, who carry out the day-to-day work and probably will be primary system users, surely need to be interviewed. So too do their supervisors, and their supervisors' managers, possibly at several levels depending upon the size and complexity of the problem and organization. I recommend *starting with the highest level position* one can get access to and working down, because the higher positions often can set the context and identify others who may also need to be interviewed. In contrast, the workers at the operational level may not be aware of all the other players who also may be affected. Furthermore, there may be many other types of people who may not be directly involved with the system but whose information also is necessary, or at least helpful.

In my experience, most systems projects are for an organization's own use, as opposed to creating software for sale. On the other hand, most authors and speakers seem to refer mainly to creating commercial software to be sold to some undetermined users. In such cases, individuals from a product or marketing department usually are considered the source of requirements. *The need to identify business requirements and the methods for doing so are the same for internally and externally used systems.* However, projects for external use invariably start at a disadvantage because product and marketing folks not only are not real users of the intended product, but they also may have very little meaningful familiarity with the external purchaser's stakeholders and their real requirements.

✖ Warning

If you are expected to rely on surrogate sources of requirements, such as your own organization's marketing staff members, or high-level managers who purport to speak for lower-level people who actually do the real work, *make every effort also to get in touch with individuals who really will be using the system or otherwise have a direct stake in it*; recognizing the high likelihood that your sources will not know the real requirements, be sure to *use the Problem Pyramid and more of the 21+ ways described in this book to test that requirements are accurate and complete.*

The most common interview format is one-on-one. Usually interviews are face-to-face, but interviewing can be conducted over the telephone, by video conferencing, and even in written correspondence such as e-mail. It's common for ineffective interviewers to interview a group of several people at once, such as everyone who works in the same group or function, since it seems more economical. Avoid this method because it usually results in only superficial information. Nobody in the group gets sufficient opportunity to be heard, and presence of others can have a censoring effect. (Note, facilitated group sessions such as JAD and focus groups are often very effective, but they are not merely group interviews.)

I have found it very effective to have two interviewers speak with a single interviewee. Interviewer costs are twice as much, and it can be intimidating, but such interviews often yield more useful information than the one-on-one format. Each interviewer acts as a double check on the other, picking up on issues that otherwise may slip through and improving the thoroughness of notes. While two-to-one is effective, having more than two interviewers just adds to expense and may interfere with interview effectiveness.

Keeping notes also can be problematic. The more one writes, the less he or she tends to pay attention to what is being said. If you're a person who has difficulty taking good notes during the interview, consider an approach used by some physicians and therapists. They take no notes during the interview, but pay very close attention. When the interview ends, they quickly write or dictate all they can remember. It's a skill that takes practice to become proficient. Alternatively, use a second interviewer or a tape recorder.

✖ Warning

Be sure to *gain prior permission to tape record an interview*. Some people do not want to be taped, for whatever their reasons. Also, be careful of relying on technology. It has a way of not working, and too often the time is not taken to listen to and transcribe the tape-recorded session into readable form. Be sure to *pay attention* to what is said so that you can write your notes later if the tape recording turns out not to work for any reason.

The keys to effective interviewing are planning and controlling the interview. Planning an interview includes qualifying the interviewee and identifying the topics to be covered. Most interviewers are ineffective because they just show up without any idea what they are trying to learn. In order to plan appropriate questions, it helps to *qualify the interviewee*, which means identifying what one should expect to learn about from them. Their role, level within the organization, and amount of experience provide good guidance. Also it's often helpful to know where they stand politically with respect to issues that may be raised, such as if they advocate a particular course of action.

It's generally wise to start the interview by *qualifying yourself* and gaining rapport. Explain why you are there and what you hope to learn about. It's courteous and can be helpful to send a note prior to the interview explaining these objectives and possibly including questions you'd like to discuss. However, I've found that despite such preparatory efforts, few interviewees give much thought to the meeting until the interviewer arrives. Yes, encourage preparation but don't rely on it. Predefined questions are only a part of what a good interview covers. Don't be like the ineffective interviewers I've seen who are rendered practically immobile when they discover the interviewee had not done the requested preparation, or it didn't cover the right things.

Your own role, level, and experience determine how much the interviewee can expect you to understand. Be pleasant and considerate, especially of the interviewee's time. Many authors suggest breaking the ice by commenting on something you see in the interviewee's office or workplace that gives you a hint about that person's interests, such as photographs, a set of golf clubs, or a trophy.

✖ Caution

Superficial discussions presumed to be building rapport invariably seem contrived and actually can harm rapport by projecting insincerity. If you must use them, be brief.

Interview techniques and tips

The interviewer controls the interview by asking and listening, not by telling. Remember, two ears and one mouth. The interviewer is there to learn what the interviewee knows and thinks. People like to talk about things of interest to them, and they don't especially find value in talking about something just because it's of interest to someone else.

The interview needs to reveal, from a *what* rather than *how* standpoint, all of colleague Len White's "Four E's of Requirements," as cited by fellow colleague Carol Dekkers [4]:

- Expressed (what they tell you they want);
- Expected (what they want but didn't tell you);
- Elusive (what they need but it's not clear how to give it to them);
- Exciting (what they didn't know they could get it but it will make them very happy).

✖ Warning

There is no set of magic questions that reliably reveal expected, elusive, and exciting requirements. Effective interviewers discover these often-unrecognized and unarticulated requirements by listening, analyzing, and digging past the expressed requirements.

Moreover: Real people don't always present things in the well-organized logical fashion that many authors' examples and sound-bite television have led us to expect. You have to be a detective and find the meaning.

Background, rationale, and emotions help us understand why people do things or perceive them as they do, which can be as important as facts and figures. *Interviewing is interpersonal,* which can be hard for people more accustomed to interacting with machines. *Don't assume you know what they are going to say. People talk about things they think are important, so look for why they think what they are talking about is valuable to know; and if you don't understand, ask.*

Ask *open-ended questions* to get things going. Open-ended questions give the interviewee the opportunity to set the direction, which ordinarily will be toward things the interviewee considers important. They invite a longer and more thoughtful response than *closed-ended questions*, which usually can be answered with a "yes," "no," or some short fact requiring only a few words. Effective interviewers use good *follow-up (or probing) questions*; ineffective interviewers don't. Sometimes raising hypothetical solutions can be helpful, but be careful not to overdo it or turn the interview into telling the interviewee what you've already decided the requirements are (or more likely what the product design should be).

Listen actively. There are many books, articles, and seminars on active listening. They all advise maintaining eye contact, leaning forward toward the other person, nodding periodically, summarizing from time to time, and repeating back what the speaker has said. This gives the interviewee ways to tell whether you understand what has been said.

✖ Caution

Conventionally prescribed active listening actions can backfire because they can make you appear to be understanding, even when you're not. To warrant the interviewee's trust, actually do pay attention, analyze what you are hearing, and respond meaningfully.

It's also a good practice afterward to send the interviewee a written summary of the interview. It's courteous and provides a chance to confirm understanding; but I'll be the first to acknowledge that sending follow-up memos could be done more regularly.

Ask questions that focus on understanding what the problem/opportunity/challenge is, how to measure it, what the objectives are and how to tell they've been achieved, what the "as is" process is that is creating the current results, and what the "should be" might include. To *find the value* that will be obtained when the requirements are satisfied, ask:

> ‣ What do you do?
> ‣ What are key business and temporal event triggers?
> ‣ How?
> ‣ What's it for?
> ‣ What are you trying to accomplish?
> ‣ What gets in your way?
> ‣ How should it be? (Caution, this invites product design. Pursue business *whats*.)

‣ Why? Why? Why? Why? Why? (I have heard this question attributed to Toyota Motors and to Ishikawa, the inventor of the "fishbone" diagram, who may have coined the "Five Whys" at Toyota. One supposedly can learn the root cause of any problem by asking, "Why?" no more than five times. *Caution*: you quickly can sound like a two-year old.)

Advanced interview skills

In contrast (I fear) to systems, there is an industry that very much values interviewing skills: sales. Truly effective sales people are not the fast-talking glad-handed huckster stereotypes who trick people into buying things they don't need. Rather, long-term sales success goes to salespeople who help buyers get what they want, which generally entails an extraordinary ability to ascertain and enable the buyer to recognize what they want. That is, *salespeople succeed—and are directly rewarded—based largely on their ability to discover buyers' real requirements, mainly through interviewing.*

Not surprisingly, therefore, much of the best thinking and writing about effective interviewing is directed toward salespeople. Some of the work comes from classic psychology, but I didn't become aware of it until I was long out of psychology graduate school and started looking "where the money is." Without claiming to convey anywhere near all the lessons that routinely turn interviews into sales dollars, I do want to share briefly a few techniques that are well-known in the sales community and encourage you to extend your reading into the sales realm.

Effective salespeople have learned to *identify and use prospects' various preferred modes of communication*. That is, each human being has particular attributes of communicating that they are most comfortable with. When using these modes, the prospect receives and conveys information more effectively. The salesperson gathers more accurate and complete requirements, and the prospect is more confident in the salesperson.

In short, people are more comfortable talking with other people like themselves. Naturally good communicators unconsciously shift their communication style to that of their listener. Psychologists and sales experts have studied such good communicators, isolated these techniques, and train salespeople to employ the methods consciously.

Several key techniques involve picking up on and adopting externally observable speech style and habits of the other person whom you want to connect with. For instance, a person from the southern United States typically speaks more slowly than a person from New York City. Someone from Mississippi ordinarily would be somewhat uncomfortable being interviewed by a New Yorker, unless the New Yorker slows down his speech.

Similarly, it's helpful to emulate the receiver's pronunciation, being careful not to seem to be mocking. For instance, southerners tend to emphasize the first syllable of the word "insurance," whereas northerners tend to emphasize the second syllable. Also, people tend to use certain terms and phrases over and over, so use those particular words rather than one's own terms that mean the same thing. For instance, in Minnesota people park their cars in a "ramp," which is a "parking garage" to easterners.

Many people are visual. That is, they use terms such as, "I see what you mean" and "It looks good to me." Other people are auditory and say, "I hear what you mean" and "It sounds good to me." Yet others are kinesthetic and say, "I sense what you mean" and "It feels good to me." Shift your imagery to the listener's dominant modality and they'll find you easier to understand and communicate with.

Consider all the years of formal education directed toward use of native language (that's English classes for English speakers). Overwhelmingly, such education is directed toward teaching people to use suitable vocabulary with proper grammar and meaningful organization. Yet, a famous study by Professor Albert Mehrabian [5] found that only 7 percent of meaning is conveyed by the actual words used. The study found that the listener gets 38 percent of meaning from tone, such as pace and inflection. Contrast the different meanings conveyed by these same words with different emphases:

- I think you can do it.
- *I* think you can do it. (Maybe nobody else thinks you can do it.)
- I *think* you can do it. (I'm not sure you can do it.)
- I think *you* can do it. (I think you, but maybe not someone else, can do it.)
- I think you *can* do it. (I think you can, but maybe won't, do it.)
- I think you can *do* it. (I think you can do it, but maybe not understand it.)
- I think you can do *it*. (I think you can do it, but maybe not something else.)
- I think you can do it? (I don't really think you can do it.)

Mehrabian found the most meaning, 55 percent, is conveyed by body language. Take the same, "I think you can do it," coupled with arms crossed and turning away from the listener with a frown ("I don't really think you can do it"), compared to facing them and emphatically pointing toward them with a big smile ("I really do believe you can do it").

An additional sales technique is called "mirroring" and involves emulating the listener's body language. If the other person leans forward and rests her head on one hand, you do the same. If the person leans back and crosses his or her legs, you do it too, and so forth. Communication improves.

Personality types

The other major category of improved communication techniques involves internal, psychological styles of thinking. Each person has particular ways of interpreting the world, and effective communicators learn to get in sync with the other person's ways of interpretation. BSM Consulting's www.personalitypage.com [6] describes at length the most widely known method for characterizing personality types, the Myers-Briggs test, which measures four personality type dimensions:

- "Our flow of energy… *I*ntroverted or *E*xtraverted."
- "How we take in information… *S*ensing or i*N*tuitive."
- "How we prefer to make decisions… *T*hinking or *F*eeling."
- "The basic day-to-day lifecycle that we prefer… *J*udging or Perceiving."

BSM Consulting reports for example that more than a third of people fall into the patterns of ISFJ, INFP, and ENFP. Only 2.2 percent of people are ENTJ (the visionary), but they earn the highest average incomes, while the more common INFP (the idealist) people's incomes are lowest on average. A typical software developer probably would be ISTJ (the duty fulfiller), introverted, trusting concrete senses rather than instincts, logical and objective, and organized, purposeful, and structured. Consider how difficult a software developer might find interviewing an opposite ENFP (the inspirer), who might seem disorganized and flighty.

Tony Alessandra describes a simpler and easier way to remember personality classification based on two dimensions: openness and directness [7]. These form quadrants describing four common personality patterns which others have likened to types of birds:

1. *Socializers* (peacocks) are high in directness and openness. They tend to be fast-paced and spontaneous, people-oriented idea people. They would be in professions such as sales.

2. *Directors* (eagles) are high in directness and low in openness. They tend to be businesslike, results focused, and impatient. Many executives are likely to fit this category.

3. *Thinkers* (owls) are low in directness and openness. They are detail-oriented systematic problem solvers but not necessarily strong on people skills. They are attracted to disciplines such as engineering and accounting.

4. *Relaters* (doves) are low in directness but high in openness. They are warm, supportive, and relatively unassertive, especially concerned about avoiding conflict. The caring professions, such as nursing, tend to attract these types of people.

While all these ways of characterizing an individual overgeneralize to some extent, each provides a convenient way to quickly understand a lot about how a person interprets the world. Recognizing the other person's thinking style can give us guidance in how best to communicate with him or her so he or she is more comfortable, and in turn we can appreciate better what that person says. Together these factors help an interviewer discover data about requirements more accurately and completely. For many people in the systems world, such approaches may be new. I've tried to present only a brief introduction to a few and refer you to the original sources and sales literature in general to learn more, such as about your own style and how it interacts with others.

ElecTech case interviews

To learn more about the ElecTech order entry system business requirements, Ann Analyst briefly interviewed the following key stakeholders: sales manager, order processing manager, and manufacturing manager. Each interview is transcribed below and is followed by analysis of Ann's interviewing techniques.

✍ Exercise: Analyze real interviews

Read each interview in its entirety. *Don't skip this and don't fall into the trap of just passing over the words mindlessly. That's how interviewers act when they don't really listen.* Your purpose is to learn more about ElecTech's order entry system business requirements as well as about interviewing techniques.

Before proceeding, follow one of the simplest and most-often ignored practices of effective interviewers: write down some key questions you would want to ask each of the interviewees. Even though you are not conducting these interviews, such advance preparation will help you to learn more about both the case's requirements and about what Ann does and does not do well.

Interview with ElecTech Sales Manager

SM: Hi, nice to meet you. Thanks for coming. What can I do for you?

Ann: We're fixing the order entry system problem. Can you tell me what's wrong with it?

SM: What are you referring to?

Ann: The kinds of problems you have entering orders with the computer system.

SM: I don't have any problems with the computer system. I don't enter orders myself.

Ann: Who does enter your orders?

SM: I don't get orders. I manage a region with about 50 salespeople. They get orders.

Ann: What kinds of problems do they have entering orders with the computer system?

SM: None that I'm aware of.

Ann: (long pause) I've been told there's a problem with the order entry system. Is there one?

SM: I haven't heard about any problems with the computers.

Ann: What about customers not buying our products?

SM: That's definitely a problem. Is that why you're here? What do you think we can do?

Ann: The Web is the way to go, especially with Web Services and .NET.

SM: You're sure? How will that get customers to buy our products?

Ann: The Web is where the action is. Our customers are all high tech, so they should use it.

SM: I have 50 salespeople who are dying on the vine. They are paid on commission and don't make anything unless they sell products. They break their backs finding prospective customers, working with the prospects to identify which of our products the customers would benefit from, and then having the sale fall through. How would the Web fix that?

Ann: The Web is so convenient.

SM: My salespeople create awareness of need in the customers, most of whom have no idea that they need our products. Why would they go to our Web site in the first place?

Ann: We should advertise and write articles about the products so customers know.

SM: We do advertise and our products are regularly featured in articles which repeatedly describe our products as the highest quality, truly world-class excellence.

Ann: Maybe the ads need to be different or placed in better locations. Maybe they should be on TV and the Web. Perhaps we should get a famous sports star to be a spokesperson.

SM: That's the way the ads are now. Ads only create a general awareness of a company. It's the salespeople's knowledge that finds the prospects, figures out the proper product configurations, and makes the prospect aware how the product will benefit them.

Ann: Shouldn't good salespeople be able to sell great products?

SM: After the salespeople have gone all through the sales cycle and gotten the prospect to the edge of closing the sale, the prospect invariably asks, "When can I get it?" The salespeople look on the lead time report that manufacturing sends out each month and tell the prospect that an order will ship in say 4 to 5 weeks. The prospects routinely tell the salesperson they need the product sooner and that our competitors can ship in 3 weeks.

Ann: But don't the customers care about how high our product quality is?

SM: Some do, but many say that quality doesn't matter if they don't have the product to use.

Ann: How can competitors ship quicker? Is it because they don't have such high quality?

SM: Quality may take longer. I really don't know how the competitors manage to ship in 3 weeks. They're not very willing to tell us their secrets. In the past, we'd sometimes be able to hire their former sales-people who could give us some inside insights on how the competitors operate; but these days we're losing salespeople to the other companies.

Ann: Maybe the competitors charge less for their products or pay salespeople more.

SM: Some of their products may be less expensive, but lead time usually is what we hear about. Salespeople mainly make money on volume of sales. The commission rates are probably pretty close. If higher commissions rates were the issue, salespeople would be selling lots of our SuperProducts. Competitors offer products similar to our regular lines, but we're the only ones with SuperProducts, which provide far greater capabilities. We can charge a lot more for them, and we've initially sweetened the pie even more by increasing the commission rate, but our salespeople don't even seem to try selling them. The sales cycle is just too long and products are too complex. We even provide field engineers to do a site survey and make sure the configurations are correct. But, they stick with simpler to sell—still complex to configure—regular products. We're losing our chance to lock up the highly attractive SuperProduct market before the competitors enter it.

Ann: Maybe sales contests and trips to resorts would help?

SM: We've tried that many times. We analyze all sales in spreadsheets every month and target opportunities for incentives as we calculate commissions. There are a lot of smart people in this company, and we've tried everything we can think of to no avail. That's why you're involved.

Ann: What about the phony orders I've heard about?

SM: We know salespeople place orders early when they think a sale is going to land soon. If the sale does come in, we don't have real good ways to know the order was placed early; and frankly, we can cut the salespeople slack there. However, when the order doesn't come in or comes in different, then we hear about it and take action against big abusers.

Ann: My time is up. Any other ideas before I have to leave?

SM: No, I've told you what we need.

Here are a few comments on Ann Analyst's interviewing techniques. Ann didn't seem to have qualified the sales manager beforehand, and thus apparently had no idea that he doesn't personally enter orders into the computer, which made her initial questions about computer data entry off-base. She didn't even seem to know how the company advertises its products. Ann also was taken aback when told there was no problem with the computer system, which still is what she (and probably her manager) conceives must be fixed, even though the Problem Pyramid identified "customers refusing to buy" as the real problem (of course, the computer system could need to be fixed too).

To some extent, the sales manager was interviewing Ann; and Ann kept offering solutions, not just for technology she presumed should be used but also for topics she probably doesn't know much about, such as advertising and sales contests. Even if Ann is familiar with these topics, she's supposed to be finding out about the requirements, not proposing solutions, which is premature until the requirements are known.

Ann didn't ask many open-ended questions, such as about the typical process salespeople use to make a sale ("What do you do?" and "How?"). Fortunately the sales manager offered some of this information in response to a slightly different question, or actually a somewhat confrontational conclusion that the salespeople ought to be able to sell the products. Ann didn't follow-up any of the sales manager's comments related to the salesperson's perspective on what the system is for; that is, how does selling really work (rather than just the need for more sales), what needs to be accomplished to make sales, and what gets in the way (besides confirming that customers resist long lead times).

Understanding the "as is" situation from the perspective of the stakeholders is key to getting the real requirements right. Ann might have benefited from being more attuned to the sales manager's personality type and its focus on people. Technical analytical types like Ann tend not to recognize the importance of information that can't just be programmed, such as the role of sales commissions. The reasons people do things usually are very important but may not be of interest to technical folks. The most technically elegant computer system won't work if it doesn't get money quickly into the salespeople's pockets.

To Ann's credit, she did ask a few good probing follow-up questions about customers' interest in quality and competitors' behaviors. On the other hand, Ann never asked *why* and missed some follow-up opportunities, such as about how sales were analyzed. Perhaps she made a conscious decision to ask instead about phony orders to make sure she'd cover her planned topics in the remaining time available. If she had additional questions to ask, she could have scheduled a subsequent interview, and she could have inquired who else the sales manager would recommend she talk to.

Interview with ElecTech Order Processing Manager

Ann: We're fixing the order entry system problem. Can you tell me what's wrong with it?

OPM: The system works fine. It's a lot better now that salespeople can enter orders out in the field. Before, when they mailed or faxed in the orders, legibility and missing information were big problems. The computer has pretty much eliminated those issues.

Ann: Can you explain what all these people do?

OPM: Orders that come in from the field are printed here in O/P at Headquarters. First, our customer specialists check the order to make sure the customer number is correct or assign a number to a new customer. We have over 50,000 enterprise customers on file. They are constantly merging and changing their names and so forth. Salespeople often deal with subsidiaries and don't have any way to know the parent's customer number. Our specialists keep the data accurate in a way 300 salespeople scattered around the country never could. Also, each delivery location is stored separately on our database. Some orders have as many as 200 delivery locations. Salespeople don't have the time or knowledge to get all those locations and their subcustomer numbers correct.

Once we know who the customer is, then the order goes to a contracts specialist to determine whether the order is covered by a contract. We have many contracts with parent companies. They usually offer discounts for purchasing particular dollar volumes, or number of units in a product line, or some combination. Only the contract specialists can keep track of all the variations. If a contract is involved, the specialist updates the cumulative purchase quantities in the contract and applies any earned discounts.

Then the order goes to a pricing specialist who checks for any prices that are different from list price and are not covered by contracts. Salespeople have a tendency to think they can get the sale if they can just offer a little lower price. As with many companies, salespeople here are not authorized to offer special prices, which they call "deals," without prior approval of a sales manager or vice president. If there's a lower-than-list price and no approval, the pricing specialist chases the salesperson for the paperwork....

Ann: That's fine, thank you. What about the computer system?

OPM: I was just getting to it. Once we know who the customer is and what the pricing is, then the order goes to an order entry specialist. Each of the six regions has two or three O/E specialists. The salespeople don't always deal with the same individual, but they get to know and work closely with a small group. The O/E specialist actually enters the order into the computer and then is the contact person for that order thereafter.

Ann: Is all this papershuffling the reason it takes so long to ship orders? How long does it take?

OPM: My people work very hard and do an excellent job in difficult circumstances. If orders come in clean, they get moved through right away. Of course, bigger orders are going to take longer than smaller ones. Many orders are not clean and need to be corrected. Any delay time is mainly waiting for salespeople to get back to us with the correct information. Salespeople make lots of mistakes. Products are very complex and hard to configure. Salespeople get options and product numbers wrong. We have a technical specialist engineer who reviews all Super-Product order configurations and any others that an O/E specialist is concerned about. Many mistakes are just carelessness. For instance, O/E specialists themselves spot things like ordering five units and only four chassis, or orders that are headed to Europe but don't include European power supplies. They may spot conflicts like configuring two female couplings together, but these can slip through.

Ann: Don't you have any statistics on how long it all takes?

OPM: It's my job to be on top of what goes on in my department. These are people, not just numbers. Everyone is busy and working very hard.

Ann: If I were to help you set up some tracking, do you think your people would be able to help me figure out how much time is needed to process orders?

OPM: I'd be glad to help. I'd hope you'd also be able to show how sales' mistakes delay us.

Ann: Do the sales managers know about all these mistakes? Why don't you just tell them you won't process orders with so many errors in them?

OPM: I meet with my counterparts regularly. They are aware of these issues. I have no authority to control them. My people's job is to process the orders we've got, not to refuse them.

Ann: Which of these is your biggest problem and how should we fix it?

OPM: Actually, our biggest problem comes after the order has been entered. The O/E specialists spend most of their time checking the status of orders and making changes to them. Salespeople constantly are asking to expedite orders, which means my people have to go to extraordinary lengths to find ways to get manufacturing to ship an order sooner. Often it's by shifting a product in progress to a different customer, then finding a product to replace the shifted one, and so on. Also, salespeople are constantly phoning with changes to products. They always claim it's because the customers changed their minds; but we know it's usually because the salesperson made a mistake or booked an order before knowing for sure what was needed. Sometimes, though, it's actually the customer calling with a change, like maybe they need an additional unit or perhaps fewer units.

Ann: Thank you for your time and information.

Again Ann started with a fairly limiting question about what's wrong with the order entry system. Then she did shift to a more open-ended question about what people do but cut off the order processing manager's answer. Ann's papershuffling comment did follow up a bit, but could have been perceived as judgmental and possibly could have provoked defensiveness. Depending on tone, the question about keeping statistics also could sound confrontational, and it continued Ann's prior papershuffling theme rather than probing information the order processing manager raised about errors in orders. Even when Ann offered to help gather statistics, she didn't seem to pick up on the order processing manager's motivation to use the measures to send a message to sales.

Ann heard about things that she didn't have any reason to suspect existed, such as the fact that order entry specialists spend most of their time supporting orders after they have been entered. Ann failed to probe this topic either, possibly due to lack of time.

Many interviewers, especially more technically oriented ones, tend to lose patience with somewhat lengthy responses such as the ones the order processing manager gave. It's common to feel the speaker is rambling and either tune out or interrupt as Ann did to direct the discussion back to points that the interviewer wants to cover. Sometimes, indeed, speakers do ramble off-track (discussions of golf and grandchildren usually qualify), but most of the time the problem is not with the interviewee.

✖ Warning

Don't follow your normal inclination to tune out what the interviewee is saying or interrupt when you hear yourself say to yourself, "Why doesn't this fool shut up about this blah, blah, blah and start talking about what I want them to talk about?" Learn to sense when these behaviors occur and use them as a red flag to jolt you into awareness that you were about to miss something very important. Instead, ask, "Why don't I understand why the speaker thinks this is important?"

Interview with ElecTech Manufacturing Manager

Ann: We're fixing the order entry system problem. Can you tell me what's wrong with it?

MM: Nothing that I'm aware of. Orders come up from order processing, get printed and distributed to my manufacturing planners who are respectively responsible for the 9 product lines. Based on factory capacity and raw materials availability, the planner determines when an order can be shipped and enters the ship date in the computer. That puts the order into the manufacturing schedule and causes confirmations to be printed and sent to the customer, sales, order processing, and to us.

Ann: Why do orders ship so late?

MM: Orders don't ship late. In fact, my shipping people give me a regular report which shows again and again that on average shipments go out ahead of scheduled ship dates. This one shows we're shipping 6 days early. It's not always that much, but it's always pretty good.

Ann: Could I have a copy of that report?

MM: Sure.

Ann: What about the factory's capacity?

MM: We have the most sophisticated manufacturing lines in the world. That's one of the reasons, along with superb engineering of both products and how we manufacture them, that we're able to produce the incredibly high-quality products that earned us our reputation for world-class excellence.

Ann: So how do the planners decide which products to build at any given time?

MM: Now we "build to order." We don't build a product unless it's been ordered. Let me explain how this is superior to our old "build to stock" method. Based on sales forecasts, which we'd always have to massage, we used to schedule the factory line to produce at one time all of a particular product that we'd expect to need for an upcoming time period, say a month. This allowed us to use our factory equipment most efficiently, by minimizing set-up and tear-down time. The finished products went into a warehouse. Whenever someone ordered one of those products, the order could be filled immediately. That was the good news. The bad news was that it took forever to fill the 80 percent of orders that were for products that weren't in the finished goods inventory. Also, a lot of the products that had been manufactured never did get sold; or by the time they were sold, they had to be rebuilt to current engineering change levels before they could be shipped. Scrap and rework were costing us a fortune. Now they're essentially zero. Moreover, we're not paying to maintain a finished goods warehouse, and we're not carrying the costs of products waiting to be ordered. We can charge less for our products and still make a profit.

Ann: Do shortages of raw materials affect when an order can ship?

MM: No. We're really excellent at having adequate raw materials when we need them while at the same time minimizing costs of goods sold. Like all leading manufacturers, we've adopted the Japanese just-in-time (JIT) methods. Again based on sales forecasts, we enter into contracts where our suppliers agree to supply us certain quantities of raw materials over a given time period. We refine those quantities quarterly, monthly, weekly, and ultimately daily. That is, every day the suppliers deliver to our factory floor just the materials we'll be needing to make the products scheduled for manufacture that day. Again, we have eliminated the cost of operating a raw materials warehouse and minimized raw materials carrying costs.

Ann: Doesn't that expose you to shortages when forecasts are wrong?

MM: Yes, that's why it would be great if the sales managers and salespeople learned to forecast what they sell or sell what they forecast. We have to massage their figures and build in a certain safety stock tolerance, but usually it's a small overhead compared to the cost of shortages. Occasionally we'll get an unexpected order for a product that uses some raw material we hadn't anticipated, which could take up to

10 weeks to receive. Most of the time, though, shortages will be only minor blips. Ironically, big orders for the same product can mess us up the most, because they use up the period's total quantity at a faster pace than the supplier is prepared to deliver; and in turn they can tie up the line so other orders get delayed.

Ann: Do you have any ideas why competitors can ship orders in 3 weeks and we can't?

MM: I'm not so sure competitors really do ship all orders in 3 weeks, especially not of products that match ours in quality and complexity. I think the 3 weeks refrain may be a convenient excuse that salespeople are using. You know, somebody heard it once, and now everybody claims to hear it all the time. Maybe the competitors have better salespeople and more disciplined practices. You have no idea how many orders the planners have to kick back because salespeople have specified configurations that are outright impossible. Realize that a manufacturing facility can produce the most by maintaining a stable flow. Every time a salesperson changes an order or tries to expedite, we have to go out to the line, find the item, pull it off, perhaps damage it trying to remove components, and then put it back at the appropriate place on the line where the changes can be made. This doesn't affect just that one order, it interferes with every order being manufactured on the line; and this happens many times a day.

Ann: Thank you. This has been very informative.

Almost all of Ann's questions followed up to some extent on what the manufacturing manager had just discussed. Ann's question about forecasting errors leading to shortages was especially perceptive, and she asked for a copy of the shipping date report which was mentioned. Note that twice Ann led with presumptions, that orders ship late and that competitors ship in 3 weeks, which the manufacturing manager disputed. Possibly because of time shortage, Ann did not probe more on topics such as changes to orders.

Some commonalities across interviews also are instructive. Note that everybody (sales, order processing, and manufacturing) believes they are doing the best job they can. It's only human nature to assume that problems are due to someone else's dropping the ball. Note also that the *existence* of problems like those at ElecTech generally is well-known within a company, and, at least at the higher levels, people from various departments do talk with each other about such issues. However, even though companies are full of smart, capable people who really do know how to do many things well, and despite having tried all manner of solutions, they still may not be able to solve all their problems.

Gathering data in conjunction with interviews

On interviews, it's common to collect examples of existing forms and reports, such as the manufacturing manager's shipping report. Table 8.1 shows the average and a few of the entries from a sample report.

When needed data does not currently exist, such as measures of how long it takes to process orders, special efforts may enable collecting the data. Table 8.2 shows the averages and a few of the entries from one of several samples that the order processing manager assisted in collecting. This report lists the Julian dates (e.g., January 1 is day 1 of the year, December 31 is day 365), which within the same calendar year make arithmetic calculations easy. Thus, day 69 is March 10 and day 75 is March 16.

We see from this sample of orders that on average it takes about 5 days for order processing to enter an order. The Revision 1 Acknowledgment is the initial confirmation that is printed when the manufacturing planner assigns the order's shipping date, which takes about another 5 days. The Revision Number at time of shipping is 1 for orders that have not changed. An order with a Revision Number of 4 has been changed three times, and on average half the orders are changed. This report corroborates the manufacturing manager's report of shipment occurring prior to scheduled ship date, although this sample is early by only 4.5 days on average.

Table 8.1 Manufacturing Manager's Shipping Report

Scheduled Ship Date	Actual Ship Date	Days Late or Early
4/17	4/17	0
4/17	4/16	−1

4/24	4/10	−14
4/27	4/30	3
Average		−6.2

Table 8.2 Julian Date at Key Order Processing Points

O/P Receives Order	Order is Entered	Cust's Want Date	Revision 1 Acknowledgment Printed	Revision 1 Ship Date	Revision Number	Last Scheduled Ship Date	Actual Ship Date
69	75	100	79	100	2	107	107
89	93	105	97	114	1	114	100
-----	-----	-----	-----	-----	-----	-----	-----
77	84	76	85	114	2	114	114
43	51	51	54	57	4	85	57
76.0	80.8	96.2	85.4	109.8	1.5	114.7	110.2

Interviewing is an especially essential skill for discovering requirements. Keys to effective interviewing are planning what to ask about, using open-ended questions to let the interviewee set the direction, listening actively (and most importantly, intelligently) to truly hear and understand what is said, and following up with probing questions to learn more. Learning why people do things, which stems from how they perceive situations, and appreciating that often there are multiple conflicting perceptions of the same objective situation, are as important to the real requirements as step-by-step procedures.

References

[1] Gottesdiener, E., *Requirements by Collaboration: Workshops for Defining Needs*, Boston, MA: Addison-Wesley, 2002.

[2] Robertson, S. and J. Robertson, *Mastering the Requirements Process*, Harlow, England: Addison-Wesley, 1999, p. 72.

[3] Beyer, H. and K. Holtzblatt, *Contextual Design: Defining Customer-Centered Systems*, San Francisco, CA: Morgan Kaufmann Publishers, 1998, p. 8.

[4] Dekkers, C., e-mail communication to Quality_Plus_Measurement_Forum@ yahoogroups.com, May 8, 2002.

[5] Mehrabian, A., "Professor Albert Mehrabian's Communication Model," http://www.businessballs.com/mehrabiancommunications.htm, August 2003.

[6] BSM Consulting, "Information About Personality Types," www.personality page.com/info.html, August 2003.

[7] Alessandra, T., P. Wexler, and R. Barrera, *Non-Manipulative Selling*, New York: Simon & Schuster, 1987, pp. 14–27.

Formats for analyzing requirements

It's better to light one small candle than to curse the darkness.

—Chinese proverb

Someone once described the effect of a candle in a dark room as expanding the amount of darkness of which one is aware. That's perhaps a pretty heavy thought for as late as Chapter 9, but it's a key theme:

> *Analyze what we do know to become more aware of what we don't know.*

Data versus information

Data by itself has little value. Information comes from adding meaning to data. Information has potential value, which becomes actual value only when the information is used. *This chapter describes a number of formats for analyzing data in order to add meaning, turn the data into information, and identify what else needs to be known.*

Technical people know and use many of these techniques in the normal course of development, although probably more often in respect to designs rather than business requirements. While each of these formats could be considered another of the ways to test requirements, finding issues generally is a by-product of the formats' primary purpose of promoting understanding. Therefore, I'll not be starring or numbering these methods, and I have not tried to describe every possible format that can be used to help understand requirements. Consequently, your favorite technique may not be described; however, I think I've included a suitable sampling. Also, since these

125

techniques generally are well-known, I have not gone into great detail explaining them.

Many of these methods are graphical and may be considered modeling. While valuable for helping understand requirements, these are not by themselves appropriate formats for documenting business requirements. These *modeling formats are better suited for communicating designs*, which is another tip-off that authors who prescribe using models to define requirements actually are talking about high-level product design system requirements, rather than business requirements.

I've intentionally not described object-oriented (O-O) techniques, including the Unified Modeling Language (UML). For those who want to learn more about these methods, there is no shortage of books which can be found easily at your favorite bookseller. Despite the claims of advocates that these methods are intuitive, I find that people who are not already initiated devotees seldom grasp or gravitate of their own accord to these models. Moreover, each new release of UML notation seems to grow even more ponderous. O-O and UML are widely praised, somewhat less widely used, and indeed are becoming standards for a significant portion of system development. Along with all the other formats I haven't explicitly described, if you find them helpful, or if your organization promotes their use, by all means use them.

Most people think of data as only being numbers, typically in a columnar spreadsheet-like format. With requirements, though, *notes from interviews and document reviews are the most common forms of data*.

Ineffective requirements definers gather data but don't analyze it, and especially don't use analysis to recognize what else they need to know. In my experience, a too typical behavior of interviewers is to put their interview notes in a folder somewhere and never look at the notes again. Let's get some practice doing what effective requirements definers do: review, analyze, and learn from their data.

✍ Exercise: Identifying what we don't know

Reread the three interviews and accompanying documents in Chapter 8. What else do you need to know and how might you find it out?

When experienced professionals attending my seminars go back to examine their notes of the interviews with the ElecTech managers, they ordinarily become aware of the need to learn about issues such as:

- ▸ What exactly is order processing doing that takes 5 days to enter an order?
- ▸ What exactly are manufacturing planners doing that takes 5 days to schedule shipment of an order?
- ▸ How are salespeople trained?
- ▸ How does the product numbering scheme work?

- Which items do sell and in what frequencies?
- Which errors do salespeople make most on orders?
- What types of changes are made to orders and in what frequencies?
- How are sales commissions calculated?
- Do competitors actually ship comparable products in three weeks; and if so, how?

With perhaps the exception of the last question about competitors, it should be possible to find answers within ElecTech to all of the above questions by interviewing, reviewing procedural and other documentation, and observing operations or documenting workflow timings (as the order processing manager already has done). For instance, tracking and analyzing a number of representative orders would probably reveal considerable information about the nature and reasons for corrections and changes.

If we had not asked the simple question about what else we need to know, most of the above topics probably would not be addressed further. It should be obvious that without such information, the requirements would likely be deficient and soon start creeping in these directions. It's also likely that ordinarily the creep would be considered inevitable and attributed to the users not knowing what they wanted. Clearly, much of such creep can be avoided.

Sorting, summarizing, segmenting, and showing

Meaning comes from sorting, summarizing, segmenting, and showing data. For example, averages are a way of summarizing that makes voluminous detail meaningful. Sorting can suggest segments, relationships, and patterns (or trends) within the data, especially when shown graphically. Many useful ways to segment data are naturally occurring, such as by customers' geographical location, industry, or size. The tracking report prepared by the order processing manager segmented based on key processing milestones; and the summarizing averages made the detail more meaningful.

Sometimes segments that don't occur naturally nonetheless can reveal important information that otherwise would not have been evident. Data mining hunts for such segments within masses of data; but non-naturally occurring segments often can be identified productively without the need for sophisticated techniques such as data mining. Table 9.1 shows an example of non-natural segmenting, based on the time between when order processing receives an order and when the customer wants it.

It was reasoned that orders which customers wanted soonest would be the ones whose actual shipment dates would slip farthest from desired. Indeed, orders wanted within the first 10 days were shipped an average of 16 days later than wanted.

However, when ElecTech had an additional 10 days (want date 11–20 days after order processing received the order), slippage *increased* to almost

Table 9.1 Shipment Slippage and Time to Customer Want Date

	Percent of Cases	Want Date (Days After O/P Receives Order)	Ship Date (Days After O/P Receives Order)	Slippage
Want Date 0–10 Days After O/P Receives Order	11.8%	3.3	19.3	16.0
Want Date 11–20 Days After O/P Receives Order	35.3%	13.7	34.5	20.8
Want Date 21–30 Days After O/P Receives Order	23.5%	23.9	27.0	3.1
Want Date 30–90 Days After O/P Receives Order	14.7%	43.4	56.8	13.4
Want Date 90+ Days After O/P Receives Order	14.7%			
Average		20.2	34.2	14.0

21 days. This is a most unpredictable finding. While precise data was not available to explain this unusual result with certainty, the considered opinion was that orders wanted immediately (within 10 days) got the most attention, at the expense of these orders that were wanted a bit later.

Note that orders wanted 21 to 30 days indeed were shipped almost on time, slipping only 3 days. These orders were the ones the current process was set up to handle: orders that would ship in 4 to 5 weeks. Chances are that a segment of orders wanted 28 to 35 days, as opposed to 21 to 30 days, after order processing received the order would have shipped right on time.

Interestingly, the trend takes another unpredicted shift, as slippage again increases for orders wanted 31 to 90 days out. The most likely explanation for such increase was that these orders may be more likely to be diverted to satisfy other orders which were wanted sooner. While this analysis produced some interesting results, it's probably most valuable as an example of non-naturally occurring segmenting and raises questions about:

▸ Why the slippage did not continue linearly in the expected direction?

Structuring business rule language

Business rules constitute a significant component of business requirements. To a considerable extent, business rules can translate directly into system requirements and then into code, but only to the extent that the business rules are identified fully and accurately. In a typical organization, business rules are found in a wide variety of formats. Some are explicit; whereas many business rules must be pieced together from partial rules found scattered about, often existing only implicitly within the personal knowledge of perhaps several different individuals.

Even when business rules are clearly labeled and stated explicitly, they most commonly are in narrative form, which inherently is subject to misinterpretation. For example, consider the information Ann Analyst gathered about determining the price for ordered items. The order processing manager conveyed business rules but did not characterize them as such and did not frame them as business rules logic. From a business requirements standpoint, the order processing manager's communication was perfectly normal and reasonable; but a technical person probably would have described it as "not knowing how to say" the requirements properly (to guide programming).

To make sure the business rules are recognized and understood, several formats can be applied. The first is called "structured English" and is similar to pseudocode used by program designers. Structuring physically lays out the logic that narratives tend to obscure. Nonprogrammers usually find structured English understandable and helpful for clarifying business rules. Here is how the technique could be used to portray some of the pricing rules buried in the interview:

> If the client enterprise has a contract with ElecTech, and
>> If the purchased products are covered by the contract,
>>> Then add the new purchase to contract totals-to-date
>> If total-to-date purchases satisfy contract criteria,
>>> Then apply the contract's discount to this purchase.

Organizing the rule in this format helps identify additional questions, such as:

- What are the various types of criteria found in contracts?
- What are the various ways discount amounts are calculated?
- How should an overlooked order qualifying under a contract be processed after the order has been entered?

Cause-and-effect graphing

Dick Bender is the leading proponent of a technique called cause-and-effect graphing (CEG), which portrays the business rule logic graphically. (Note, the term "cause-and-effect graphing" is applied to at least two other formats. The best known of the formats is the familiar Ishakawa fishbone diagram, which is one of the fundamental tools of TQM. Yet another format I'm not personally familiar with but, I am told, is used in electrical engineering to depict logic circuits.) For Bender, CEG as described here is mainly used in conjunction with his automated BenderRBT tool for designing a minimum set of rigorous tests that exercise all feasible functional logic variations [1].

CEG shows the logic as paths between nodes, which are represented by circles, and a few key operator symbols: "∨" means *or*, "∧" (the Greek character lambda, an inverted "V") means *and*, and "~" (tilde) means *not*. Colleague and Bender associate Gary Mogyorodi was kind enough to use BenderRBT to generate a CEG similar to that shown in Figure 9.1 for the above pricing example.

The cause-and-effect graph in Figure 9.1 reads similarly to the structured English:

> If the customer has a contract *and*
> > the contract covers the purchase,
> > > Then accumulate the purchase totals to date
> > > If the purchase qualifies for a discount
> > > > Then apply the discount
> > > Else Quit (don't apply a discount).
> If the customer does not have a contract *or*
> > the contract does not cover the purchase
> > > Then Quit (don't apply a discount).

While even this simple example starts appearing somewhat complicated, graphing does offer some advantages. First of all, graphing can reveal complexities that may have been hidden by the words alone. Second, the graph tends to force awareness of the Else conditions that weren't explicitly articulated in the structured English. Third, as the logic grows in complexity, only a graphical technique such as CEG may be able to capture the implications. Fourth, graphical techniques are especially valuable for communicating with people who speak different languages. Fifth, when used for testing (especially with the almost-necessary assistance of a tool such as Bender's BenderRBT), infeasible paths and unobservable intermediate conditions can be identified, which in turn may indicate the need for requirements adjustments.

This technique raises questions, such as:

> • Whether anything additional should be done when there is a contract that does not cover the purchased items.

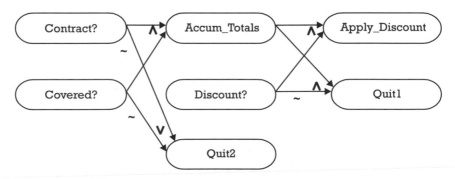

Figure 9.1   Cause-and-effect graph from BenderRBT.

Decision trees

As with so many of these techniques, the term "decision tree" is applied to several different formats. The format depicted in Figure 9.2 is relatively simple and informal. It's laying out graphically the presumed sequence of decision choices involved in identifying the appropriate customer. (Another common, more formal decision tree format resembles that of organization charts as shown in Figure 9.5.)

Here's how to read Figure 9.2. If the customer number is not known, then perhaps the customer could be identified by the subsidiary company's name; if not, then maybe by the name of its parent company; and if not by number or name, then possibly by street address. If the customer cannot be identified as an existing customer, then the customer may be added to the system and assigned a customer number. Once the customer has been identified, its descriptive information (address, telephone, etc.) can be seen.

Without the graphic, one or more of the decision choices would be more likely to be overlooked. For instance, the diagram helps create awareness of choices such as finding the customer by the name of the parent company and by street address. Even using a graphic, though, doesn't guarantee noticing all choices. For instance, many seminar participants overlook the choice of quitting, even though the diagram shows it clearly.

This technique presents questions such as:

▸ Whether there are additional ways to identify customers.

▸ How to differentiate customers with the same or similar names.

▸ What to do when two customers merge.

Decision tables

A decision table is another commonly used, convenient format for clarifying business rule choices. Programmers frequently use decision tables, since they translate directly into programmable logic. Some automated code-generation tools structure their input in the form of decision tables.

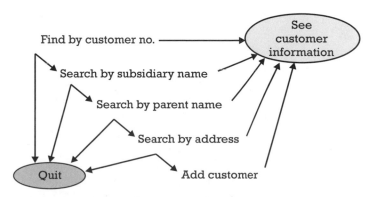

Figure 9.2   Decision tree for identifying a customer.

As with many of these formats for analyzing data, decision tables come in several different formats. All formats show the outcomes of combining two variables, one indicated by rows and the other by columns. Some formats simply indicate true-false or present-absent for each resulting row-column cell. The format shown in Table 9.2, tends to be a bit more flexible because the outcome is written in words in each cell.

When a decision cannot be determined, the affected cells can be left blank, or they can be filled in (as shown) with presumed decisions, and then reviewed with suitable stakeholders. Filling out the decision table below raises questions such as:

‣ What price to charge when both a contract and special pricing deals are present?

‣ What to do if a price on the order is actually higher than the list price?

Entity relationship diagram

Entity relationship diagrams (ERDs) are fundamental to data modeling and object-oriented design. The diagram depicts how many times one entity (something that exists in the real world) occurs relative to some other entity. Trying to define ERDs in meaningful words that don't just repeat "relationship" and "entity" is almost impossible, so it's easier simply to look at an example, such as Figure 9.3.

Figure 9.3 says that a customer makes zero to many orders, but a specific order is received from one and only one customer; and an order contains one to many products, but a specific product is included in zero to many orders. This example is fairly trivial but makes ERDs understandable.

Trying to draw more specific and detailed ERDs for the ElecTech case reveals the need for more information and raises questions such as:

‣ How many contracts can a parent company have?

‣ How many product lines can be covered in a contract?

‣ Are all of a parent company's contracts applicable to all its subsidiaries

‣ How many sales people can sell to a particular company and to a particular company location?

Table 9.2 Decision Table

	Price on Order		
Contract	Equal to List Price	Below List Price with Approval	Below List Price with No Approval
Contract Covers Order	Contract price	Lower of Deal or contract price	Contact salesperson
Contract, But Doesn't Cover Order	List price	Deal price, notify approving executive	Contact salesperson
No Contract	List price	Deal price	Contact salesperson

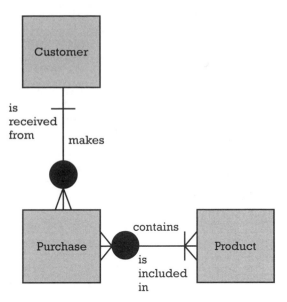

Figure 9.3   Entity relationship diagram.

Data models

The data model depicted in Figure 9.4 probably looks familiar to most people involved with system development. It's similar to the table descriptions used by database management systems. While the format is essentially the same, there's a big difference. A database table description, which sometimes is referred to as a "data dictionary," is a *design* document describing the *physical* implementation of the data in the database.

In contrast, when the same format is used with *requirements*, it's describing *conceptually* what the data elements are, how they seem to cluster, and how the clusters interrelate. Conceptual requirements data models need to precede design of the physical database. Since they have the same format, translation from requirements to design usually is straightforward.

Figure 9.4 describes six of the main clusters of data related to an order. The clusters would contain some additional data elements, such as telephone numbers, which I've left out for the sake of keeping the example moderately readable. Here's how to read the data model example as shown. A customer is uniquely identified by his CustID (customer identification number). Each of the customer's delivery locations is identified by a unique LocID (location identification number) for the CustID. Salespeople are identified by a unique SlsID (salesperson identification number), which is included in the order along with CustID and a unique OrderNo (order number). Products are identified by a unique ProdID (product identification number). The ProdID for each individual product ordered for a specific location is identified by a unique OrderLine for the OrderNo, which also identifies POQty (quantity) of the product ordered and the CustID and LocID of the location to which the product is to be delivered.

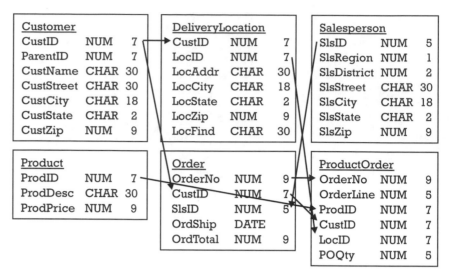

Figure 9.4 Data model.

Preparing the data model raises numerous additional issues, such as:

‣ What size and format of data elements actually are needed for the business to function effectively?

‣ What other data elements are needed for the business to function effectively?

‣ What other clusters of data also relate to orders, and what data elements need to be associated with them?

Organization chart

Most of us are no strangers to organization charts. Ordinarily such charts are mainly important for seeing where one sits within the overall status hierarchy and to whom one reports. However, organization charts can also be very helpful for understanding requirements, and especially for understanding who the stakeholders are or may be. Figure 9.5 shows an organization chart for ElecTech's order processing department.

The organization chart in Figure 9.8 shows only the number of positions in each role. More detailed versions of organization charts would list the names of the individuals in those positions.

Some questions that this organization chart raises include:

‣ What do all the administrative assistants do?

‣ Where in the organization, and to whom, does order processing report?

‣ What is the organizational status of the order processing manager compared to the status of the sales managers and the manufacturing manager?

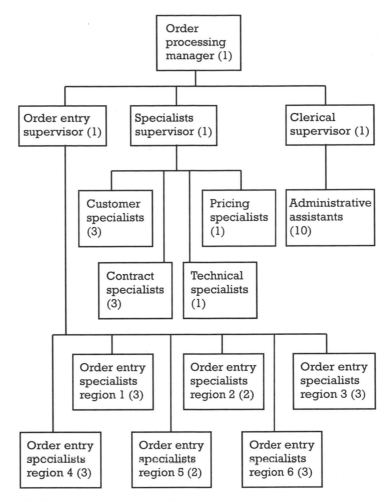

Figure 9.5   Order processing organization chart.

Responsibility matrix

Often people's responsibilities for various functions are not identical to their job titles, levels, and positions within the organization. In such cases, it can be helpful to use a responsibility matrix, like the one in Figure 9.6, to identify which persons are primarily, secondarily, and not responsible for particular functions.

As Figure 9.6 shows, for example, the salesperson is primarily responsible for creating special pricing deals. Since the sales manager must approve the deal, the sales manager's role is secondary. Similarly, the order processing pricing specialist checks the special pricing, which also is a secondary role. The involvement of the other positions is at most incidental with regard to special pricing deals. Note also that there can be only one role with primary responsibility, but there can be one or more positions having secondary responsibility for any given function.

The responsibility matrix format raises questions, such as:

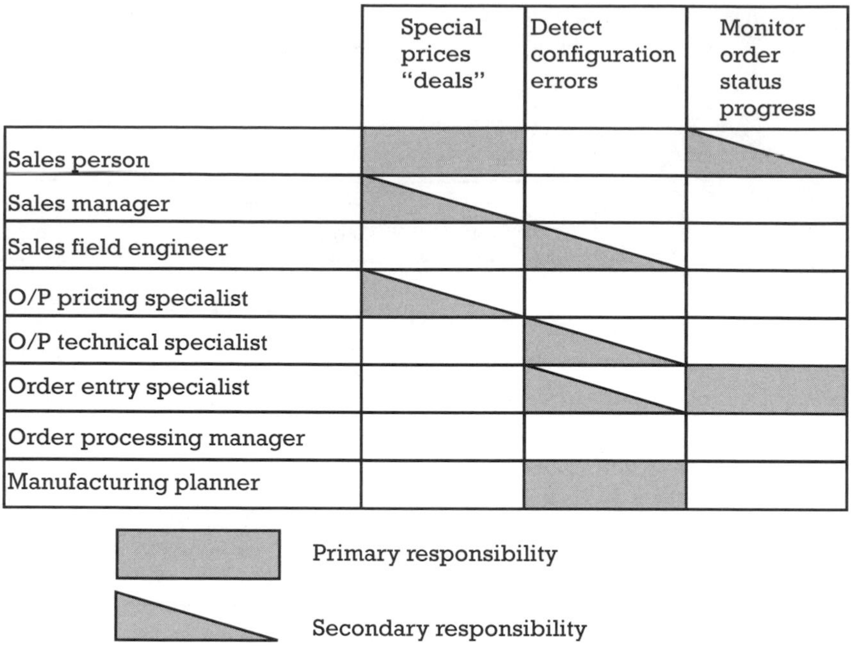

	Special prices "deals"	Detect configuration errors	Monitor order status progress
Sales person	Primary		Secondary
Sales manager	Secondary		
Sales field engineer		Secondary	
O/P pricing specialist	Secondary		
O/P technical specialist		Secondary	
Order entry specialist		Secondary	Primary
Order processing manager			
Manufacturing planner		Primary	

Primary responsibility

Secondary responsibility

Figure 9.6   Responsibility matrix.

▸ Why is the salesperson not considered even secondarily responsible for detecting configuration errors?

Flowchart

When analyzing a process, perhaps no format is more helpful than a flowchart. The advantages of a flowchart are that it shows the sequence of the process' action steps (depicted by rectangles) and the effects of decision choices (depicted by diamonds) on the sequence. Flowcharts are very commonly used to portray physical design of systems, in which case additional symbols usually are used to designate specific types of inputs and outputs, such as printed reports or database (disk) files.

Flowcharts have fallen somewhat out of favor for several reasons. In the old days, say the 1960s, many systems organizations mandated that programmers draw detailed flowcharts of program logic before actually coding the programs. Back then, developers were cheap relative to the costs of computer time, so making extra efforts to get the program design right before coding were accepted to some degree. However, programmers (including me) frequently balked at what they considered extra busywork which interfered with the coding they enjoyed most. As technology made it easier to code programs and cheaper to let the computer find errors, flowcharting fell by the wayside. Many programmers do resort to flowcharts to solve thorny logic problems.

Two other factors also contributed to flowcharting's lack of popularity. As with many of the analysis formats, flowcharts can be drawn at varying levels of detail. For instance, a high-level flowchart could describe an entire system on a single page, whereas a detailed flowchart could extend over many pages depicting the logic of a single program within the system. However, flowcharts gained the reputation of being used only for detail, which tended to make them tedious, hard to read, and hard to keep up to date. Nontechnical people especially seemed put off by flowcharts, partly because of the amount of often-confusing detail.

Regardless, flowcharts have made a bit of a resurgence and are usually the technique chosen by my seminar participants to understand the business process. Figure 9.7 shows a conceptual (as opposed to physical) flowchart of actions followed by the order processing customer specialist as part of the order entry process.

Note that this entire flowchart in Figure 9.7 might appear on a higher level flowchart as a single action, perhaps entitled "Identify Customer." This flowchart could itself be drawn in greater detail. For instance, the "Locate Customer" action is moderately high-level and could actually consist of a number of more detailed actions, such as, "Find by Customer Number," "Search by Name," and "Search by Address."

Figure 9.7 says that if the customer specialist determines that the customer is identified appropriately (by correct CustID) on the order, the customer specialist is finished processing this order and passes it along to the contract specialist (which I've identified with a double rectangle indicating a predefined process, but I could have used a rectangle or other symbol such as an oval terminator or a vertical-arrow-like off-page connector). If the customer already is known to ElecTech, and thus has a CustID, but that

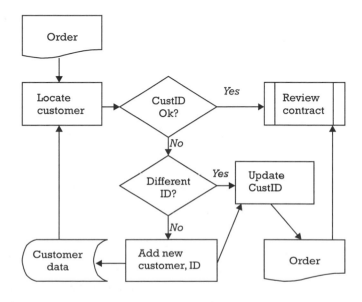

Figure 9.7 Customer identification process flowchart.

CustID was not already on the order, the customer specialist puts the proper CustID on the order and forwards it to the contract specialist. If the customer is new to ElecTech, the customer specialist assigns the new customer a CustID, adds the customer to ElecTech's customer records, puts the CustID on the order, and forwards it to the contract specialist.

Note that the flowchart in Figure 9.7 shows two separate symbols for what is really the same "Order," which obviously could cause confusion. Some people might try to position the "Order" symbol so that it is both input to the "Locate Customer" action and updated by the "Update CustID" action, and others might draw a dotted arrow between the "Order" on the left side and the "Order" on the right side. Unfortunately, some may find that either of such efforts to reduce the confusion actually can result in greater confusion. The difficulties increase with the complexity of the process portrayed.

Flowcharting helps understanding of the process and also identifies further issues, for example:

- What other clues do customer specialists use to identify a customer who is currently known to ElecTech?

- How should an existing customer be identified if they merge with or are acquired by some other existing customer?

- What are the circumstances where a customer specialist needs to get further information from the salesperson in order to identify a customer correctly?

Data flow diagram

Data flow diagrams come out of the structured analysis and design methodologies. While various authors employ variations of how the symbols are drawn, all share a fundamental simplicity that I find causes many people to prefer data flow diagrams, especially nontechnical people. I also contend (only partly facetiously) that nontechnical people resist flowcharts' sharp corners, which can seem threatening, whereas data flow diagrams have friendlier shapes (especially when drawn with graceful swooping French curves, which cause the diagrams to look like flowers).

Data flow diagrams are the simplest charting technique, using only four symbols. The square or box represents an external entity, someone outside the system, who ordinarily provides inputs and receives outputs. The arrows show the flow of data, inputs and outputs. The rounded rectangles (sometimes referred to as "bubbles") are where processing takes place, where inputs are transformed into outputs. The open rectangles are data stores, where data are kept. When data flow diagrams depict designs, processing bubbles are usually computer programs and data stores are usually databases. When portraying requirements data, though, symbols are conceptual rather than physical.

The advantage of data flow diagrams is that they show all the pieces and their relationships to each other without getting immersed in the intricacies of sequence and decision logic that characterize flowcharts. The disadvantage of data flow diagrams is that they don't show such logic.

As a convention, a data flow diagram occupies only a single page, which also can enhance understandability. To display greater detail, each individual processing bubble is expanded into its own data flow diagram, which is also limited to one page, and so forth until the set of diagrams is down to a sufficient level of detail for one's purposes.

Many requirements authors put great stock in a context diagram, which is simply the highest level data flow diagram. It has one processing bubble, usually titled "the System." Its context relates to the various external entities interacting with the system. I find that context diagrams invite misinterpretation, since "the system" can mean anything and everything, which translates to meaning nothing. Therefore, I personally avoid context diagrams and prefer to show the same information at one lower level of detail, where everyone can tell better what main processing the system includes.

Figure 9.8 shows a moderately detailed data flow diagram, which might be an expansion of a higher level diagram's processing bubble entitled "Process order." Note that the "Identify customer" bubble's logic is described by the flowchart in Figure 9.7.

Figure 9.8 shows that the order comes from the salesperson. Customer data from the order is used to identify the customer in ElecTech's customer records, add the customer to the customer records and assign a CustID if necessary, ascertain the customer's correct CustID, and update the order with the CustID when it is not already present.

Product and customer data are used to update contracts and determine contractual discounts, which are updated on the order. Product and customer data also is used to identify potential deal special pricing, which is confirmed by a vice president or sales manager, and if approved, the discounted special price is updated on the order. When customer and pricing have been verified and updated on the order, the processed order is entered and sent to manufacturing to be scheduled, manufactured, and shipped. During order entry, the salesperson may provide clarifications in response to questions.

The data flow diagram format raises many questions, such as:

- How are special pricing deal approvals recorded and communicated with the order sent by the salesperson to order processing?

- How does the order processing pricing specialist identify the vice president or sales manager from whom to seek approval of a special pricing deal?

- What is the sequence of actions when an order is changed, especially when the change affects purchase totals qualifying for contractual discounts?

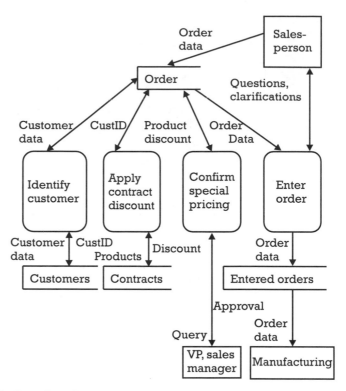

Figure 9.8   Data flow diagram to process an order.

Each of the above techniques provides different CAT scan angles for analyzing requirements data. Each helps with understanding, and each reveals
additional issues that need to be addressed in order to discover the requirements more fully. Ineffective requirements definers tend not to do such
analysis and therefore fail to become aware of gaps in the requirements
which invariably turn into creep. Effective requirements definers do analyze
their findings, both to understand what they do know and to identify what
they still don't know but need to discover.

Reference

[1]   Bender, R., *BenderRBT*, Queensbury, NY: Bender & Associates, 2003.

Key to completeness

It ain't over 'til it's over.
                    —Yogi Berra

One of the most common questions I'm asked about defining requirements is, "How do I know when I'm done?" Developers and managers are under pressure to stop defining requirements and get on with producing program code. At one extreme is the risk of "analysis paralysis," where the project becomes mired in endless requirements discovery and never delivers any working software. At the opposite extreme is the too real and expensive creep rework from, "You start coding, I'll find out what the requirements are."

In hindsight, many project managers realize they had stopped defining requirements prematurely, before adequately understanding them. However, at the time of stopping, they probably felt confident that they indeed had defined the requirements sufficiently. We can learn two important lessons from this oft-repeated scenario:

1.   Current common methods of deciding on-the-fly when requirements are "good enough" may not themselves be good enough to rely on.

2.   Projects haven't learned the lesson of, and in fact keep denying, point #1.

This chapter describes some key techniques for telling more reliably, in the midst of requirements discovery, when in fact the requirements are reasonable to implement.

In addition to the formats described in Chapter 9, I also find a format called a process map valuable for understanding requirements, especially in ways that help tell whether we're done. I'm not suggesting that a process map should be the only method used, or even that it always should be used; but it's an important method to consider.

Figure 10.1 shows a process map of the ElecTech order processing process. Many people refer to this format as "swimlanes," because the diagram has a column (or lane) for each key player, such as sales or manufacturing. Swimlanes highlight handoffs, which often are a source of delays and difficulties. Although process maps don't necessarily include time-scaling, I find it adds further meaning.

Figure 10.1 is especially important because it shows us something that none of the other requirements discovery and analysis so far has revealed: the *customer view*. Remember Chapter 3 said that *the real process needs to be*

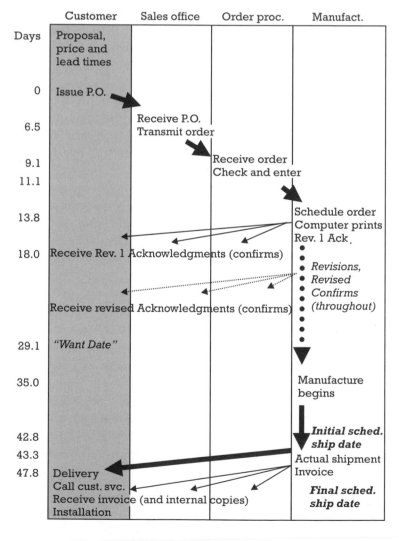

Figure 10.1 ElecTech order processing process.

defined, from the beginning to the full end result—when it works right from the customer's perspective.

Importance of customer view

From ElecTech's customers' standpoint, the process begins when the customer places the order. However, everything that we've seen from ElecTech acts as though the process starts when order processing receives the order. Figure 10.1 shows that customers think the process has been going on for nine days before ElecTech considers it to begin.

Similarly, a customer's view would say the order is completed when the customer *receives* it, not when ElecTech ships the order, which is when ElecTech treats the process as ending. This gap was estimated to be about five days. Thus, for customers the real process takes seven weeks, whereas ElecTech operates on the presumption that the process lasts only five weeks. The net effect is that *the customer's view of the process includes some two weeks that ElecTech's presumed process view doesn't recognize.*

If ElecTech were to act in a typical manner and take actions to address its unreal presumed process, they probably would expend considerable time and resources to cut two weeks out of the process. At best, it still would be taking five weeks for customers to receive orders. Consequently customers probably still would refuse to buy from ElecTech. In other words, the real problem would not be solved, and ElecTech wouldn't have a clue why their efforts had not succeeded.

But wait, there's more to the customer's view. Not only are orders shipping on average about two weeks after the customer's "want date" for the products, but an order isn't done until it works right. The customers get no value from just receiving the ElecTech product until they actually are able to use it. The complexity of these products means they usually need to be installed by trained personnel. Therefore, when an order arrives, a customer must contact ElecTech's customer service department and schedule a service engineer to come install the products which have been received. Because they weren't taking the customer's view, ElecTech was totally unaware of this necessary step. Customer Service wasn't recognized as a part of the order process and had no idea when orders were due. Besides being very inconvenient for customers, installation delays were estimated to extend the real order process at least a week to a total of eight weeks.

Many manifestations of silos

This is a real-world case that happened to a company with a reputation for world-class excellence. Any organization can, and most do, fall into the trap of silo thinking. ElecTech's presumed order process was clearly a silo, focusing on intermediate internal steps without recognizing the steps' place within the overall context customers perceive.

Let's examine some more aspects of the real order process as shown in Figure 10.1. The manufacturing planners schedule orders by about day 14, which is when the initial (revision 1) acknowledgment confirmation is printed and sent to customers. (Note: these figures differ a bit from the sample of data shown in the order processing manager's report summarized in Table 8.2. Figure 10.1 is based upon a larger, more reliable sample.) Thus, customers are in the dark for more than two weeks before they receive acknowledgment of their order from ElecTech. Subsequent modified acknowledgments are issued whenever orders change throughout the remaining period prior to shipping (not just at the particular points that the diagram may seem to suggest). Again, it's easy to understand why customers may not be eager to buy from ElecTech.

Figure 10.1 also shows that manufacture of the order doesn't begin until day 35. Why is there a three-week delay from when the order is scheduled until manufacturing actually starts? The most common response is that the delay must be due to waiting for raw materials. However, the manufacturing manager said that raw materials ordinarily were available as needed, so materials are not the reason.

Then what could possibly be going on during this three-week period? Nothing! It's just a delay. But why? Perhaps you recall that the manufacturing manager also described the importance of maintaining a smooth manufacturing process. One very effective way of keeping the manufacturing flow smooth is to have a backlog of work, say three weeks' worth, to buffer any disruptions.

Would a customer be willing to pay, let alone pay extra, for a three-week backlog buffer? I don't think a customer would find the delay to add value, nor would salespeople or the company itself. The delay serves only manufacturing, suboptimizing their silo without being aware it's at the expense of the others. Of course, reducing sales ultimately is to manufacturing's disadvantage too, but like most of us wrapped up in the day-to-day, they are not in a position to see the real broader effects of their actions.

You may recall that the manufacturing manager's report summarized in Table 8.1 showed orders consistently shipped several days prior to their scheduled shipment dates. Figure 10.1 puts this data in context by showing that shipments still lag customer want dates by about two weeks. Without attributing intent, it is clear that the manufacturing planners consciously set shipment dates they knew they could beat. A silo!

Another aspect of the order process warrants discussion, even though Figure 10.1 does not reflect it specifically. Salespeople have a very strange and complicated way to describe products in sales orders. Perhaps an analogy will help us understand why. Consider how you would buy an automobile from a dealer, say a Toyota Camry (which I've chosen because it's supposedly the largest seller). The dealer would sell you one Toyota Camry, with a handful of key options delineated, such as color and engine size.

Let's say instead the dealer described your purchase as: 1 chassis, 2 axles, 4 fenders, 4 wheels, 4 brakes, 4 brake pads, 4 doors, 4 door windows, 1 front windshield, 1 back windshield, 1 muffler, 1 exhaust pipe, 2 floor mats

6 spark plugs, etc. Would you have any idea whether you'd end up with a Toyota Camry, let alone one that actually runs? Yet, this type of parts list was essentially what ElecTech salespeople were required to write as customer orders, which easily resulted in errors. Moreover, each confirmation acknowledgment simply repeated the list of parts, which confused and perturbed customers, especially since the reasons for order revisions were not indicated.

Clearly this parts list order format did not benefit customers, salespeople, or ElecTech. So why use it? Who would it benefit from requiring nontechnical sales people to write orders in terms of engineering specifications for the products to be built? Only manufacturing—the detailed parts list made it easier for the manufacturing planners to schedule the manufacture of the various components of an order. Another silo!

Updating the ElecTech Problem Pyramid

In Chapter 7, we prepared a Problem Pyramid which identified ElecTech's real problem as "Customers refuse to buy products of recognized world-class quality" and identified causes of the problem as:

> ‣ Lead times greater than 3 weeks;
> ‣ Late/wrong/incomplete orders;
> ‣ Complex products;
> ‣ Clumsy processing;
> ‣ Phony, changed orders.

Based on the additional analysis, especially the process map, it should be clear that the causes need to be expanded to include:

> ‣ Not accounting for the customer's view of an order's duration;
> ‣ Manufacturing's backlog buffer delay to start producing orders;
> ‣ Confusing and error-prone parts list order format.

If ElecTech had proceeded to design and implement a system to solve just the causes identified initially, they would have been highly unlikely to solve their real problem. They may well have made improvements, but possibly too little to matter. Moreover, their well-intentioned but short-of-the-mark efforts quite possibly could have exhausted time and resources necessary to make the meaningful turn-around the company needed. It seems quite apparent that the updated list of causes is far more likely to lead to solving the real problem and get customers to stop refusing to buy.

This makes sense with respect to the ElecTech case, but it's not just limited to the case. It applies to your real world situations too. The keys to having reasonable confidence that the real requirements have been defined adequately are:

- Use the Problem Pyramid and the guidelines for evaluating it to identify the real problem, measures, "as is" causes, and "should be"
  requirements.
- Identify the process from beginning to the full end-result—that it
  works right—from the customer's perspective.

Only now that we've identified Blocks 1–4 of ElecTech's Problem Pyramid, the real problem and its key causes, are we ready to start defining the
real requirements.

Formats for documenting requirements

Write no more than is helpful—and no less.

In olden times, the phrase "It is written," conveyed special meaning. When so few people could read and write, committing something to writing put sort of a stamp of finality and authority on it. Once written, it was to be believed and not argued with.

Similarly, requirements gain a form of respect from being written, at least partly because so often our projects proceed without requirements in writing. *Requirements need to be written*. The other side of the coin is the fear of too voluminous requirements. Many organizations have experienced requirements documents that seem to take on a life of their own, becoming mainly an exercise in busywork yielding verbiage for its own sake.

Not only do more requirements take more time to prepare, but volume itself can interfere with understandability; the thicker the requirements document, the less likely it is to be read at all, let alone in its entirety. Therefore, *the writing needs to be in as concise and organized form as possible that includes necessary information while also promoting understanding*. Form affects whether those involved actually read the writing.

Requirements are the "should be" Block 5 of the Problem Pyramid. This chapter describes four of the most commonly used formats for documenting and communicating requirements: generic unstructured individual requirements, IEEE Standard 830-1998 for Software Requirements Specifications, use cases, and hierarchical itemized deliverables.

Generally agreed-upon contents

In general, all four formats share some common characteristics. Ordinarily, requirements documentation is prefaced with the requirements' goals, objectives, and expected value. This may be supplemented with explanation of the current situation background that prompted the definition of requirements. Requirements documents also generally identify the scope, context, and environment. Scope not only says what *is included*, but also what is *not included*, where stating such exclusions is necessary for understanding.

It's important to recognize that there are at least *two types of scope*: the scope of the requirements and the scope of implementation projects to accomplish the requirements. In my experience, few projects recognize this distinction; and they typically define the project scope before they necessarily have sufficient information about the real requirements scope. For instance, Ann Analyst's boss defined the scope of Ann's assignment as "replacing the order entry system." In contrast, *the appropriate scope of requirements is the real problem as defined by the Problem Pyramid.*

The heart of any requirements document is the set of specific requirements. One point on which I believe all requirements authorities agree is that *requirements should be itemized*, rather than be in narrative form. Each requirement is a separate item, and each item is a separate requirement. Itemizing makes it easier to tell what the requirements are and to trace each requirement backwards to its source and forward to where it is used in design, code, tests, and user instructions. Some authors also acknowledge that itemized requirements can be *hierarchical,* although many are silent on the subject.

Similarly, authors may not explicitly address use of narrative formats, although narratives often are used to provide explanations and convey workflow and linkages among items. Some authors do explicitly include models or graphical formats in the requirements, whereas others may treat such material as supplementary to the textual items.

Requirements often are characterized as being of the following types, which many authors treat separately within a requirements document:

- Functional requirements related to the application purposes;
- Nonfunctional requirements, such as quality factors and performance levels that some consider not to be related to the application purposes;
- Interfaces with which the application must interact, including environment;
- Constraints on the delivered product;
- Constraints on project and/or delivery process.

Generic unstructured individual requirements

One common format for requirements is simply to list each individual requirement without describing any hierarchy or other explicit relationships among the requirements. For example:

R001: The system shall identify the product number of each item ordered.

R002: The system shall issue a confirmation to the customer when a shipping date is assigned.

The advantage of the unstructured approach is that it's low overhead. Its weaknesses are that without an organizing structure, it's easier to overlook requirements and become hard to manage. The three other approaches described below provide greater structure.

IEEE Std. 830-1998 for Software Requirements Specifications

The Institute of Electrical and Electronics Engineers (IEEE) is an international association of more than 300,000 professionals that, among other activities, defines standards for a wide variety of things electronic, such as microwave ovens and information systems. One of their most widely known standards is Std. 830-1998 Recommended Practice for Software Requirements Specifications [1], which suggests the following format:

Table of Contents

1. Introduction
    1.1 Purpose
    1.2 Scope
    1.3 Definitions, acronyms, and abbreviations
    1.4 References
    1.5 Overview
2. Overall description
    2.1 Product perspective
        2.1.1 System interfaces
        2.1.2 User interfaces
        2.1.3 Hardware interfaces
        2.1.4 Software interfaces
        2.1.5 Communications interfaces
        2.1.6 Memory constraints
        2.1.7 Operations

Many organizations use the IEEE standard, which certainly does provide a very thorough set of requirements elements to address. One risk of such an apparently exhaustive set of topics is that it can lull requirements definers into overlooking any topic not specifically designated, such as usability. To prospective users, the standard's biggest disadvantage probably would be that including all the topics in a document could be considered high overhead. Consequently, many organizations might be unlikely to expend the effort other than for large systems.

I'll suggest the IEEE standard poses several more substantial but less likely to be recognized issues. First and foremost, the standard is not quite appropriate for documenting business requirements. Instead, *the standard very clearly is documenting system requirements* (which we're using broadly to include software requirements). We need look no further than the title,

"Software Requirements Specification," which not only says it's "software requirements," but also says it's a "specification," which is a term denoting design. Section 2 indicates that these are the requirements of a product, which also is characteristic of system requirements. Moreover, Section 3.2 functional requirements speak in terms of input, processing, and output (IPO), which is a systems rather than a business way of viewing the requirements.

Pigeonholing

The IEEE standard brings to light two topics which also are used by some other formats and warrant separate highlighted discussion. The first of these is a technique which I call "pigeonholing." Pigeonholes refer to part of a desk or a type of filing cabinet. Each pigeonhole typically is a box that is open on one side, and ordinarily there are a number of such pigeonholes together, with each pigeonhole being used to hold materials pertaining to a separate matter. For example, pigeonholes might be used in an office to hold incoming mail, where each person's mail is in a separate pigeonhole.

The IEEE standard essentially creates a separate pigeonhole for each topic. While being valuable for assuring a topic is addressed, accumulating the information separately in a pigeonhole makes it difficult, and perhaps unlikely, to relate the pigeonholed information to the context (usually the functional requirements) in which it is supposed to apply. When the two related pieces of information are stored physically apart, it's hard to know the pigeonholed portion even exists, let alone keep aware of it.

Nonfunctional requirements

Moreover, pigeonholing leads to treating topics such as nonfunctional requirements as though they existed in the abstract. For instance, pigeon holing essentially limits the questions one could ask about reliability to, "How much reliability is needed?" It's obvious such a question has no meaningful answer because the pigeonholed items don't exist in the abstract. They only have meaning with regard to functions and constraints.

Consequently, *I find the term "nonfunctional requirements" inappropriate and misleading*. That's why I prefer to call these various attributes of functionality "quality factors" and integrate them with other aspects pertaining to required functionality, including constraints on the functionality and how it is produced.

Use cases

By far, use cases are today's most commonly favored format for documenting requirements. For many organizations and authors, use cases are the requirements, and the requirements are the use cases. This section is intended only to introduce and position use cases relative to business requirements, not to explain them exhaustively. I'll refer you to colleague

Alistair Cockburn's *Writing Effective Use Cases* [2], which in my opinion provides a very cogent, insightful, and readable explanation.

The term "use case" was coined by Ivar Jacobson [3] and first gained prominence in the object-oriented world, although usage has spread to all parts of systems development. Even before Jacobson formalized and popularized use cases, I and many others had used similar user-centered methods for years without calling them use cases.

A use case describes a step-by-step event scenario from an actor's perspective of how the actor interacts with the system. An actor ordinarily is the user but also could be another system or piece of hardware. Jacobson describes use cases as representing an implementation- and environment-independent transformation from the requirements specification and mentions that use cases can be expressed in terms of problem domain objects. In my experience, organizations typically treat use cases as an alternative to requirements specifications and by "system" mean the system to be implemented rather than the problem domain. I find few references to problem domain use cases but was pleased to hear Software Development East 2003 Conference fellow presenter Jim Heumann of Rational Software (IBM) contrast "business" and "system" use cases [4].

Use cases actually have three common formats: narrative, one-column, and two-column. Here are very basic bare-bones examples of how each of the respective use case formats might portray the same scenario for an actor, the order processing customer number specialist, identifying an order's customer.

Use Case: Narrative Format

Look up the customer in the customer file based on the customer number indicated on the order. The system displays the customer's data or a "not found" error message. If not found, search the customer file first by customer name, then by telephone number, and finally by customer address. If the customer still is not found, assign a customer number and add the customer to the customer file.

Use Case: One-Column Format

1. Look up the customer in the customer file based on the customer number indicated on the order.

2. The system displays the customer's data or a "not found" error message.

3. If not found, search the customer file first by customer name, then by telephone number, and finally by customer address.

4. If the customer still is not found, assign a customer number and add the customer to the customer file.

Use Case: Two-Column Format

U1. Look up the customer in the Customer File based on the customer number indicated on the order.	R1.1 Display customer data. R1.2 Display "not found" error message.
U2. Search by customer name.	R2.1 Display customer data. R2.2 Display "not found."
U3. Search by telephone number.	R3.1 Display customer data. R3.2 Display "not found."
U4. Search by customer address.	R4.1 Display customer data. R4.2 Display "not found."
U5. Assign customer number.	R5 Add to customer file.

Beyond the basic step-by-step sequence, which usually includes exceptions (like "not found"), many use cases also identify additional information, such as triggering event, preconditions, risk, criticality, importance, and frequency. For the above examples, the trigger event might be receiving an order; a precondition which must be met for the use case to apply might be that the customer name and address is supplied with an order. The use case might also indicate an alternative course of action when the precondition is not satisfied.

Reflecting their origin in the programming field, some use cases are like subroutines and are incorporated by reference within other use cases. For instance, "Search by customer name" might represent a separate use case whose steps are repeated in use cases for a variety of events. In addition, a basic use case can have extensions, other use cases that are applied in conjunction with this use case under certain circumstances. For example, perhaps sometimes when adding a customer to the customer file, a credit check also is performed, and there would be another use case describing the credit check steps.

Use cases offer a number of advantages. Merely breaking out the narrative steps in the one-column format improves understanding, and the two-column format is even more understandable. Both users and developers find the step-by-step sequence and relative concreteness easy to understand. The format can be used to capture and analyze data about requirements too. Programmers can much more reliably translate use cases into programs that work the way the use case describes, compared to the traditional situation where programmers guess on the fly how the user should use the system.

Use cases can be hierarchical. That is, a step in a use case can refer to a subsidiary use case which contains greater detail. A beneficial by-product of use cases is that they seem to translate very readily into test cases, which then can be executed to demonstrate whether the use case indeed has been implemented. The two-column format is essentially the same format as a test case specification, which describes input and expected results in words. Of course, applicable data values are needed to execute the test case and compare against actual results.

Use cases also have a number of weaknesses, perhaps the greatest of which is the too common tendency of some advocates to treat use cases with almost religious zeal, which often does not brook even the possibility of weakness or limitation. Fortunately not all authors fall prey to this trap. For instance, Cockburn says that use cases are the behavioral requirements but acknowledges they don't cover requirements such as external interfaces, data formats, business rules, complex formulae, performance targets, and process requirements [5]. I've found that relatively few use cases even attempt to address such matters, and then usually by pigeonholing each topic in a separate section, which can severely impact readability and still often results in overlooking the linkages.

Much to the chagrin of many use case experts, in practice use cases often are written inappropriately. For instance, frequently use cases are nothing more than user instructions for a GUI, such as "click this box, pull down this list, double click on the entry, tab forward, and key in a certain value." Also, many use cases describe mainly the "happy path" and overlook exceptions and alternatives, even though use cases are supposed to describe all the paths an event can take. Furthermore, the fact of (and sometimes hoopla associated with) using use cases can obscure realizing when a use case does nothing more than describe the "as is" instead of the "should be."

However, there's a much more significant and almost totally unrecognized issue:

Use cases can be but seldom are business requirements. Use cases are touted as *user* requirements but usually are *usage* requirements.

Although use cases can be used to describe the problem domain, such problem domain or "business use cases" (which I *would* consider to be business requirements) are exceedingly rare. Rather, use cases usually are a form of system requirements that describe the *usage* of the product that is expected to be built or otherwise acquired.

The use case definition process almost always goes straight to focusing on questions about how the user wants the computer system to operate, not what the user needs to accomplish, which leaves it subject to assumption and oversight. In fact, *many use case writers include only those steps that they expect to be automated.* Real business requirements include all that the business requires, regardless of whether it's expected to be automated, which clearly is an issue of design, not of requirements. When one omits steps presumed to be manual, there will be little chance of ever automating those steps. For instance, it's easy not to notice that the order entry system use case examples above do not include manual steps, such as:

- The specialist judges whether the displayed customer is in fact the customer who is to receive the order.

- The specialist uses accumulated business knowledge, books, and other noncomputer sources of information to identify the customer's identify.

A step-by-step use case format can be valuable for gathering data about requirements and describing the product's system requirements in ways that enhance understandability and implementation success. While use cases can be used for documenting business requirements, ordinarily they are not. Use cases usually describe usage of a product, which is more likely to be successful when its design is based upon system requirements that satisfy appropriately defined business requirements.

Seven guidelines for documenting hierarchical itemized deliverables

The format that I've found most suitable for documenting business requirements is a hierarchical list of itemized business deliverable *whats* that contribute to value when delivered. Following are seven guidelines for preparing it.

1. *Go top-down* (level by level, starting with the "big picture") *in the user/business language, focusing on end results/outputs whats of the "should be" business model, addressing in an integrated fashion* without pigeonholing:

   a. Strategy, mission, and competitiveness;

   b. Business functionality and business rules;

   c. Management information and controls;

   d. Operational effectiveness and workflow preferences;

   e. Performance levels and quality factors (which often are called "ilities," because so many of the quality factors end in "ility," such as usability and reliability);

   f. Interfaces and environment compatibility and constraints;

   g. Project-related constraints, including deadlines and resources.

2. *Identify everything (as much as possible) the business needs to solve its problem.*

   Business requirements should be inclusive. Too many real requirements are identified and then discarded because of well-intentioned but premature efforts to cut scope. A business requirement is still a business requirement, regardless of whether there is time or money to accomplish it. Include routine functions, even though they may seem obvious, as well as those that are exceptional, unusual, and ideal. Include both needs and wants, since wants won't be likely to be satisfied unless they are recorded, and since wants have a way of becoming needs.

3. *Anticipate change and support.*

    Much of what is called "creep" is due to changes which were much more predictable than people realized they could predict. While the *specific* future changes are not known, ordinarily the *nature of likely changes and the variables affected can be anticipated to a large degree.* Business requirements for being able to address such changes can dramatically reduce the impact when the specific changes do occur. Similarly, ongoing operation and support are essential for any system and can be, but seldom are, anticipated as requirements.

4. *Break down each item to a suitable level of detail.*

    Each requirement should be taken down level by level until it is clear, complete, testable, and able to stand on its own, from the perspective of people in the user/business community. Requirements vary in the number of levels they need to be broken down. If you must skip part of the definition process due to lack of time, it's preferable to shortcut the time-consuming driving down to detail rather than cutting steps 1–3, which identify the higher-level topics that eventually need to be detailed.

5. *Supplement as appropriate with narratives, diagrams, and examples.*

    Such supplemental information is not the requirements, and care should be taken that it enhances but is not essential for communicating meaning. *The most important supplement is a high-level conceptual design relating to top-level requirements.*

6. *Prioritize and weight meaningful groupings.*

    Being attentive to interdependencies and conflicts among requirements, it is most effective to limit prioritization to major functions and higher-level groupings. Efforts to prioritize too many items at too low a level of detail often prove counterproductive. There are two major approaches to prioritization:

    a. Rate each requirement individually, either in categories such as mandatory, desirable, or ideal; or rate with a numeric weighting, such as from 1 = low to 10 = high. These approaches seem simple but tend to result in unreliable ratings, frequently with everything turning out to be top priority.

    b. Prioritize in a manner that forces distinctions among the choices. This method yields more reliable ratings but is harder, partly *because it's necessary to be aware of the full set of choices so they can be compared to each other.* For workability, the set of choices must be kept limited, typically to no more than 10 or 15, so use this method with high-level groupings. The simplest method is ranking. While ranking indicates which requirement is more important than another requirement, ranking alone doesn't tell how much more important one is than the next. A method I call the "hundred-point must system" provides both measures. Each rater is given 100 points to distribute among all the choices in proportion to the importance they assign to each choice. They must assign all 100 points and must assign at least one point to each choice. It's best to have multiple raters and discuss wide variations before averaging final ratings.

7. *Every item is an observable deliverable* what *that contributes to value.*

Regardless of level of detail, one must be able to say in yes-no binary fashion whether a requirement has or has not been delivered by the system. The way to assure this is to make each requirement an observable deliverable. Since projects are accomplished by successive deliveries, *defining business requirements in terms of deliverables sets the stage for project success.* Each deliverable must contribute to achieving the Problem Pyramid Block 3 goal measure value or benefit.

Figure 11.1 shows the hierarchical structure of an itemized deliverable business requirement. *The top-level item is one of several top-level items that taken together are the Block 5 "should be" of the Problem Pyramid.* Each lower level set

Top	1. At the time of taking an order, reliably ascertain the date the order actually will ship.
First	A. Indicate the quantity of products which can be ordered for shipment (open slots) for the next ten shipment dates.
	B. Reserve the next available manufacturing slot which enables delivery by the date the customer requests.
	C. Provide the salesperson easy access to accurate current product availability information.
Second	a. For each product.
	b. For each configuration (combination of products).
	c. For all configurations which the salesperson indicates must ship together.
Third	1) Assume (default) the entire order.
	2) Allow the salesperson to identify groupings.
	3) Warn of products with technical dependencies.

Figure 11.1 Hierarchical itemized deliverable levels.

of items essentially redefines the item above it. For example, the top-level item is redefined in greater detail by the first-level items designated A, B, and C. Together they describe what is meant by the top-level item, or what the top-level item consists of.

Similarly, item 1.C is redefined by, or consists of, the set of second-level items designated a, b, and c. (Items 1.A and 1.B each would have similar second-level a, b, and c items, but I have not shown them in Figure 11.1.) Each item ultimately is decomposed down to as many lower-level subitems as necessary to be clear, complete, testable, and able to stand on its own within the context of the hierarchy from the perspective of people in the user/business community.

Each lower level need not decompose into exactly three items. I've simply used sets of three subitems for the sake of example. Each lower level must contain at least two subitems, otherwise the lower level adds no further meaning. A level generally should not contain more than seven to nine subitems, and preferably no more than about five subitems. These limits are based on a well-known psychological concept, "the magic number seven, plus or minus two," which represents the human mind's typical span of control.

✪Hierarchical itemized business deliverable *whats* that contribute to value (test method #25)

At each level of detail, business requirements should meet the format test of being hierarchical, itemized, in business (as opposed to technical) language, deliverable, *what* (as opposed to *how*), and contribute to providing value when delivered. Note that this test can be used with any of the four documentation formats, since even individually written requirements still could be grouped, and thereby satisfy the hierarchy criterion.

✍ Exercise: Define top-level requirements

Figure 11.1 shows one of the top-level business requirements that taken together constitute the Block 5 "should be" requirements of the Problem Pyramid. *Before proceeding (because you'll learn more by doing), write two of the remaining top-level requirements and break one of them down into its first level A, B, C.*

Experienced systems professionals I encounter generally presume it is easy to write top-level business requirements, until they actually try to do it. Then they frequently discover it is very hard, partly because they are not accustomed to thinking at the big picture top levels and partly because they are not accustomed to defining deliverable *whats*.

One of the most common pitfalls people encounter when first trying to write real business requirements is the tendency to phrase them in terms such as "improve," "reduce," "eliminate," "streamline," and "speed up." Such terms are measures, not the *whats* that will produce the measure when delivered. Thus, for example, rather than a requirement to "cut the order lead time to three weeks," the real business requirements identify *whats* that when accomplished will result in orders reaching customers within three weeks.

In accordance with the seven guidelines, top-level business requirements for ElecTech follow. Note that no sequence is implied. That is, for example, requirement 1 is not necessarily expected to take place before requirement 2; 1.A is not expected to occur before 1.B, and so forth. I have not felt compelled to use magic words or begin each item with "The system shall." You can if you like or must, but I find the hierarchy creates a meaningful context more economically. Please further note that:

▸ Each item meets the "hierarchical itemized business deliverable *whats* that contribute to value" test.

▸ Together these represent the Block 5 "should be" of the Problem Pyramid that reasonably address the Block 4 causes and are likely to prodivide the desired benefits by meeting the Block 3 goal measures.

Top-Level Business Requirements

Objectives: Implement a replacement for the existing order processing system within six months. The new system should be of sufficiently high quality that it no longer is a factor in losing sales and may even become a competitive advantage, reducing cycle time to less than three weeks. It also should reduce administrative, manufacturing, and inventory expenses by reducing the number and extent of order revisions and cancellations. Specifically, the new system should:

1. At the time of taking an order, reliably ascertain the date the order actually will ship:

   A. Indicate the quantity of products that can be ordered for shipment (open slots) for the next ten shipment dates.

   B. Reserve the next available manufacturing slot that enables delivery by the date the customer requests.

   C. Provide the salesperson easy access to accurate current product availability information.

2. Enable the salesperson in the field to enter an order either at the time of, or shortly after, the customer issues the order:

   A. Capture all necessary data and validate at the time of entry.

   B. Accurately identify proper customer and delivery location numbers, or capture sufficient data to assign them reliably.

   C. Transmit the order to the central computer system either at the time the order is written or by midnight that night.

D. If any discrepancies are detected in the central system, automatically send a notice to the salesperson immediately.

3. Help the salesperson write up an order that correctly identifies all the suitable product numbers by:

A. Making the salesperson aware of all options for a base or SuperProduct;

B. Allowing configurations to include only allowable options;

C. Assuring that necessary option choices are identified.

4. Enable the salesperson at the time of taking the order to identify existence of customer contracts including:

A. Types of products covered (and therefore not requiring a separate purchase order);

B. Bulk purchase discount categories and percentages/prices;

C. Current purchases per category and prices to which entitled;

D. Indication of approved contract pricing on the order.

5. Provide indication of special pricing approvals on orders:

A. Enable the salesperson to identify authorizing manager.

B. If prior authorization is not indicated, automatically route a request for authorization to the appropriate manager.

C. When authorization is received, update the order to show it.

6. Enable the salesperson or O/E specialist to inquire directly about all details of current order status and shipment date.

7. Provide a controlled process whereby the salesperson in the field may modify or cancel orders directly so that:

A. Information is validated at the source.

B. Changes are coordinated with manufacturing schedules.

C. Changes are coordinated with contracts.

8. Create customer confirmation notices that are:

A. Easily understood, containing only necessary information.

B. Produced only at appropriate times from the customer's view (and not at inappropriate times, such as for purely internal changes);

C. Informative about the action or change causing the notice.

9. Maintain appropriate sales records, including:

A. Sales per salesperson by product and by customer;

B. Commissions due, paid, and adjustments;

C. Sales relating to contests.

Scope that doesn't creep

Many seminar participants indicate that in their organizations, project scope statements are similar to the objectives paragraph of the top-level business requirements. When a project's scope is stated merely in terms of objectives, nobody has any idea what the project actually will and will not deliver; and creep is inevitable. On the other hand, *project scope does not creep nearly so much when it is defined in terms of deliverable top-level requirements.*

The scope of the requirements is the full Block 5 "should be" of the Problem Pyramid, as shown above for ElecTech. The project to implement the requirements may address only a subset and thus have a scope that may be somewhat smaller than the Problem Pyramid scope of the requirements, but still should be phrased in terms of the top-level requirements that the project proposes to deliver.

High-level conceptual design

Business requirements are a *list* of itemized deliverables. As such, no interrelationships or flow among requirements is implied. However, a valuable aid to understanding comes from supplementing the business requirements with diagrams that show interrelationships and flow. I refer to such diagrams as high-level conceptual designs. While many diagramming techniques can be used, I generally find data flow diagrams effective. Figure 11.2 is a data flow diagram depicting all the pieces needed for one possible way to deliver the ElecTech order processing top-level requirements. Because of the number of

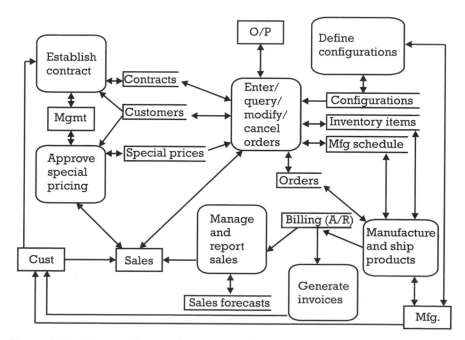

Figure 11.2   ElecTech high-level conceptual design.

elements on the diagram, for the sake of readability I've omitted labeling the data flows. (I don't think this omission is critical, since data flows at this high level generally are identified rather gratuitously anyhow, such as "customer information.")

Here's how to interpret the diagram. It's usually a good idea to start with the customer (and it's amazing how often the customer is left out of high-level conceptual designs, which may be a tip-off to problems). The customer gives an order to a salesperson, who enters the order right away, which takes a big step toward cutting the lead time to three weeks. Salespeople also can query, modify, and cancel orders—as can order processing specialists, though they'll be involved with far fewer orders.

When working with an order, customer and contract information may also be accessed and possibly updated; and special pricing information may be accessed. Management is responsible for establishing contracts with customers and approving special pricing. Configuration information also may be accessed, and the manufacturing schedule, inventory items information, and the order itself may be accessed and possibly updated.

Manufacturing is responsible for maintaining configuration information. Manufacturing also accesses and updates the manufacturing schedule, inventory items information, and the order itself. When manufacturing ships products to customers, it also generates billing information, which is used to generate and send invoices to customers. The orders and billing information are used by sales management for sales forecasts and sales reporting, including commission calculations, some of which also goes to salespeople.

A high-level conceptual design is a transitional document between business requirements and system design. It's probably the only design document that nontechnical people can understand and work with comfortably. It's also like a scorecard that helps define implementation projects, since ultimately each of the pieces in the diagram must be accounted for, either existing already or being implemented.

Iterative requirements negotiation without analysis paralysis

Business as well as technical people should be able to understand and evaluate the adequacy of both the itemized business requirements and their associated high-level conceptual design. As shown in Figure 11.3, through a series of iterations, these should be reviewed and revised until all key stakeholders agree the Problem Pyramid reasonably represents the real problem and real requirements which when delivered are likely to achieve the goal measure and provide real value.

Only after an inclusive set of real top-level requirements has been identified and agreed upon is it appropriate to begin considering implementation project constraints, such as budget, deadline, and available resources. Based on meaningful estimates of cost, time, and other considerations to implement a system that meets the business requirements, it is common for

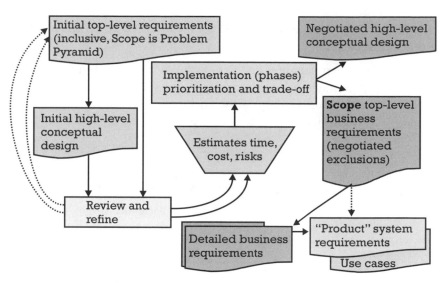

Figure 11.3 Negotiating requirements.

the decision makers to elect to spend only enough to implement some subset of the requirements.

That subset (which could be the full set) of top-level requirements forms the scope of the implementation project. Only those business requirements need to be defined in greater detail at the present time. Once the applicable business requirements have been defined in detail, then a product can be designed to meet the business requirements. The product design includes high-level and detailed system requirements, which are external views of what the product does. In addition, the product design includes use cases describing actors' views of how the product operates to meet the product system requirements.

Analysis paralysis occurs when requirements discovery becomes endlessly mired in detail; but it won't occur with this approach because initial iterations involve only top-level requirements and can be accomplished relatively quickly.

✖ Warning

Although top-level requirements can be defined quickly, some time is required. It is easy to presume they can be defined in a brief meeting, perhaps only with the project sponsor or a JAD session with key stakeholders. The more important participants (think they) are, and the more convinced they are that they already know what is required, the more such sessions are prone to produce product system requirements—which not only are not business requirements, but have a way of turning out not to be right. Often, as Ann Analyst's experience demonstrates, this occurs because the real problem and requirements are not readily apparent. Usually, more extensive (than expected) data gathering and analysis are needed to discover top-level business requirements, but the effort is still much less than when also trying to define detailed requirements.

Estimating time and effort to implement the requirements

Invariably one needs to estimate the cost, time, resources, and risk needed to meet the requirements. Invariably too the estimates turn out to have little relationship to reality. In my experience, estimates are wrong for several reasons:

- Business requirements themselves are not a suitable basis for project estimates.
- Estimates are not calculated in an appropriate, reliable manner.
- Politics, games, and focusing on single data points out of context supersede meaningful management decision-making.

Business requirements are deliverables which themselves have no cost. Their cost is entirely attributable to the resources and effort needed to produce the deliverables. What someone would like that to cost is totally irrelevant to what it really will cost. Thus, reliably estimating the cost of meeting business requirements takes the following steps:

- Develop a high-level product design to meet the high-level business requirements.
- Define the tasks needed to produce the product.
- Estimate the resources, effort, and duration needed to perform the tasks.

The job of an effective project manager is to find a suitable way to implement a system which meets the business requirements within the necessary time frame. Until such a workable approach has been identified, budget and resource issues are not relevant. The project approach that can deliver the needed results will take a certain amount of resources and time. Neither that necessary resource cost nor time, nor the real business requirements, is changed by wishes or availability of resources.

Only after a workable approach has been identified is it reasonable to adjust the other project variables in order to fit within constrained variables. Such adjustment could mean adding time or budget, or implementing differently, although often it involves reducing the scope of the implementation project. Realize that project scope changes do not at all change the scope of the requirements, which frequently is reflected in subsequent implementation projects ("Phase 2") to deliver the remaining business requirements.

Detailed requirements

Those top-level business requirements chosen for implementation need to be defined in detail. This may take additional data gathering and analysis. To avoid analysis paralysis, it's a good idea to approach the detail iteratively.

For each top-level requirement, define perhaps three lower levels and then review with affected stakeholders to determine whether the detail is on track and whether further detail (and more data gathering) is needed. An example of more detailed ElecTech business requirements follows.

Detailed Requirements

1. At the time of taking an order, calculate as reliably as possible the date the order actually will ship.

C. Provide the salesperson easy access to accurate current product availability information.

   a. For each product.

      1) Base products and options.

      2) Identify quantities of finished goods on-hand.

      3) Indicate total quantity which can be produced.

         a) By want date.

         b) By any specified date.

   b. For each configuration (combination of products).

      1) Formatted with respect to

         a) SuperProduct, modified by its base products.

         b) Base product, modified by its unique combination of options.

      2) Coordinated with verification that configuration is feasible and contains necessary options.

      3) Calculating total quantity across subordinated individually identified quantity per delivery location and delivery date.

   c. For all configurations which the salesperson indicates must ship together.

      1) Assume (default) the entire order.

      2) Allow the salesperson to identify groupings.

         a) Configurations which must arrive at the same time.

         b) At same or multiple delivery locations.

      3) Warn of products with technical dependencies.

         a) Products which must be present for an ordered product to function properly.

         b) Products which depend on the ordered product being present for them to function properly.

Some of these items already may be defined at as low a level of detail as necessary, whereas others may need to be broken down still further. Note that at each level of detail, the business requirements still must meet the "hierarchical itemized business deliverable *whats* that contribute to value" test. Note also that the context of the hierarchy adds meaning and is much more succinct than a format which endeavors to include within each individual item sufficient (and often redundant, e.g., "The system shall...") information for the item to stand alone.

The next two chapters describe additional ways to test whether the business requirements are accurate and complete. When testing top-level requirements, one often must make a judgment as to whether the top-level requirements reasonably and foreseeably lead to detailed requirements that satisfy the test.

References

[1]   IEEE, "Std. 830-1998 Recommended Practice for Software Requirements Specifications," June 1998.

[2]   Cockburn, A., *Writing Effective Use Cases*, Boston, MA: Addison-Wesley, 2001.

[3]   Jacobson, I., et al., *Object-Oriented Software Engineering, A Use Case Driven Approach*, Wokingham, England: Addison-Wesley, 1992, pp. 126–130.

[4]   Heumann, J., "How to Move from Business Use Cases to System Use Cases," *Software Development Best Practices 2003 Conference*, Boston, MA: September 18, 2003.

[5]   Cockburn, A., *Writing Effective Use Cases*, Boston, MA: Addison-Wesley, 2001, pp. 13–14.

Finding overlooked requirements

Rule 1: The customer is always right.
Rule 2: If the customer is ever wrong, refer to Rule 1.

—Stew Leonard's Dairy Store

Stew Leonard's Dairy Store is a small Connecticut supermarket chain that is legendary for fanatical customer service and, not coincidentally, for earning the grocery industry's highest profits per square foot of shelf space. The two rules are inscribed on a large rock in front of each store. Stew Leonard "found religion" about customers when a woman announced she'd never return to the store, after Stew argued with her that some eggnog she'd bought was fine even though she thought it "wasn't right." Stew did the math. He'd lost a customer who probably spent $100 per week, 52 weeks a year, for perhaps 10 or more years, plus the dollar he'd finally grudgingly refunded for the eggnog, because he could not accept that the customer cared about what she thought, not what Stew thought.

I mention this story because *requirements are the customers', what they think, not what we think the customers need or ought to want*. When we forget this fundamental fact, we overlook requirements—bunches of them. This chapter describes numerous ways to identify requirements that have been overlooked and become expensive creep. We'll apply each of the ways to the top-level business requirements defined in Chapter 11. Even though those requirements seem reasonable (many seminar participants describe them as better than they are accustomed to), we'll find that each CAT scan angle reveals overlooked requirements that normal development and other angles miss.

Let's start by examining what we mean by system quality:

- Fits system specs;
- Runs efficiently;
- Doesn't blow up;
- Follows standards;
- Uses current technology;
- Uses modern techniques;
- Can be easily modified:
    - Without changing program code, or
    - When code does change.

Most systems professionals I encounter agree the above list pretty well describes what they usually mean by system quality. What then is the following list?

- Does what needs to be done correctly;
- Performs adequately;
- Functions reliably and consistently;
- Is easy to use;
- Is supported quickly and correctly;
- Is delivered on-time and in budget.

Oh, that's what others, such as, customers and management, mean by "system quality." Which list is correct? They both are, but *the customers' view is most important, because the technical view doesn't matter if the customers' view of quality isn't first satisfied.* When one side acts as if theirs is the only meaning of system quality, and the other side doesn't seem to care about it, they presume the other side doesn't care about quality, which causes resentment and additional problems. Both sides do care about quality, but in different ways; and both sides need to know the full story, that system quality involves both lists.

✖ Warning

An analogous situation exists within the requirements and testing communities. Conventional testing of requirements focuses almost exclusively on the form issues addressed in Chapter 4, such as whether a requirement is worded sufficiently, specifically for its implementation to be testable. In contrast, the business side is most concerned that business requirements are identified (i.e., not overlooked) and accurate, neither of which is assured by the emphasis on form. Just as with the two views of system quality above, the customers' or business view of requirements is primary; the technician's concern with matters of form is secondary and doesn't matter much if requirements are overlooked or wrong. Overemphasizing form not only can result in requirements that miss the boat, but also can divert time and resources from finding important issues while losing the business people's confidence and cooperation.

This chapter describes a number of ways to test that *identify overlooked requirements*. Chapter 13 presents a number of additional ways to test that requirements are *accurate*. As with the various ways to test requirements form discussed in Chapter 4, each of these ways is essentially a topic, guideline, or checklist to be used in a review or inspection, whether formal or informal, individual or group. Each way serves as a different CAT scan angle revealing issues that other ways to test the requirements missed. It's not either-or. Rather, use as many of the ways of each type as you find fruitful for your particular situation. The more ways used, the more potential problems will be detected.

As with all testing, the *purpose of these tests is not to define the requirements but to* confirm that the defined requirements are accurate and complete, where test discrepancies *indicate the likely existence of omissions and inaccuracies*. Conventional requirements definition and testing techniques routinely produce and seldom detect such requirements issues. For greatest payback, the test methods in this and the next chapter concentrate on higher levels within the requirements hierarchy. Overemphasis on detail distracts.

Once alerted to probable errors and omissions in indicated areas, one applies the various requirements discovery techniques described in the preceding chapters. The approach for addressing overlooked and incorrect business requirements is the same as Figure 11.3 describes for initial discovery. That is, first identify top-level business requirements and then iterate selectively top-down to expand them into detailed business requirements. At higher levels, less specific verbiage is not only acceptable but advisable. It's only at the more detailed levels within the hierarchy that many of the form tests—such as assuring wording is specific, objectively operational, and testable—become more pertinent.

✪Users, customers, and stakeholders (test method #26)

We use the term "business requirements" rather than "user requirements" because parties other than users also can have requirements. A *user* is anyone who physically uses the system (in the broadest sense of the term, not just a set of computer programs). Similarly, following from Total Quality Management's broad definition, a *customer* is anyone internal or external who uses or is affected by the work or work product. A *stakeholder* is anyone whose opinion of the work or work product matters. All users are customers, but there can be customers who are not users. All customers are stakeholders, but there can be stakeholders who are not customers.

Therefore, stakeholders are the group which includes customers and users, and *requirements are the stakeholders'*.

✍ Exercise: Identify stakeholders

Identify the ElecTech case's stakeholders.

Of course, the main stakeholders already identified are salespeople, order processing specialists, and manufacturing planners. Also, let's not forget end-customers who buy ElecTech's products and for some, their parent and related companies too. Who else? How about: sales managers, field engineers, sales office support staff, manufacturing managers, factory workers, shipping staff, shipping companies, purchasing personnel, raw materials vendors, customer support staff, product designers, manufacturing designers, billing and accounts receivable staff, payroll staff, IT (including analysts, programmers, managers, help desk, documenters, testers, computer and network operations) staff, senior management, marketing staff, internal and external attorneys, regulators, competitors ("disfavored stakeholders"), and probably a few more. The seemingly adequate business requirements overlook almost all of these stakeholders and consequently overlook all of their requirements.

It's helpful to think of requirements of stakeholders as falling in any or all of three quality dimensions. Thus, even when a stakeholder has been identified, all their requirements for a particular quality dimension will be overlooked if it is overlooked. After briefly describing each quality dimension, we'll present a powerful method for applying them to reveal overlooked ElecTech order processing requirements.

✪ Quality dimension: Quality of design (test method #27)

The first, *quality of design, identifies what it needs to do*. This quality dimension deals with making sure required functions, capabilities, and performance levels needed by all stakeholders have been identified and defined appropriately, accurately, and completely with meaningful common understanding. As suggested by its name, quality of design also goes beyond the business requirements to assure that the design suitably meets the requirements; that costs, benefits, and schedules are accurate; and that trade-offs are reasonable and based on adequate information.

✪ Quality dimension: Quality of conformance (test method #28)

The second quality dimension, *quality of conformance, deals with how it's produced*. Business requirements include assuring that products will conform to design and apply suitable standards and conventions; that workers use expected skill and care and apply defined methods and tools; and that management uses appropriate practices. Quality of conformance is especially concerned that the product is delivered on time and in budget.

✪Quality dimension: Quality of performance (test method #29)

The third quality dimension, *quality of performance, addresses how it's delivered*. Remember, value depends on delivery. Business requirements include that the product is available as needed for use, works in the intended manner reliably and accurately, and handles the workload adequately. Quality of performance recognizes that delivery is ongoing and extends to assuring the product is supported and maintained responsively.

Strawman technique

One of the biggest difficulties in testing requirements is that there is no prior definition of "right" (expected results) to compare against the actual results—the requirements which have been defined. To get around this somewhat significant limitation, we use a technique called a "strawman." *A strawman is a reasonable guess of what requirements might be, an approximation of possible expected results to compare against the actual results.* Because these guessed requirements are only "straw," they'll crumble easily when inappropriate and challenged.

There is no assurance the strawman requirements are right. However, *when what the strawman expects is reasonably present in the defined requirements, we have a basis for confidence that the requirements have addressed the topic. When the expected strawman requirements are not reasonably present, it doesn't mean the defined requirements are wrong but does indicate the need to examine them more fully.* For maximal benefit, endeavor to focus on the highest risks.

A big advantage of the strawman approach is that it forces creating concrete examples, which are much more reliable for spotting problems than simply asking whether a topic is addressed suitably. Those defining requirements presume they've been thorough, so simply asking doesn't help them become aware of oversights the way concrete examples do. Moreover, using strawmen in a sampling manner can save time. That is, if we apply a strawman to one or two key aspects of a topic, it often signals whether the topic has been addressed at all, and we don't need to apply strawmen to all the topic's aspects.

To see how a strawman works, let's use one to check the combination of stakeholders and quality dimensions. For a strawman stakeholder, let's pick billing and accounts receivable staff and make some reasoned guesses as to their requirements for the several quality dimensions.

For quality of design, billing and accounts receivable might have requirements such as:

- Customer and billing address are identified accurately.
- Ordered products are clearly, accurately, and understandably identified.
- Pricing accurately reflects contractual and deals discounts.
- Credit terms are established prior to accepting the order.
- Depending on the customer, a subsidiary may or may not share the parent company's terms.
- Schedule partial payments based on partial order deliveries.
- Order confirmation includes applicable legal terms and conditions.
- Positive indication of delivery is received shortly after delivery.

The business requirements, which seemed so adequate, would appear to address only the first three of the eight strawman likely requirements. Note that since the business requirements are only top-level, it is necessary to make judgments as to whether they would be reasonably likely to address the strawman requirements when driven down to detail. In this case, there is no indication these additional issues would be identified.

For quality of conformance, billing and accounts receivable strawman requirements might include:

- The company's billing codes are used appropriately.
- Mechanisms are included to assure all orders are recognized, filled, and billed.
- Orders can be received and billed in accordance with Electronic Data Interchange (EDI) standards.
- Suitable audit trails are provided.
- Cutover from the old system occurs at the scheduled time.

The business requirements do not seem to include or reasonably anticipate any of these requirements. Note, some of these also could be considered quality of design issues.

Quality of performance billing and accounts receivable strawman requirements might be:

- Modify customer name and billing address after an order has been placed.
- Modify billing amount after an order has been placed.
- Support new and changed billing codes.
- Provide research capabilities to assist resolving billing questions and disputes.
- Allow designating portions of or entire orders as suspended due to a dispute.

The business requirements also do not appear to address any of these requirements. We could apply the strawman technique to one or more of the other nonkey stakeholders, but we probably are safe in generalizing from the results with these strawmen that requirements need to be discovered for all the nonkey stakeholders.

✪Addressing quality factors (test method #30)

Table 12.1 lists a number of quality factors (or "ilities"), which are often overlooked and turn into creep, sometimes I suspect because referring to them as "nonfunctional requirements" can lead to inadequate pigeonholed definitions. Difficulties can result because some quality factors refer to external application features, about which users would be more concerned, whereas others relate more to internal engineering and would be more evident to technical folks.

To judge whether quality factors have been addressed adequately, we again use a strawman, but with an additional consideration. Since quality factors don't exist in abstract pigeonholes, we also must identify a user and usage situation to which the quality factor pertains, and we need to be sure to define strawman quality factor requirements in more specific, objective, operational terms. For example, the ElecTech salespeople are key users, and usability probably would be a key quality factor. For the usage situation of entering an order, some strawman usability requirements might be:

▸ Allow entering an order quickly (say no more than one minute per product) by providing intuitive workflow and minimizing the amount of data that must be entered.

▸ Prompt possible choices and immediately check data to prevent and detect clerical errors (so that at least 50 percent of orders have no clerical errors).

▸ Provide customers sufficient information to enable their immediate verification that their orders are accurate.

▸ Provide easy access to understandable explanatory assistance.

Table 12.1　Some Quality Factors ("ilities")

Application Features (External)		Engineering (Internal)	
Usability	Availability	Efficiency	Maintainability
Reliability	Appearance	Reusability	Manageability
Correctness	Performance	Portability	Manufacturability
Security	Supportability	Testability	Traceability
Integrity	Cost-effectiveness	Style	Documentation
Usefulness	Adaptability	Structure	Interoperability
		Flexibility	Understandability

Since these are strawman requirements, they may not be ones real sales-people would identify. However, they do seem reasonable. It's questionable whether the business requirements that seemed so adequate a chapter ago would be likely, even when driven down to detail, to address these straw-man requirements. Note that for the purpose of identifying overlooked requirements, general terms such as "easy access" are suitable. There's no point in trying to get more specific about what "easy access" means when the whole topic has been overlooked. Therefore, it would be advisable to go back and further investigate salespeople's usability requirements. Also, it's probably safe to generalize that we should ask other key system users too, and at the same time ask about other quality factors that would be pertinent to their key usage.

✪Aligning strategic, management, and operational needs (test method #31)

Most requirements definers focus on operational needs, such as those of the salesperson to carry out his day-to-day work activities. Initial requirements data gathering is far less likely to reveal needs of the operational people's managers and is especially unlikely to recognize the company's strategic requirements that may be relevant to the problem at hand. Again we create strawmen of reasonably likely requirements for these commonly over-looked categories. Moreover, since the requirements of one often conflict with those of the others, we need to align the requirements as much as pos-sible to reduce contention.

For example, sales managers might have the following strawman requirements:

- Report each supervised salesperson's call activity (name and address of customer contacted) to the sales manager every day.

- Provide summary totals of number of calls, qualified leads, and orders per salesperson per period (weekly, monthly, quarterly, yearly, and with respect to prior year-to-date) and in total for all supervised salespeople.

- Report sales by product line to existing and new customers per super-vised salesperson and in total per period.

- Report sales pursuant to contracts, special price deals, and at list price and compare the profitability of each individual sale and in total per salesperson and in total per period.

Keeping and reporting all this information would take a lot of a salesper-son's time, which would conflict with the salesperson's need to spend time calling upon prospective customers. Even if automated, it may necessitate the salesperson's providing extra information, such as about sales calls, which would not be a part of his normal ordering operations. To align the conflicting requirements, for instance, might suggest the need for the system also to support the salesperson's calls to prospects and customers. Neither that requirement, nor the management reports above, seems to be addressed by the business requirements. More needs to be discovered about managers' requirements.

ElecTech senior management might have the following strategic strawman requirements:

▸ Allow focusing sales efforts on prospective companies in specific industries and/or specific geographic locales.

▸ Support sales of complementary products manufactured by strategic business partners who may be identified in the future.

Neither of these possible strategic requirements is addressed by the business requirements, which suggests that senior management's strategies haven't been, and need to be, identified and related to the problem at hand. Of course, executives will continue to exercise their prerogative to shift strategies and priorities seemingly arbitrarily and truly unpredictably, but these techniques can reduce the prevalence of such changes.

✪Technology requirements versus design (test method #32)

Although it's common for technology references to be designs, business requirements can include technological needs. Usually, one can tell designs because they describe in detail specifics of matters such as: screen and report layouts, database structure, internal structures, coding techniques, naming conventions, and specific modules and interfaces.

In contrast, technological business requirements are "one-liners" identifying preferences and constraints, such as: environment, operating system, network, database management system, interface protocols, adherence to internal or external standards, languages, and tools. Sometimes too, organizations have buzzword business requirements that someone feels must be met, even though they (and others) may have no idea exactly what the buzzword means.

Some strawman technological requirements might be:

▸ Allow access via the World Wide Web.

▸ Use the company's existing operating system, network, database management system, programming language, and development tools.

▸ Conform to the company's internal GUI standards.

▸ Provide "seamless e-commerce, 24/7."

The business requirements do not appear to address any of these, so technological environment preferences probably need to be examined further.

✪Including commonly overlooked deliverables (test method #33)

Experience shows that certain key elements very often are neglected in implemented systems. Their oversight ordinarily leads to problems and rework. Part of the reason for such omissions may be that system designs frequently do not include such elements either, which in turn may be due partly to being overlooked in business requirements. Some examples of possible strawmen for these commonly overlooked deliverables are:

- *Backup and recovery*—maintain sufficient copies of work products to enable replacing any that are damaged or lost within a reasonable time period.

- *Security*—assure that only authorized parties are able to access information that is confidential, only authorized parties are able to create or modify information that is confidential or relied upon, and unauthorized access attempts are detected and addressed by either preventing the attempt or restricting it and its harm.

- *Distribution*—provide prescribed methods, procedures, and tools to all who need to use them in a manner sufficient to enable their complete and suitable use.

- *Installation*—enable all who need to use prescribed methods, procedures, and tools the means to make use of them easily and quickly once they are provided.

- *Training*—assure that those who need to use prescribed methods, procedures, and tools have the knowledge and skills necessary to use them effectively.

- *Documentation*—provide suitable means for authorized parties to access information about the meaning and use of prescribed methods, procedures, and tools, as well as their background and underlying concepts.

- *On-line help*—provide quick, easy, and unobtrusive access to such documentation in conjunction with using the prescribed methods, procedures, and tools in a manner that minimizes interruption of ongoing work.

The business requirements do not seem to mention any of the above strawman commonly overlooked deliverables and probably should.

✪Interfaces with other systems (test method #34)

Business requirements define the interfaces that are needed and their key elements. System requirements and design define the specifics of accomplishing the interfaces. Some examples of possible strawman interfaces are:

- Provide to the billing system within one day of delivering products and/or services to customers sufficient information to charge the customer, including: customer identification, description of all products and services delivered, including dates and locations to which delivered plus any pertinent additional explanatory descriptions, pricing for each item provided, and description and amount of any applicable discounts.

- Provide to the marketing system on request the names, addresses, and contact information for customers and prospective customers in designated geographic regions, in designated industries, with designated current technology environments, or who currently have, have expressed interest in, or have been identified as possibly having interest in designated ElecTech products.

Neither of these strawman interfaces is mentioned in the business requirements, which suggests that more information is needed about required interfaces.

✪Third-party access and auditing (test method #35)

A common source of changes to implemented systems occurs when some unanticipated users need access in specialized ways. Following are some examples of possible strawman third-parties who may need access.

- Provide the company's internal and external auditors the means to easily and unobtrusively sample designated financial records used and maintained in conjunction with customer orders.

- Maintain suitable records of requests and responses to requests including prior senior management and company legal department authorizations, by governmental agents for disclosure of information about customers meeting certain demographic criteria and/or those ordering designated products; provide such information pursuant to disclosure limitations prescribed by senior management and/or the company legal department.

While it is possible such types of third-party access may not be required, it seems unlikely, and the business requirements give no indication that the topic had been addressed, so it at least probably warrants inquiry.

✪Conformance to laws and regulations (test method #36)

For many highly regulated industries, such as those involved with health care and insurance, a major portion of business requirements involves conformance to laws and regulations. However, all organizations may have some such needs, which often are overlooked and turn into costly creep, along with the possibility of fines and penalties. ElecTech might need to conform to strawman laws and regulations such as:

- For designated products and customer usage, assure that applicable safety-related options and instructions are included within the configuration.

- Assure that designated products are not sold to customers, or customers having designated association with other organizations, which lack necessary certifications or otherwise have been identified by governmental authorities as ineligible to buy said types of products.

Again, it is possible that such legal and regulatory conformance strawman requirements would not really be true for ElecTech, but today's safety and security environment makes such requirements increasingly likely. The business requirements do not seem to address such needs, which deserve at least an inquiry.

Each of the 11 starred ways to identify overlooked requirements is a CAT scan angle which revealed likely problems in the set of business requirements that seemed so adequate a chapter ago. One not-so-apparent consequence is that data models need to be adjusted to include additional elements to support such overlooked requirements. Systems professionals I encounter generally acknowledge that applying these same tests to their own systems at work, even those already in production, would reveal overlooked requirements and thus help avoid the expensive and disruptive rework creep that ordinarily would occur.

Checking requirements accuracy and completeness

Everyone is ignorant, only on different subjects.
—Will Rogers

Chapter 4 described a number of ways to evaluate requirements form, which is the most common way to test requirements. One of the reasons form is a relatively weak type of testing is that form can be evaluated by someone who is essentially ignorant of the subject domain. Chapter 12 described more powerful tests that reveal groups of overlooked requirements. Performing these tests takes more subject-area knowledge than testing requirements form, but can tolerate some ignorance making "strawman" reasonable guess approximations of "right" that were not necessarily correct. This chapter describes various ways to test requirements accuracy and completeness that do rely on the evaluator to know the right answer.

✪Importance and criticality (test method #37)

Important features add major value, such as through reducing cost, increasing revenue, and/or making more satisfied customers. In a manner sort of similar to a strawman, analyze the business case (but not the written requirements document) to identify the key sources of value to be delivered. The written requirements must be sure to address them. For example, key sources of value include:

> ▸ Scheduling manufacture of products for delivery by the customer's want date;
> ▸ Facilitating accurate configuration of even the most complex products;
> ▸ Providing customers timely, understandable, and meaningful communications;
> ▸ Promoting sales, especially of SuperProducts;
> ▸ Assuring economical adequate availability of raw materials.

The top-level requirements 1, 3, and 8 clearly address the first three. However, promoting sales may need additional attention, since requirement 9 is merely to maintain sales records, and the requirements do not mention raw materials.

Critical features are necessary for the system to work. Some examples would be:

> ▸ Orders have to be recognized and put in motion within a very short time of the customer giving the order.
> ▸ Orders actually have to be delivered, installed, and work correctly on the customer's want date.
> ▸ Problems have to be identified as soon as they occur and preferably should be detected before they become big.

Top-level requirement 2 deals with timely recognition of orders. However, the requirements do not seem to cover feedback confirming successful installation nor ongoing monitoring mechanisms to anticipate and identify problems.

✪ Clarifying application feature quality requirements (test method #38)

Quality actually consists of two components:

> ▸ *How much*, how many relevant functional capabilities are provided.
> ▸ *How well*, at what level each capability is provided, where some minimum level of quality is necessary to say the capability has been provided at all, and where there may be a more desirable and even an ideal level that could be provided.

Most requirements definitions concentrate only on how much, which inevitably leads to presumptions about how well. Consequently, it's common for mismatches to occur when the user expects one level of quality and the developer provides a different level. Note, providing a Rolls Royce when a Volkswagen is expected often is just as much a mismatch as the reverse; and each situation can cause "not what I expected" creep.

Thus, the requirements testing issue is not so much the specific desired level of quality, but rather whether the choices have been identified so that the customers can consciously choose the level most suitable to them. The customers' choices should be based on their perceived value relative to expected costs and risks, which can only be estimated reliably after the choices have been identified. I use a simple framework I call Engineered Deliverable Quality to guide informed definition of minimum (good), desirable (better), and ideal (best) quality levels for a few key features. For example, let's consider some attributes of the quality levels that might be associated with order confirmations:

Minimum:

> Printed, black and white, text, on preprinted multipart forms;

> Mailed to the customer within one day of receiving the order;

> Basic identification of customer, product, and key configuration options;

> Comments identifying nature of and reasons for any changes.

Desirable:

> Printed in color, text and graphics, on plain 8½ × 11-inch paper;

> Handed to customer at time of receiving order, or mailed within one day if not in customer's physical presence;

> Basic identification of customer and product/options, plus diagrams of the configured product;

> Comments identifying nature of and reasons for any changes, plus highlighting changed portions.

Ideal:

> At customer's preference, conveyed in one or more of the following manners:

>> Printed in color, text and graphics, on plain 8½ x 11-inch or A4 paper;

>> Handed to customer at time of receiving order, or mailed within one day if not in customer's physical presence;

>> Faxed;

>> Sent in e-mail text and/or as a formatted attachment;

>> Transmitted electronically in a format compatible with customer's Accounts Payable system.

> Basic identification of customer and product/options, plus diagrams of the configured product and of the customer's site installation;

> Comments identifying nature of and reasons for any changes, plus highlighting changed portions and indicating prior values.

While it's possible driving the top-level business requirements down to detail might address some of these topics, there is no reason to believe such quality-level choices have been or would be identified. When quality levels appear not to have been addressed for sampled key features, then it probably would be wise to use the Engineered Deliverable Quality technique to solicit additional stakeholder information about *how well* expectations for the functional capabilities that are most important to them.

✪Guidelines and conventions (test method #39)

Many organizations encourage or mandate adherence to a standards manual, which probably mainly prescribes guidelines and conventions. Guidelines are suggested, nonmandatory, presumably best practices. Conventions may or may not themselves be best practices, but they provide value because they are *standardized* methods and specifications, agreed upon ways for everyone to do a job which thereby reduce the learning curve and potential confusion.

An automotive example of a guideline might be: drive in the same lane except when passing another vehicle. An example of a convention might be: in the United States, one drives a car on the right side of the road, whereas in British countries, one drives on the wrong (joke!!, actually the left) side of the road. Neither side is inherently superior, but it is important that everyone in the country drives on the same side of the road.

There is no indication that ElecTech has guidelines and conventions or that they are to be used. However, such requirements often exist but may be implicit and known only within the development side. It's a good idea to make expected adherence explicit and evident to both business and technical sides, since such constraints can impact delivery.

✪Engineering standards (test method #40)

Unlike IT standards manuals, which typically prescribe "thou shalt" absolutes, *engineering standards define how to do it well* in terms of tolerances, acceptable degrees of variation from correct. *The tighter the tolerance, the higher the quality.*

Figure 13.1 shows an example of physical tolerances, let's say for a bolt that is supposed to be exactly 12-inches long to hold the wing on an airplane. In contrast to ordinarily one-directional absolutes, tolerances recognize that sometimes it can be just as bad to be too high as too low. If the bolt is too short, the wing will fall off, but if the bolt is too long, perhaps it interferes with hydraulics controlling the flaps. One vendor (shown by the dotted lines) produces 12-inch bolts that are from 10 to 14 inches long, a tolerance of 4 inches. A second vendor (shown by the solid lines) makes 12-inch bolts that vary from 11 to 13 inches, with a tolerance of only 2 inches. Which bolt would you prefer on the plane you're in? I'd certainly

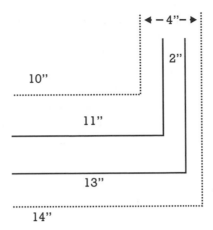

Figure 13.1 Tolerances for a 12-inch bolt.

choose the solid-line vendor, since their bolts have tighter tolerances, which means they are closer to correct, and thus higher quality.

Engineering standards typically describe the minimum (least demanding) tolerance which must be met in order for the standard to be met, target or desirable tolerance, and ideal tolerance. Engineered Deliverable Quality uses similar concepts, but applies to specific application features; whereas engineering standards apply across applications. Both can define tolerances for a variety of characteristics, for example:

▸ *Dimensions*—for information systems, dimensions could include size and weight of devices that salespeople reasonably could carry, which are at best implied in the business requirements. Dimensions also could include volumes, such as number of customers, which was not reflected in the requirements either.

▸ *Physical properties*—such properties could be technical, such as protocols and physical interfaces; they also could relate to the environmental conditions under which the salesperson must operate, including matters such as telephone access. Neither seems to be foreseeably mentioned in the business requirements.

▸ *Appearance*—appearance often refers to GUI format standards, but also could pertain to readability and layout of confirmations. The business requirements do not seem foreseeably to address appearance characteristics.

▸ *Performance nature and level*—the most notable performance level mentioned in the business requirements is delivery on the customer's want date, where delivering late creates obvious problems of the customer's not having the products when needed, but delivering early also could create problems, such as delivered products getting in the way or being subject to loss or damage.

Preferably, characteristics and tolerances are measured as quantifiable *metrics* (or variables), which tend to be easier to understand and evaluate. However, as seen with the Engineered Deliverable Quality example, characteristics also can be described in terms of present-absent *attributes*. Engineering standards ordinarily also depict the types of tests suitable for detecting defects, as well as the kinds of defects which could occur and their seriousness, that is, the extent to which the defect causes the standard not to be met.

Furthermore, failure to meet an engineering standard has inherent significance that the standard usually identifies, and people tend to be more likely to abide by standards, especially those with critical importance. In contrast, the most common consequence of failing to meet guidelines and conventions is usually some kind of administrative sanction, which sort of acknowledges implicitly that the guidelines and conventions may lack true

---

Engineering Standard: Data Entry

Definition:	The individual entering data into the system must be able to do so efficiently and with a high degree of accuracy.
Criticality:	MAJOR. Overly time-consuming or inaccurate data entry significantly reduces system effectiveness.
Minimum:	1. Entry is field-by-field.
	2. Each field is discete and clearly identifiable.
	3. Entry is positioned automatically to the beginning of the field.
	4. All data fields are submitted to relevant editing prior to being relied upon.
	5. A means is provided to delete or correct erroneous entries.
Target:	1. Each data field is accepted only after passing relevant editing at the time it is entered.
	2. Where practical, field values are filled automatically.
	3. Data fields are formatted automatically (e.g.,right-justify numerics).
	4. All data filling, formatting, and interpretations are displayed and can be modified at the time of entry.
Ideal:	1. Where practical, entry is automated, such as barcode scanning.
	2. Where appropriate, the end-user enters and verifies the data.
Defects Major:	1. Field value cannot be entered as operator intends.

	2. Incorrect format, range, or other editable value is accepted.
	3. Operator cannot tell what value to enter.
	4. Entry duration significantly interferes with reasonable workflow.
Minor:	1. Operator must manually accomplish format or spacing of entered field, (e.g., entering fill characters to right-justify a field).
	2. Operator must manually position to the beginning of a field.
	3. Error messages do not clearly indicate what is wrong.
	4. Workflow is clumsy or inefficient.
	5. Nonobvious coded values are not displayed back.
Incidental:	1. Obvious coded values are not displayed back (e.g., M-Male).
Tests:	1. Observation.
	2. Operator reports.
	3. Automated capture of input and displays.
	4. Usability laboratory hidden videotaping.

inherent significance and, in turn, probably contributes to their frequently being ignored. Following is an example of an engineering standard for software.

While this is only a basic example of an engineering standard for software, it seems fairly reasonable for most data entry situations. You may find it needs some adjustments to fit your environment. Participants in my seminars generally agree that data entry which doesn't meet the standard's minimum characteristics would not be adequate, and that data entry meeting the target and ideal characteristics would be respectively of higher quality.

When I ask what level of data entry should be required, "ideal" is chosen almost automatically. However, *the appropriate quality level is the customer's choice and depends on the situation and needs*. For instance, salespeople probably need relatively high levels of data entry quality for entering orders, since they do it frequently and errors could cause significant impacts. The business requirements don't seem to, but should, reflect the characteristics associated with required quality levels, if only by reference to the engineering standard. If you think engineering standards would be useful, I suggest starting with just a few, for your organization's most critical functions.

✪ Balancing conflicting requirements trade-offs (test method #41)

It's common for some requirements to conflict with others. The most desirable solution is to find ways to resolve the conflicts so that both requirements can be met. In other instances, though, it's necessary to choose one requirement over a conflicting one. Two elements are essential for making meaningful choices:

▸ The conflicting requirements and the existence of conflict must be recognized.

▸ Selection of one choice should be based upon balancing the full trade-offs.

Many conflicts aren't recognized until they turn into creep and rework, as it often is hard to become aware of conflicts among requirements. Techniques such as Engineered Deliverable Quality and engineering standards are especially effective at forcing recognition of otherwize overlooked conflicting requirements. Furthermore, concretely identifying the choices provides the basis for adequately estimating the information needed to balance trade-offs meaningfully. The stakeholder is the one who must choose, balancing the overall benefits against the overall costs of the respective choices.

When choices are described fairly specifically, the stakeholder is in a position to judge the respective benefits, and the developer is able to estimate reasonably reliably the relative cost, time, technical feasibility, risk, and other management considerations of delivering and operating with each choice. Also, too, it's important to identify other requirements that may be affected by the choices and their implications. Since no conflicting ElecTech business requirements have been identified, there are no trade-offs.

✪ Work out business rules (test method #42)

One of the best ways to determine whether a business rule has been understood correctly is to work out examples, typically with paper and pencil or a spreadsheet. Often trying to apply the rule concretely proves impossible or produces an incorrect result, thereby making apparent the need for additional information. The worked-out rule also can be saved to use as a test case when the system is delivered. For example:

▸ Business requirement 9.C involves maintaining records of sales relating to contests, but sufficient information is not yet available to determine how to identify contests and related sales.

✪Determine rules regarding corrections (test method #43)

In operation, all systems encounter situations where it's necessary to correct data that already has been entered into the system; yet the need for and rules governing such corrections frequently are not defined and turn into creep when the system can't handle the corrections properly. Business requirement 7 explicitly does address changing orders. However, the business requirements do not appear to deal with other corrections, such as:

> • When a customer in fact has been improperly identified and either:
>> • Notifies the company prior to delivery, or
>> • Receives and returns a delivery they did not order.
> • When Manufacturing does need to revise a shipment date due to internal factors.

✪Identify data retention and purging (test method #44)

Especially after a system has been in operation for a while, data grows beyond immediate needs. Some of that data may need to be retained for a specified period of time, either for legal and/or business purposes, and some of the data may be suitable for purging. Retaining unnecessary data can impede performance, both human and automated, but purging data inappropriately can create far larger problems when a need for that data surfaces. The ElecTech business requirements do not address these issues.

✪Identify historical data archiving and access (test method #45)

Similarly, when data needs to be retained but is expected to be accessed only infrequently, that data becomes a good candidate for being moved to secondary archived storage. When such needs are not anticipated in business requirements, they often appear to be changes to requirements and generally can prove quite disruptive. The ElecTech business requirements do not address archiving, and consequently they also are silent on who should be able to access archived data and under what conditions.

✪Map to manual procedures (test method #46)

A key characteristic that distinguishes system from business requirements is that system requirements almost never identify requirements which are expected to be accomplished via manual procedures. However, business requirements need to identify all the business' needs, regardless of expected means of implementation. When they are so identified, they have a chance of being automated appropriately, whereas failing to identify such requirements virtually assures they'll be overlooked in system designs. They turn into creep and expensive redesign and rework when the need for them becomes apparent after the system's implementation. Some likely manual procedures that the business requirements do not seem to address include:

- Determining who the customer is and whether he or she should be considered the same as some different-named customer that already has a customer number;
- Forecasting sales;
- "Massaging" sales forecasts to create just-in-time raw materials commitments.

✪Anticipate parameters of likely changes (test method #47)

As discussed previously, conventional wisdom says that requirements changes are both inevitable and unpredictable. In fact, *a large portion of supposedly unpredictable changes can be predicted* and thereby create far less disruption when the changes actually occur. When one examines changes that have occurred in the past, ordinarily many of them tend to cluster into groups with common elements. While the specific changes cannot be known in advance, frequently it is possible to identify those elements that are likely to change in certain definable ways. The real business requirements should include the ability to address such types of changes quickly, easily, and reliably. The ElecTech business requirements could, but do not, address likely changes, such as:

- Adding product lines;
- Changing salesperson territory definitions.

✪Review test cases (test method #48)

In Chapter 4, writing test cases was described as a way to assure testability, which in turn was one of the ways to test the form of requirements. While necessary, testability in no way assures that requirements are correct. However, those same test cases that were written in part to show testability (and in part to use later with the finished system to demonstrate that the requirements have been delivered) also can be used to evaluate content correctness. The secret is to have the users and other key knowledgeable stakeholders who did not write the test cases review them. While users generally are not as effective as often presumed at reviewing requirements, because they were the source of the requirements (and it's hard for one to spot his own mistakes), they can be very effective reviewing test cases written by some-body else. Let's take the following test case for example:

Inputs: Product Number 123;
                      List price $1,000;
                      Quantity ordered 10;
                      Contract price $900 after purchasing 10;
                      Number purchased previously, 1;

Expected Results: 10 Product Number 123 @ $900, Total Price = $9,000.

This test case shows that the requirement had been misunderstood. In fact, it should have:

Expected Results: 9 Product Number 123 @ $1,000;
                      1 Product Number 123 @ $900;
                      Total Price = $9,900;
                      Number purchased previously, 11.

✪Prototype (test method #49)

Chapter 8 discussed the strengths and weaknesses of prototyping as a requirements *discovery* technique. I contend that prototypes are better suited for *testing* requirements that have been defined already. A prototype demonstrates a partial implementation of a design presumed to deliver the business requirements. Whereas attention traditionally focuses on the delivered prototype, which usually is reacting to design issues, it's the prior effort of trying to figure out the prototype that is perhaps more likely to reveal business requirements issues. For example, I'd suggest trying to pro-totype the following business requirement would reveal significant ques-tions as to how approvals are solicited, communicated, and related to particular orders:

Provide indication of special pricing approvals on orders.

✪Simulate workload performance (test method #50)

A common cause of creep occurs when a system goes into operation and turns out not to be able to handle the workload acceptably. Simulating workloads can help assure that the business requirements provide sufficient definition to guide designs that perform adequately. To simulate, pick a key type of business transaction, mock it up on paper or with a coded prototype, try out a few sample transactions to get representative timing and volume estimates, and multiply that times the number of transactions expected in given time periods. For example, assume the following simulated timings and volumes:

One minute to locate an existing delivery address;
Two minutes to determine an address is not known and add it;
A maximum order has 200 delivery addresses, assume 75 percent are new;
Total time just to identify delivery addresses =
    $(50 * 1) + (150 * 2) = 350$ minutes.

Simulation reveals a significant business problem with salespeople's handling orders that go to a large number of different delivery locations. Further definition is needed *from a business perspective* and then from a product system requirements standpoint.

✪Requirements walkthroughs (test method #51)

Chapter 2 identified the use of formal technical reviews as a procedural approach that applies to all the remaining ways to test that business requirements are right. Inspections are reviews guided by topics lists such as represented by these various ways to test requirements. Walkthroughs are reviews guided by the material being reviewed and, even when conducted informally (which they often are), can reveal content correctness issues.

✖ Warning

Requirements walkthroughs are subject to several traps. First, walkthroughs follow the flow in the materials being reviewed. However, business requirements are a list of deliverables, which by themselves do not have an inherent flow. Thus, either what is being walked through is a design (which does have inherent flow) or some additional information is needed to indicate flow, such as a high-level conceptual design.

Second, the purpose of a review is to find the potential problems; but it is very common for walkthroughs to be educational sessions to enable participants to understand the system. An educational mindset causes reviewers to find much less than when seeking problems. Increasing the review's formality, including emphasizing its purpose to identify potential problems, can help avoid these traps.

Walking through the high-level conceptual design might reveal issues, such as:

▸ What is the role of order processing now that salespeople primarily enter and update orders?

✪Joint application development (test method #52)

Like prototyping, JAD was described in Chapter 8 as a requirements discovery technique, but JAD also can be (though less frequently) used to evaluate the adequacy of requirements that already have been defined. A facilitated review by the stakeholders might reveal the following issue with the business requirements:

> Where's the customer service department and how do they know when to install delivered products?

✪Defining acceptance criteria (test method #53)

The Proactive Testing Life Cycle described in Chapter 1 depicts two independent paths: acceptance testing and technical testing. Each path provides a different, major CAT scan angle for detecting problems. Technical testing primarily is the responsibility of the technical side and is mainly concerned with demonstrating that the developed system conforms to the design. Acceptance testing is the responsibility of the business/user side and is aimed at demonstrating that the developed system meets the business requirements.

For greatest effectiveness, the bulk of acceptance test planning should occur prior to system design and involves identifying requirements-based tests and acceptance criteria. We've already identified the dual uses of tests based on requirements (including use cases) for testing both form and content of requirements. *Acceptance criteria are defined by the stakeholders without referring to the defined requirements and represent what must be demonstrated to the stakeholders before they will be willing to stake their jobs on using the delivered system.* Acceptance criteria are defined with respect to five areas:

1. What *functions* the system must perform;

2. *How much* must be shown to give confidence it works;

3. *How well,* how system quality will be assessed;

4. *By whom,* who should perform tests for confidence we can use it;

5. *In what manner,* testing format for confidence the system works.

Some examples of acceptance criteria might be:

> Accurately calculate sales commissions and contest awards.

> Provide historical tracking of products and configuration options purchased, by product and by customer, along with all correspondence with the customer both before and after the purchase.

The business requirements do address the first acceptance criterion, but not the second.

✪Match against an independent mini definition (test method #54)

A relatively expensive but powerful way to assure important requirements are addressed is to prepare an independent mini definition of requirements. Like a strawman, the mini definition serves as an approximation of the right answer to compare against the actual requirements that have been defined. The difference is that a mini definition is expected to be accurate, whereas a strawman just guesses about possible requirements.

Let's say two analysts spent one month preparing the requirements definition being tested. Another analyst who was not involved might spend two days gathering data and writing the mini definition. Two days is enough for the headlines, identifying the top requirements, but not to learn much about even the second and third levels down. The full requirements definition, therefore, will contain much information that is not in the mini definition, but everything in the mini definition should be in the full requirements. Examples of requirements which might be in a mini definition but weren't in the more complete requirements definition include:

- ▸ Handling orders that the customer determines are incorrect after delivery;
- ▸ Expediting orders by transferring products from one order to another (which may still be appropriate under certain special circumstances).

✪Match against an independent "canned" definition (test method #55)

"Canned" definitions of requirements, such as from a text book or specifications for a commercially available software product, can serve as less expensive but less specific approximations of right. For example, there are many order processing software packages for sale. Each has many features which probably would be required by any order processing system; but none would be likely to have all the unique capabilities needed by ElecTech. Some of the requirements evidenced in a standard software package that don't seem to be addressed in ElecTech's business requirements include:

- ▸ Interfacing with standard word processing and spreadsheet application software products;
- ▸ Identifying delivery variables, including special instructions about where and when to deliver, preferred carrier, and optional express service.

✪Independent expert validation (test method #56)

One of the most common methods organizations employ to check requirements is engaging an expert consultant, someone who has suitable subject area knowledge and is independent of the process that produced the requirements being evaluated. One doesn't have to be a world-renowned expert, or know a lot about the subject initially, to perform this role capably. One doesn't even have to be a professional consultant or work for an outside organization.

While (I am not unbiased and) do feel outside consultants can be good choices, very often, independent people with suitable knowledge can be found within the organization, perhaps working on allied projects or in related areas, such as internal audit. They also can be found in academic institutions or through professional associations. Moreover, one can develop reasonable expertise relatively quickly with some concerted research and good analytical skills. An independent expert's evaluation will be facilitated by preparing a mini definition of requirements and other checklists before looking at the requirements to be evaluated.

✍ Exercise: Your independent expert review

At this point, you probably know more about order processing and ElecTech than you ever expected. You are independent of the requirements and have developed a reasonable subject area expertise. What still hasn't been identified as missing or wrong?

You might have come up with still-unidentified issues such as:

▸ Getting feedback about customer needs from customer service representatives:

  ▸ Installing the ordered products;

  ▸ Servicing the products after installation.

▸ Interfacing with the company's financial accounting systems.

✪Two independent reviews (test method #57)

Sometimes organizations need to have a way to gauge confidence in the adequacy of their requirements, especially if they've used some of the test methods described and found a few problems. One technique that can be helpful is a variation on validation by an independent expert. This approach is twice as expensive, because it involves having two independent experts independently evaluate the business requirements, ordinarily after the initial requirements definition has been tested and revised accordingly.

While the specific issues each expert identifies do need to be addressed, the main purpose of this technique is to compare the two experts' findings. The more their independent reviews identify only minor issues or the same big issues, the more confident one can be that all the main issues have been revealed. If their reviews each discover big issues but don't overlap, there's a good chance that they are drawing from a still-large population of issues that includes some additional issues nobody has yet identified. Some remaining issues are:

▸ Managing delivery of orders where the ordered products are produced at different times because of factory considerations or the customer's needs;

▸ Providing alerts when manufacturing capabilities, including prospective raw material availability, become threatened.

We have tested the business requirements from 57 different CAT scan angles, and each one continues to find problems that the others did not reveal. The industry tends to emphasize testing requirements form, which is necessary, but I believe relatively weak in comparison to the value obtained by the more powerful methods that can detect overlooked and incorrect requirements. While I suspect your independent expert review may not have detected the two additional (I'd consider moderate) issues above, I think we've probably surfaced most of the important shortcomings in the set of business requirements that seemed so adequate at the end of Chapter 11.

The next step would be to revise that document to reflect the issues identified by the various test methods. While of course you'd need to bring your own project's business requirements up to speed based on applying these various ways to test, I am not going to do that exercise in this book. Discovering the revised requirements would involve additional data collection and analysis in the same manner we've already described. Repeating such description would add pages to plow through with no significant added value.

Measuring proof of the pudding

You are responsible for your results.

Ultimately, the most meaningful test of requirements is whether they result in a solution that works. The previous chapters describe methods for discovering and testing business requirements up-front, before designing and implementing a system that presumably will meet the requirements and thus provide value. This chapter deals with some techniques for relating information from later phases to testing the adequacy of the requirements.

✪ Cost/benefit analysis (test method #58)

Although many organizations only analyze costs and benefits as part of feasibility analysis, *financial tests of project viability are appropriate at every phase* of the development life cycle. Since business requirements provide value when delivered, the cost/benefit comparison must show net benefit. Otherwise, either the requirements aren't real or are not defined adequately; or the means of delivery are unsuitable.

Costs and benefits are analyzed over the anticipated useful life of the system, typically five years, and are adjusted by present value factors to reflect future cash flows in current dollars. Benefits are shown by comparing full costs and benefits for various scenarios, at least one scenario for implementing the system and one for "no change." As shown in Table 14.1, implementing a system in 6 months that meets the business requirements should turn around the company and produce a five-year total net cash flow benefit of $89 million in today's

Table 14.1   Cost/Benefit Analysis

	Likely (6 months)				
Revenue:					
Net Sales Gain	10,800,000.000	23,220,000.000	26,703,000.000	30,708,450.000	35,314,718.000
Expenses:					
Development	1,000,000.000	200,000.000	240,000.000	288,000.000	345,600.000
Notebook PCs	450,000.000	90,000.000	108,000.000	129,600.000	155,520.000
Telephone	225,000.000	540,000.000	648,000.000	777,600.000	933,120.000
O/P Staff (10%)	−200,000.000	−440,000.000	−484,000.000	−532,400.000	−585,640.000
Net Annual Benefit	9,325,000.000	22,830,000.000	26,191,000.000	30,045,650.000	34,466,118.000
Present Value	.909	.826	.751	.683	.621
Net Present Value	8,476,425.000	18,857,580.000	19,669,441.000	20,521,179.000	21,403,459.000
				Total:	88,928,084.000
	No change				
Revenue:					
Net Sales Gain	−1,800,000.000	−3,420,000.000	−4,878,000.000	−6,190,200.000	−7,371,180.000
Expenses:					
Development	0.000	0.000	0.000	0.000	0.000
Notebook PCs	0.000	0.000	0.000	0.000	0.000
Telephone	0.000	0.000	0.000	0.000	0.000
O/P Staff (10%)	0.000	−220,000.000	−242,000.000	−532,400.000	−585,640.000
Net Annual Benefit	−1,800,000.000	−3,200,000.000	−4,636,000.000	−5,657,800.000	−6,785,540.000
Present Value	.909	.826	.751	.683	.621
Net Present Value	−1,636,200.000	−2,643,200.000	−3,481,636.000	−3,864,277.000	−4,213,820.000
				Total:	−15,839,134.000

dollars. On the other hand, if the company makes no change, it will continue to lose business, with a total profit loss of about $16 million (optimistically estimating only 10 percent lost sales per year) over 5 years.

Specific relevant sources of costs and revenues are identified, and their amounts are estimated for each of the useful life years, based on quantities of units, amount per unit, and percentage change. For example, each of the 300 salespeople average $600,000 per year sales of regular products with an 8 percent profit margin (net of directly related expenses, such as sales commissions and manufacturing costs) and $100,000 per year sales of Super-Products with a 12 percent profit, for total current sales profit of $18 million. If the business requirements are met by a system that takes 6 months to implement, sales management expects:

▸ Regular product sales should increase 50 percent (regaining the 33 percent lost from the prior year) in the next 12 months, and 15 percent each year thereafter.

▸ SuperProduct sales should increase even more, 400 percent the first year after implementation (to initial projected levels), and 15 percent in following years.

Instead of showing net revenue, it's common to show gross revenue (i.e., total sales) and then list each related cost, as well as costs that are not directly linked to specific revenue. Some costs are one-time, such as development and equipment acquisition, which should be estimated respectively by IT management and by a representative computer vendor who is willing to sell products at the quoted price. Other costs are ongoing, but are fixed, such as maintenance contracts that are owed regardless of how much the system or equipment is used. Ongoing costs also could be variable, depending on usage, such as for long-distance telephone, and should be provided by the vendor based on a profile of expected usage. Growth and inflation (a 10 percent rate has been used in the example) need to be factored in for both costs and revenue. Usually quantity changes are projected to be continual, but can be periodic (or stepwise) as the no change scenario shows for order processing staff reductions which the order processing manager projected will occur in years 2 and 4 due to reduced numbers of sales to process.

✖ Warning

Organizations typically make financial cost and benefit estimates at the beginning of a project but fail to tie back actual figures when they become known. Intermediate financial measures are valuable ways to gauge the accuracy of estimates during the development process, and comparing to final figures is invaluable for identifying ways to improve the development process, most notably improving requirements.

✪Challenge cost and benefit estimates (test method #59)

People who want to do a project have a natural tendency to overestimate benefits and underestimate necessary time, effort, and resources. Therefore, it's valuable to challenge these estimates, which in turn can help detect requirements issues. The most effective way is to assure there is a rational relationship between meeting the requirement and the claimed benefit. For example, it indeed is reasonable to believe that sales will rise when the system enables orders to be placed more simply and accurately and be delivered within three weeks. It's also reasonable to believe the effects will be even greater for SuperProducts, since their sales have been suppressed due to long lead times and complexity, which the system should improve. Similarly, since the salespeople will be doing the bulk of order entry, and the system will do much of the contract and special pricing processing, fewer order processing specialists should be needed.

Other ways to challenge these estimates involve obtaining independent estimates. One approach would be to get quotes for notebook computers and for telephone services from different vendors, and have a different project team provide costs and time for developing the system as described. Another approach is to ask a separate project team to develop its own design and estimates for meeting the business requirements. The independent views serve as different CAT scan angles, and when they produce markedly different estimates, it's frequently a signal that requirements are incomplete or unclear.

✪ Define system requirements (test method #60)

This book has emphasized the primacy of business requirements, but that's not to say system requirements don't also have value. Once business requirements have been defined from a business perspective, then it is appropriate to design a product (system) to meet the business requirements. Difficulties designing the product often indicate the need for additional or corrected business requirements.

The system requirements describe the product from an external (user) perspective, though for engineering aspects the user may be very technical or even another system or piece of equipment. Like business requirements, system requirements can be hierarchical, defined at a top level of major functions along with subsidiary detailed requirements. However, system requirements typically will be organized somewhat differently, (i.e., based on product structure and operation as opposed to the more list-like set of top-level business requirements). Many business requirements map verbatim to system requirements, though not necessarily in the same sequences and arrangements. Moreover, each system requirement should trace back to a business requirement. In addition, system requirements should meet the various tests of form described in Chapter 4.

✪ Define use cases for product usage (test method #61)

Use cases were described in Chapter 11. Use cases also need to be written in a manner that meets the tests of form in Chapter 4. One of the big advantages of use cases is that their step-by-step concreteness tends to reveal inconsistencies, inadequacies, and oversights that weren't evident from the requirements alone. Such problems may come from product design system requirements or may stem from the business requirements.

✪ Trace addressing of business requirements (test method #62)

Whether or not a business requirement is included verbatim, *the product design needs to address all the business requirements*; both in the external system requirements view, use cases describing product usage without regard to physical implementation, and also in the technical view of the design's physical implementation structure and components. Similarly, each business requirement should be addressed in the implemented code, in tests, and (where external) in user instructions. Failure of a subsequent artifact to address a business requirement may indicate a design or implementation shortcoming, or it may signal a problem with the business requirement.

The keys to tracing are:

‣ Itemizing business requirements, where each item is a separate requirement;

‣ Assigning each itemized requirement a unique identifier.

Keeping track of and tracing usage of requirements is an enormously tedious and time-consuming activity that automated tools can assist. The most commonly used tools for capturing requirements are word processors and spreadsheets, and they can be adapted to capture usage cross-references as well.

In addition, several commercially available tools are designed specifically to manage requirements and emphasize cross-reference tracing capabilities. Such tools support tracing forward to usages from the requirements and backward to the requirements from where each requirement is referenced. Perhaps the best-known such tool is Requisite Pro[1], which has the advantage of being intentionally integrated tightly with related modeling and testing tools sold by the same vendor (Rational Software, that recently became part of IBM). Compuware includes a tool with consciously more modest features called Reconcile[2] in its tool suite. Two tools which many consider the most full-featured are DOORS[3] and Caliber-RM[4], which are sold by vendors who do not also produce related modeling and testing tools, but which are designed to integrate loosely with many popular versions of these tools.

✖ Warning

Many automated tools, especially popular word processors, assign identifiers automatically, which can be very time- and error-saving. However, once the set of requirements is stabilized and ready for referencing in other artifacts, tools' tendency to automatically renumber when inserting items can totally destroy prior cross-references.

✪Monitor requirements changes (test method #63)

As development proceeds, the number and nature of requirements changes are perhaps the most direct measures of requirements quality. Effective development organizations keep track of these changes and their costs. To control creep, many organizations employ a Change Control Board (CCB) or similarly named function that is responsible for reviewing and approving proposed requirements changes before further effort is expended on such changes. Some CCBs also must approve implementation of approved changes. Having itemized requirements is key to spotting when a requirement is new or changed. Automated requirements management tools can

---

1. Requisite Pro, Rational software from IBM, 18880 Homestead Road, Cupertino, CA 95014, (800) 728-1212, (408)863-9900, www.rational.com.

2. Reconcile, Compuware Corporation, 31440 Northwestern Highway, Farmington Hills, MI 48334, (248) 737-7300, www.compuware.com.

3. DOORS, Telelogic North America Inc., 9401 Jeronimo Road, Irvine, CA 92618, (877) 275-4777, (949) 830-8022, www.telelogic.com.

4. Caliber-RM, Borland Software Corporation, 100 Enterprise Way, Scotts Valley, CA 95066-3249, (831) 431-1000, www.borland.com.

help assure that affected instances are addressed and that cross-referenced uses are updated.

✖ Warning

Mechanisms to monitor and control requirements changes are only as effective as the ability to spot the existence of a prospective new or modified requirement. Many such changes are hidden within other changes, such as to program code, tests, user instructions, or operations.

✪ Monitor subsequent defects (test method #64)

Effective software development organizations document, categorize, and analyze defects they encounter. One of the most powerful categories is defect source, the life cycle point at which the defect was injected. Note that failure to define a business requirement as well as defining it incorrectly would constitute requirements defect source injections.

While fears of finger-pointing often make defect injection categorizations controversial, the point of defect detection is straightforward. The time between the points of injection and detection is referred to as "defect age." The oldest defect is a requirements error that is not detected until production. The number of requirements defects escaping the definition process, regardless of when later detected, is a strong indicator of requirements adequacy. The age, or length of time defects stay undetected, indicates effectiveness of testing.

Summary

The relative cost of fixing later-discovered requirements defects compared to what it would have cost to fix them earlier was described in Chapter 1 as the amount of money that can be saved by (or spent on) more effective requirements discovery and testing. Especially with objective measures, but even with only subjective experience, the value is apparent of applying the concepts and techniques described in this book:

- ▸ Business requirements are the real requirements—*what must be delivered to provide value*—and need to be defined at both high and detailed levels; system requirements relate to one of several possible product designs to deliver the business requirements and provide value only to the extent they actually do meet the business requirements, which is unlikely unless the business requirements have been defined explicitly.

- ▸ The Problem Pyramid is a powerful method for identifying the real problem, its measures, the real "as is" process causes, and then the real "should be" requirements for providing value by achieving the goal measures. The Problem Pyramid defines the scope of the requirements and is not affected by project and implementation considerations, which do however affect scope of the implementation project; negotiating requirements scope and then project scope iteratively top-down prevents analysis paralysis; and defining implementation scope as top-level requirements deliverables reduces creep.

- The CAT-Scan Approach says that the more different angles are used, the more will be found, both when discovering and testing business requirements.

- Each of the 21+ (ultimately 64) CAT scan angle ways to test requirements continued to reveal issues that the other ways missed, even for business requirements that initially seemed reasonable and adequate. Major categories of tests were:

  - The "Regular Way" which is weaker than usually realized;
  - Foundation techniques that apply to all the ways;
  - Testing requirements form, which is necessary but relatively weak;
  - Finding overlooked requirements, usually in groups;
  - Checking content accuracy and completeness;
  - Testing the requirements and requirements process overall.

- Graphical techniques are helpful for analyzing and understanding requirements, but the appropriate format for documenting business requirements is hierarchical itemized business deliverable *whats* that contribute to value.

- Business requirements must address the real business process from its beginning through the full end result in the view of the customer.

Enjoy the project success advantages of discovering real business requirements.

Appendix: Summary of 21+ ways to test requirements

The "regular way"

1. User review
2. Management review
3. Supervisory review
4. Peer review
5. QA review

Foundation techniques

6. Use formal technical review
7. Predefine topics, guidelines, and specifics to examine

Topics, guidelines, and specifics to test *requirements form*

8. *Are they business requirements?*
9. Clarity
10. Deliverable *whats*
11. Testable
12. Reviewable
13. Itemized
14. Traceable
15. Ambiguity
16. Consistent, known usage of terms
17. Identifies assumptions
18. Stated in the positive
19. Identifies objectives
20. Identifies major functions and limits

21. Identifies business rules

22. Alternative consequences defined

23. Magic words

24. Complete

25. Hierarchical itemized business deliverable *whats* that contribute to value

Topics, guidelines, and specifics to *reveal overlooked requirements*

26. Users, customers, and stakeholders

27. Quality dimension: Quality of design

28. Quality dimension: Quality of conformance

29. Quality dimension: Quality of performance

30. Addressing quality factors

31. Aligning strategic, management, and operational needs

32. Technology requirements versus design

33. Including commonly overlooked deliverables

34. Interfaces with other systems

35. Third-party access and auditing

36. Conformance to laws and regulations

Topics, guidelines, and specifics to test *requirements accuracy and completeness*

37. Importance and criticality

38. Clarifying application feature quality requirements

39. Guidelines and conventions

40. Engineering standards

41. Balancing conflicting requirements trade-offs

42. Work out business rules

43. Determine rules regarding corrections

44. Identify data retention and purging

45. Identify historical data archiving and access

46. Map to manual procedures

47. Anticipate parameters of likely changes

48. Review test cases

49. Prototype

50. Simulate workload performance
51. Requirements walkthroughs
52. Joint application development (JAD)
53. Defining acceptance criteria
54. Match against an independent "mini-definition"
55. Match against an independent "canned" definition
56. Independent expert validation
57. Two independent reviews

Topics, guidelines, and specifics to test requirements overall

58. Cost/benefit analysis
59. Challenge cost and benefit estimates
60. Define system requirements
61. Define use cases for product usage
62. Trace addressing of business requirements
63. Monitor requirements changes
64. Monitor subsequent defects

About the author

Robin F. Goldsmith has been president of Go Pro Management, Inc., consultancy since 1982. He works directly with, and trains, professionals in business engineering, requirements analysis, software acquisition, and project management, quality, and testing. Previously, he was a developer, systems programmer/DBA/QA, and project leader with the City of Cleveland, leading financial institutions, and a "Big 4" consulting firm.

A published author and frequent speaker at leading professional conferences, Mr. Goldsmith was formerly the international vice president of the Association for Systems Management and executive editor of the *Journal of Systems Management*. He was founding chairman of the New England Center for Organizational Effectiveness. He belongs to the Boston SPIN and served on the SEPG'95 Planning and Program Committees. Mr. Goldsmith chaired BOSCON 2000 and 2001, ASQ Boston Section's Annual Quality Conferences, and is a member of the ASQ Software Division Methods Committee.

Mr. Goldsmith holds the following degrees: Kenyon College, A.B. with honors in psychology; Pennsylvania State University, M.S. in psychology; Suffolk University, J.D.; and Boston University, LL.M. in tax law. He is a member of the Massachusetts Bar and licensed to practice law in Massachusetts.

Index

A

Acceptance criteria
  defining, 191
  examples, 191
Accountability, accepting, 67
Accuracy, checking, 179–94
Actions, 72, 73
  defined, 72
  value-added, 76
  See also Processes
Active listening, 109
Alternatives, defining, 63
Ambiguity, 58–60
Ambiguity of Reference, 59
Ambiguous Logical Operators, 59
Ambiguous Statements, 60
Analysis formats, 125–40
  business rule language structure, 128–29
  CAT scan angles and, 140
  cause-and-effect graphing, 129–31
  data flow diagrams, 138–40
  data models, 133–34
  data vs. information, 125–27
  decision tables, 131–32
  entity relationship diagrams (ERDs), 132–33
  flowcharts, 136–38
  organizational charts, 134–35
  responsibility matrix, 135–36
  sorting, summarizing, segmenting, showing, 127–28
Ann Analyst
  business requirements (additional findings), 92
  definition, 31–33
  interviewing techniques, 115
  updated requirements analysis, 93
Assumptions, identifying, 61
ATM example, 38–40
  defined, 38

requirements, 39
Attributes
  present-absent, 184
  requirements form, 53
Awareness
  lack of, 34
  of requirements, 9

B

Bender, Richard, 59
  Ambiguity of Reference, 59
  Ambiguous Logical Operators, 59
  Ambiguous Statements, 60
Budgets
  as constraints, 35
  effective, 36
Business functions, identifying, 62
Business knowledge, 47
Business objectives, 3, 71
Business requirements. *See* Requirements
Business rules
  as business requirements component, 128
  identifying, 62
  language, structuring, 128–29
  in narrative form, 129
  working out, 186

C

CAT-Scan Approach™, 14–16
CAT scans
  angles, 16, 28, 140, 167
  defined, 14
  functioning of, 15
Cause-and-effect graphing (CEG), 129–31
  defined, 129
  illustrated, 130
  logic as paths, 130
  questions raised by, 130
  See also Analysis formats

Recent Titles in the Artech House
Computing Library

Practical Process Simulation Using Object-Oriented Techniques and C++, José Garrido

A Practitioner's Guide to Software Test Design, Lee Copeland

Risk-Based E-Business Testing, Paul Gerrard and Neil Thompson

Secure Messaging with PGP and S/MIME, Rolf Oppliger

Software Fault Tolerance Techniques and Implementation, Laura L. Pullum

Software Verification and Validation for Practitioners and Managers, Second Edition, Steven R. Rakitin

Strategic Software Production with Domain-Oriented Reuse, Paolo Predonzani, Giancarlo Succi, and Tullio Vernazza

Successful Evolution of Software Systems, Hongji Yang and Martin Ward

Systematic Process Improvement Using ISO 9001:2000 and CMMI®, Boris Mutafelija and Harvey Stromberg

Systematic Software Testing, Rick D. Craig and Stefan P. Jaskiel

Systems Modeling for Business Process Improvement, David Bustard, Peter Kawalek, and Mark Norris, editors

Testing and Quality Assurance for Component-Based Software, Jerry Zeyu Gao, H. -S. Jacob Tsao, and Ye Wu

User-Centered Information Design for Improved Software Usability, Pradeep Henry

Workflow Modeling: Tools for Process Improvement and Application Development, Alec Sharp and Patrick McDermott

For further information on these and other Artech House titles, including previously considered out-of-print books now available through our In-Print-Forever® (IPF®) program, contact:

Artech House
685 Canton Street
Norwood, MA 02062
Phone: 781-769-9750
Fax: 781-769-6334
e-mail: artech@artechhouse.com

Artech House
46 Gillingham Street
London SW1V 1AH UK
Phone: +44 (0)20 7596-8750
Fax: +44 (0)20 7630-0166
e-mail: artech-uk@artechhouse.com

Find us on the World Wide Web at:
www.artechhouse.com